Praise

"This book is a treasure trove of brilliant ideas far beyond accounting for anyone starting out or already on their way to gradually introducing the vast potential of data-centricity. Using the example of accounting and its interlinking within the company (and even outside), it describes in detail how a neutral, unbiased approach paired with the appropriate technology leads to a sustainably more efficient and continuously improving company."

Andreas Neumann
Freelance Catalyst
Former IT Innovation Catalyst and IT Architect, Siemens Energy

"Building on the seminal Resource Event Agents approach, and Data-centric Architecture concepts, Dave McComb and Cheryl Dunn have created a new, radically more efficient approach to Accounting and accounting software. This book is a great first step to solving many of the problems that plague accounting and is essential reading for all those executives and accountants that have suffered through the complexities of revenue and expense recognition, closing books, broken reporting, and months long external accounting audits."

Dougal Watt
Co-founder, Graph Research Labs

"Dave and Cheryl forge a realistic and inspiring path towards model-driven real-time accounting and reporting, based on events and commitments. They also include an excellent primer on all relevant accounting concepts, making it easy to absorb. Highly recommended!"

Philippe Höij
TOGAF Distinguished Architect
Co-founder, Graph Research Labs

"I don't usually pick up books on accounting, but Dave and Cheryl's fresh take on Accounting is a game-changer. Their application of DCA to finance is insightful, streamlining monthly closes and enhancing decision-making. Real-time data empowers businesses to adapt quickly, while automation improves efficiency, reduces errors, and frees time for strategic work."

Mark van Berkel
Chief Technology Officer and Co-Founder, Schema App

"Dave and Cheryl have dared to ask the question: *what would accounting look like if it were unburdened from 500 years of tradition still tied to paper, pen, and leather-bound journals?* While traditional accounting starts with the end goal of reporting and works backwards into the business, data-centric accounting starts with the elemental business events (whether financial reporting relevant or not) and works forward. Reframing the starting point makes you rethink the whole approach to accounting and provides the opportunity to discard debits and credits and embrace a new approach grounded in the events that drive business value."

John Clements, CPA
Retired Big-4 Assurance Partner

"In *The Future of Accounting*, Dave McComb and Cheryl Dunn make a compelling case for the complete restructuring of accounting as we know it. Even diehard traditional accountants will have no choice but to see the value their approach brings."

Justin Essink
Staff Accountant, West Coast CPA Group

Leaders Press

Published in the United States by Leaders Press.
www.leaderspress.com

ISBN **978-1-63735-220-5** (pbk)
ISBN **978-1-63735-221-2** (hcv)
ISBN **978-1-63735-222-9** (ebook)

Library of Congress Control Number: **2025917995**

THE FUTURE OF ACCOUNTING

Dave McComb and Cheryl Dunn, Ph.D.

Acknowledging Our Fact Checkers

We are indebted to the following people who have spent hours digging in and challenging the claims we made here. The version you have now has been considerably improved from the original draft thanks to their help.

Andreas Neumann
Freelance Catalyst, former IT Innovation Catalyst and
IT Architect, Siemens Energy

Dr. Willi Brammert
Managing Director, Ariadne Business Analytics

Alan Michaels
Director of Industry Research, Industry Knowledge Graph LLC and
Owner, Industry Building Blocks

Dr. Julia Smith David
Partner, Patheworks Consulting

Dr. Yaakov Belch
Senior Data Scientist, Semantic Thought Network

Dan Gschwend
Director, Data Sciences – Operations Data Strategy & Governance,
Amgen

William McCrea
Managing Director, Chief Data Officer, Franklin Square Holdings

Charles Hoffman
Co-Founder, TwinFox Platform, known as the Father of XBRL

Kelly Timmer
Affiliate Faculty of Accounting Practice, Grand Valley State University,
formerly VP-Finance – Hushpuppies & Chaco, Wolverine Worldwide

Philippe Höij
CEO and Co-founder, DFRNT

Dougal Watt
Co-founder, Graph Research Labs and Climate Tracker

Liam McGee
Founder & Chief Scientist, Kaiasm

Mark Van Berkel
Chief Technology Officer, Schema App

Michael DeBellis
Freelance AI Consultant

Dr. Phil Blackwood
Associate Ontologist, Semantic Arts

Dr. Michael Uschold
Senior Ontology Consultant, Semantic Arts

Dr. Peter Winstanley
Ontologist, Semantic Arts

Dr. Chris Harper
CPA, Assistant Professor of Accounting
Grand Valley State University, Senior Manager, Hungerford CPAs & Advisors, Co-owner, Capstone Investments, LLC

George Ibarra
Retired CFA, CPA, former Business Application Manager, Eide Bailly LLP

Dr. Dan O'Leary
Professor, University of Southern California Marshall School of Business and Leventhal School of Accounting

Geoffrey Goudy
Owner Operator, Geoffrey W. Goudy, CPA, LLC

Dan Carey
Expert Ontologist, Semantic Arts

We also express our deepest gratitude to the following individuals and teams for their invaluable contributions to this project:

Matt Faye, for your outstanding graphic design work, which brought a unique and professional visual identity to this project.

Editors and staff at Leaders Press, for your editorial expertise, guidance, and support throughout the publication process. Your dedication and professionalism were instrumental in bringing this work to fruition.

Table of Contents

Introduction

This book ushers in a sea change in the practice of accounting and the implementation of accounting systems. We are not tweaking the status quo. This book is the product of rethinking accounting from first principles. This is what accounting would look like if we designed it anew, based on what has been learned in information systems over the last 50 years.

Accounting systems, in the current state of the art, deliver historical information long after the fact and provide only a subset of the data needed for decision making. The **data-centric approach** we outline in this book delivers all the relevant information known to the organization, immediately, without manual intervention and adjustment.

A data-centric enterprise is one where all application functionality is based on a single, simple, extensible data model[1].

By applying data-centric principles to accounting—what we call *data-centric accounting*—organizations can vastly improve decision making and increase the likelihood of meeting budgets.

To date, we are not aware of any fully data-centric enterprises. We have worked with over a dozen firms who are on the journey towards becoming data-centric. One hurdle to becoming fully data-centric has been accounting, which is why we wrote this book.

This book is written for owners and managers who are interested in financial information that is more complete, more traceable, faster to obtain, and easier to verify.

For technologists seeking guidance on implementing data-centric accounting systems, we will publish a follow-on implementation guidebook, where you will be the target audience.

We hope this book will also appeal to accountants, though we pessimistically expect that many may be too invested in the status quo to welcome change. Please prove us wrong!

[1]McComb, D. (2019). *The Data-Centric Revolution: Restoring Sanity to Enterprise Systems*. Technics Publications.

Some readers will wonder, ***"Can't we just do this with GenAI and LLMs?"*** GenAI (generative artificial intelligence) and LLMs (large language models) will play a very important role in the future of accounting (and all) systems. However, starting with GenAI and LLM without getting your house in order will be a disaster.

Ambiguity is GenAI's kryptonite.

The more ambiguity (which is created by having multiple sources and versions of any data that contributes to the official accounting records), the more hallucination.

A Data-Centric Accounting Future

A day in the life of an employee in a data-centric firm looks a bit like this:

> Susan opens the daily financial reports for today (the 16th of the month) on her computer. She doesn't do this often—rapid-fire changes in real time are a bit distracting—but sometimes she just likes watching the revenue number ratchet up as the events of the day post to the big board. She switches it back to yesterday's financial report, which is stable. She thinks back to their prior system, where history was continually updated well into the next month, and realizes that if you capture an event as it enters the firm, there is rarely a legitimate need to post to prior dates.
>
> In her inbox is a note that the final project for a client requiring higher-level Cyber Insurance is complete. She might want to lower that coverage and therefore the premium.
>
> Looking at yesterday's financial statement (as of the 15th), she sees the insurance cost for yesterday and chuckles: *"Who would have thought that we could have all our expenses presented at a daily level, without any additional work? And in the old days, I'd be looking at last month's insurance expenses, not yesterday's."*
>
> She clicks on the expense, which takes her to a summary of the items that make up that amount: the E&O insurance, the Cyber Insurance, and the property insurance. As she is looking at the profit and loss for a single day, each line shows the insurance amount for that day, and a link to the policy summary and the actual policy. She looks at the Cyber line item, and the system tells her this month's premium was paid in full on the 10th (as planned) and that therefore the system is showing the second half of the month's premium as a *prepaid expense* on the balance sheet as of the 15th (without any human intervention). The insurance summary has a link to their broker, and she sends a request to reduce the coverage amount.

> She then notices a few discrepancies in the cost of goods on one of yesterday's orders. In the old days, she would have reviewed this through some flash report that was attempting to give an early warning to exceptions like this, but she reflects to herself how quaint that idea now seems. A quick review of everything else shows that things are in great shape. With that, she closes her laptop with the confidence that anything that could possibly have affected the firm has already been captured and reported. There is nothing in terms of the financial position to consider, and she can turn her attention to new business development and staff coaching.

If you are familiar with the current state of the art in accounting systems and accounting reporting, you know this is not what it looks like. Most accounting systems are a hodgepodge of partial solutions that need to be interfaced and reconciled, many of which exist merely to predict what the result will look like when the books finally get closed.

Why a Book Rather than a System

Entrepreneurs reading this intro might well ask, *"If this is such a good idea, why aren't you building a software system instead of writing a book?"*

Three main reasons: our ages, the need for verticality, and the context.

Both authors are near retirement age, and we have no illusions about the scope of what's outlined in this book. Funding, building, selling, and implementing systems based on the principles in this book will take considerable time.

As we will cover much later in the book, we know for data-centric accounting to achieve its maximum effectiveness, it will need to be tightly integrated in vertically-aligned, industry-specific systems. Current accounting systems are at least partially horizontal. That is, the same accounting system can often be used in many different industries. The accounting systems of the future will be intimately integrated with the business and therefore we believe they will be much more industry specific. That means there won't be a data-centric accounting system; rather, there will be dozens (or even hundreds) of them each targeted at different industries.

By context, we mean that the thinking in this book will be applied differently in different contexts. Each organization will build its own core knowledge graph, and its accounting will become a derivative of that.

The world has become used to *one-size-fits-all* application software, but we believe we're on the dawn of the opposite: **economical, bespoke systems.**

We are eager to see this possibility manifest.

Authors

Dave McComb built and implemented accounting systems in his days at Arthur Andersen. He is one of few people who have built two major custom ERP systems from the ground up (and in each case for less than comparable package implementations). More recently he has been helping clients redo their internal systems along the data-centric approach. Many of the concepts in this book are a result of a set of projects to implement data-centric at mid-sized professional services firms.

Cheryl Dunn is a professor of accounting at Grand Valley State University. Cheryl came to her insights regarding alternate ways of conceiving of accounting through three decades' study of REA (Resource Event Agents,[2,3]), a framework for designing enterprise databases capable of producing accounting reports and supporting many other business functions.

None of the content of this book, other than the enhancement of the cover art, was produced by GenAI.

[2]McCarthy, W.E. (1982). The REA accounting model: A generalized framework for accounting systems in a shared data environment. *The Accounting Review*, 554-578.

[3]Dunn, C., Gerard, G. J., & Grabski, S. V. (2016). Resources-events-agents design theory: A revolutionary approach to enterprise system design. *Communications of the Association for Information Systems*, 38(1), 29.

The Plan of This Book

The goal of this book is to help move the business—including government and non-profits—world from the current state, where accounting is an after-the-fact back-office operation, to a future where it is seamlessly integrated into the business itself.

The first two chapters set the stage; they introduce key vocabulary and describe the status quo as it is currently practiced.

We then transition to what will need to change, first describing the aspects of the status quo that will be retained and then noting those practices that will be discarded.

Almost all firms that adopt data-centric accounting will undergo a phased transition. Outside of a pure greenfield opportunity, it would be difficult to go directly to the proposed complete data-centric solution. Many of the concepts are new and novel, and existing systems won't have captured data in sufficient detail to import to the new system. In this book, we focus on the higher-level concepts of data-centric accounting; however, in a follow-on guidebook, we will suggest separate implementation phases.

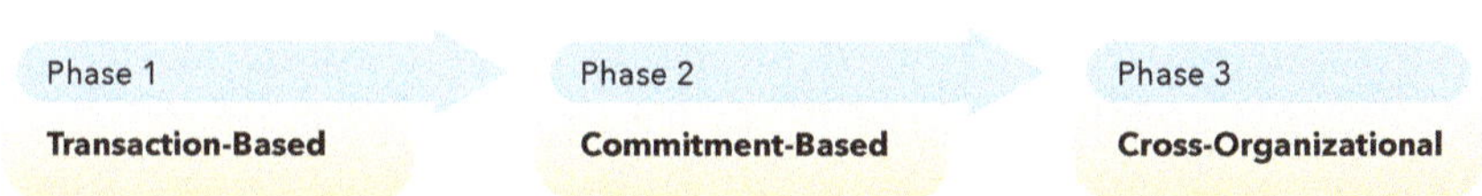

Figure 0.1: Typical Implementation Phasing

The first phase will retain many features familiar to traditional accounting systems, such as financial transactions and ledger accounts, thus accommodating data from existing systems and enabling further transition going forward. The second phase will incorporate accounting for commitments such as purchase orders and sale orders and improve accounting for economic events that occur over long periods of time while further discarding traditional artifacts. The third phase of data-centric accounting will facilitate multi-organizational settings, both for intercompany consolidated reporting and for firms to share definitions of financial commitments needed for smart contracts and more widespread supply chain sharing.

At this point, we expect many readers will find the concepts interesting but may have reservations as to how they will apply to their own unique circumstances. The last section of the book is meant to address many contextually different situations. We provide guidance on how data-centric accounting applies in different functional contexts (financial accounting versus management accounting versus tax accounting) as well as how it may vary from industry to industry.

Earlier drafts of this book had considerable information and guidelines for implementors. While we believe such guidance is important, we recognized that we have two distinct audiences—one focused on the core message and another seeking implementation details and guidance. As a result, we decided to split the earlier book into two. This book presents the motivation, core concepts, and expected benefits of data-centric accounting. A follow-on implementation guide will outline the recommended phased approach in detail.

With our plan in mind, let's turn to the status quo in accounting, starting with the most basic question: ***why do organizations do accounting in the first place?***

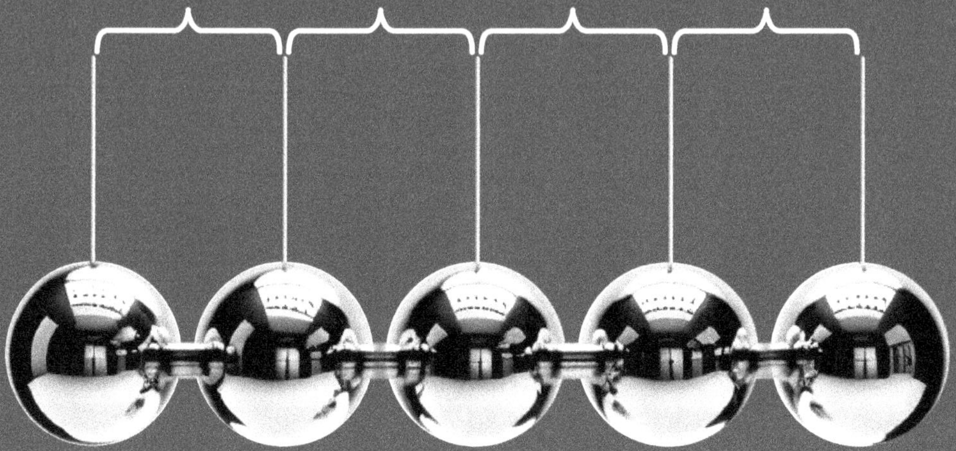

CHAPTER 1

Why Organizations Do Accounting

Sorry, but we have to do this. Before we dive deeper, we need to cover the key concepts in contemporary accounting—enough for you to fully understand the difference between traditional and data-centric accounting.

If you are not an accountant, this is likely far more than you wanted to know—but stick with us. This foundation is essential for understanding—and being able to articulate—the differences. You will need to be well-versed to stand up to the inevitable resistance you may face if you promote this idea within your organization.

If you are an accountant, you already know all this. We've simplified it, but we hope you'll agree that we have not made any egregious deletions in our trimming down the quite vast body of accounting knowledge into these few pages.

Why people "do" accounting

There are seven main reasons why people "do" accounting. These reasons have different motivations and constraints, in different settings. The relative importance of each of the seven varies a great deal from company to company, and it is the interplay of these motivations that shapes a lot of the specifics on how a given accounting system is implemented. Those seven are briefly:

1. Operational Accounting
2. Cash Management
3. Resource Valuation
4. Management and Incentive Setting for the Organization
5. Internal Control, Compliance, and Related Audits
6. Tax Minimization
7. Investor Reporting and Related Audits

1. Operational Accounting

The accounting department creates *things*. These are distinct from the *things* that the manufacturing department creates, which are often physical items such as widgets and gadgets. The accounting department creates *invoices* and *payments* and many similar things that are essential to running the organization. Operational accounting is one of the most fundamental activities of the accounting department. If you don't generate invoices and send them to your customers, you will soon run out of money. If you don't pay your suppliers, you soon won't have any suppliers.

While this is the most fundamental function the accounting department does, as we will see, this can be almost entirely automated. In most organizations, accounting feels far removed from the business events that generate its transactions, making the potential for automation hard to imagine. When we connect the dots, we will see ample opportunity to automate away most of this function.

2. Cash/Treasury Management

The accounting/finance area is tasked with predicting when cash will become available and when it will be needed. They augment this information with management of lines of credit for shortfalls or investments for surpluses. Cash management is one of the most important administrative functions in a company to ensure the ability to pay bills when they are due. Longer-term financing activities such as obtaining large loans or outside investors play into cash management but maintaining liquidity through short-term cash management is critical to any organization's success.

3. Resource Management and Valuation

Accountants are also active partners with other parts of the organization. Payroll is essentially a joint venture between the HR department and the accounting department. The accounting department needs to make sure that the cost of labor and all its burdens are properly reflected in the costs of products they manufacture. They work with operational groups such as inventory management and procurement and asset management to make sure resources are properly valued, depreciated, and protected by internal controls.

4. Management and Incentive Setting for the Organization

In any but the smallest of organizations, decision making needs to be delegated. Part of this delegation is keeping the scorecard for economic performance by the organization's various managers. Every manager could make up their own scorecard (and many do), but upper management rightly would like to have a standard way to compare different business units. They would like a scorecard that resembles the actual economic activity and value creation. This is often in the form of a departmental profit and loss statement.

The general term for this is *management accounting*, accomplished in many ways, as we'll see throughout this book and especially in Chapter 7. It is also called cost accounting partly because a significant objective within management accounting is determining accurate product costs and costs and allocations of overhead. Financial accounting (which is aimed more at investors) is far less interested in detailed cost breakdowns. Most of operational accounting that we discussed above requires very little sophistication. Invoices are based on list prices or contracts. Paying a bill requires little more than confirming its validity. But in management accounting, the complexities of accounting quickly come to the forefront. It's not enough to simply invoice a customer for the widgets you sold; you also need to know what those widgets really cost you. There are a host of issues that come along with this that we will be exploring throughout this book, including timing, valuation, classification, and the allocation of costs to various resources.

5. Internal Control, Compliance, and Related Audits

Many government agencies and jurisdictions have rules with which companies must comply. Some compliance covers non-accounting related tasks, such as quality and environmental concerns. But many compliance requirements are accounting related.

Compliance audits are often the first type of audit that most small to medium-sized companies encounter. Compliance audits may happen with respect to taxes; tax audits are occasionally necessary because often tax liability is self-reported. In this case, a tax auditor's job is to make an independent assessment of whether the information provided reflects events as they occurred.

As an organization grows, the opportunity for fraud grows, both internally and externally. One function of an internal audit department is to set up and monitor controls that minimize the possibility of fraud. Internal audit is often focused on making sure accounting controls are in place and regularly enforced.

6. Tax Minimization

The accounting function is in the best position to help the organization minimize its tax liability, which is the flip side of tax compliance. Once you have set your tax minimization strategy, you will still need tax compliance to report to the various jurisdictions.

Often strategies that minimize tax are only known to professionals who study such things. Tax accountants and tax attorneys stay abreast of current national, state, and local tax regulations and determine ways that organizations can legally minimize the amount of tax they will owe. Accelerating or postponing investments in selected types of funds or assets may affect the amount of tax owed. To adequately plan tax minimization strategies such as deciding whether to accelerate or postpone investments or discretionary expenditures, tax accountants must be able to predict with a reasonable degree of accuracy the organization's likely revenues and expenses for a given time period.

7. Investor Reporting and Related Audits

The US stock market crash in 1929 revealed the need for more accuracy and consistency in financial reporting to investors. The US Securities and Exchange Commission (SEC) was founded to protect investors from misconduct, to promote fairness and efficiency in securities markets, and to facilitate capital formation[4].

Many accounting textbooks start and end with investor reporting. This is the familiar process of compiling, vetting, and auditing a set of financial reports. The organization compiles and vets the financial reports and hires an external auditor to audit those reports. Third-party firms specialize in the practice of external audit, mostly

[4]www.sec.gov

for publicly traded companies, although private companies may need audited financial statements to satisfy some creditors. The external audit function executes procedures designed to determine whether the reported numbers accurately represent the organization's activity. Those auditors issue opinions about whether the companies' financial statements are prepared in accordance with relevant accounting standards. In the US, since the passage of SOX in 2002, external auditors also must issue opinions on the effectiveness of the companies' internal controls.

A closely held organization with one or a few investors can get by with very unsophisticated financial reports. The closely held organization is typically more interested in the first six of these accounting motivations. Even organizations that are not publicly traded have many reasons to embrace investor reporting with audited financial statements. You may be seeking outside investors. You may be applying for a loan, and the bank will undoubtedly expect to see sensible investor reports, including an auditor's opinion on the financial statements. Astute potential large customers may even request audited financial statements before committing to large contracts with you to ensure that you can deliver the contracted products, services, or payments.

Summary of Why Companies "Do" Accounting

The aforementioned represents our functional decomposition of why people do accounting. The accounting industry, however, tends to group things differently. You will often hear the distinction between *financial accounting* and *management accounting*: the former most focused on investor reporting, while the latter emphasizes internal reporting for cost containment, forming a subset of *management accounting* called *cost accounting*. What we called *operational accounting* is often referred to as *bookkeeping*. *Tax accounting* often covers both tax minimization and compliance with tax law. There is a discipline called *financial analysis*, which can be applied to either managerial or financial data and focuses on deeper drill-downs into the transactions often combined with other metrics. While our discussion emphasizes functional breakdowns, there are other common ways the field is divided.

These seven motivations summarize why companies have accounting departments. Each organization is different and will assign different weights to these aspects.

As we explore how companies traditionally do accounting, we will begin to see why some of these basic requirements are stymied.

CHAPTER 2

How Organizations Have Traditionally Done Accounting

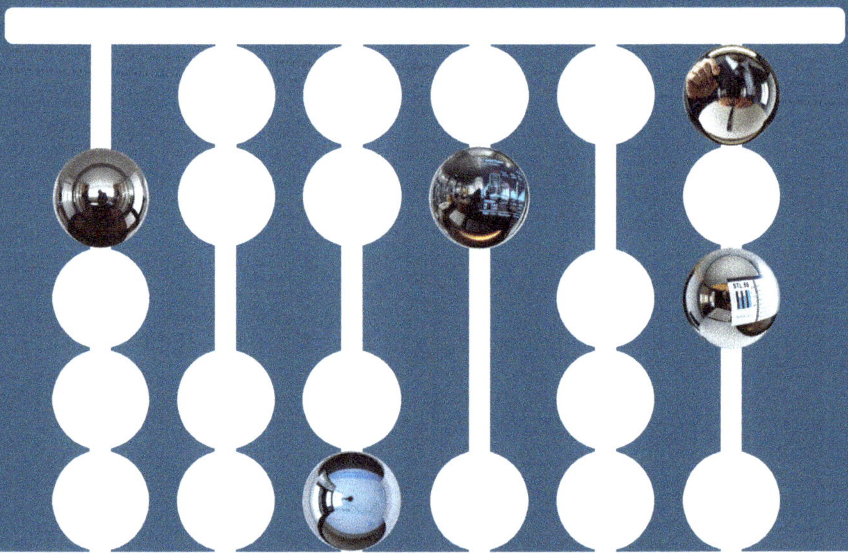

In most enterprises, accounting is a separate department. Things happen in the rest of the enterprise and eventually make their way to the accounting department. The accounting department has its own systems. These systems are sometimes fed automatically through a series of bespoke ***"system interfaces"*** often in ad hoc and partially manual interfaces. We will explore this in depth, because while having systems feed other systems may seem like a good idea at one level, at another level it is the problem.

In the book *Software Wasteland*[5], we describe an anti-pattern called ***application-centricity.***

An application-centric organization approaches each business problem independently and often implements a new application system to solve the problem at hand. While a new system may solve the immediate problem, it comes with a serious side effect. Each application system comes with its own data model. This is where the dreaded *data silos* come from. Each application database is an island unto itself. The *Systems Integration* industry represents the bridge builders in this world. Typically, 40 to 70 percent of an organization's IT budget is spent building and maintaining these very brittle interfaces. And even with all this effort, it is still difficult to get a holistic view of the enterprise.

But it doesn't have to be this way. We call the alternative ***the Data-Centric Approach*** and we describe it in more detail in *The Data-Centric Revolution*[6]. This book explains what happens when we shine the spotlight of data-centricity on the accounting function. But we're getting ahead of ourselves. First, we want to immerse you in the dismal state of most enterprise application systems.

[5]McComb, Dave. 2018. *Software Wasteland: How the Application-Centric Mindset is Hobbling Our Enterprises*. Technics Publications.

[6]McComb, Dave. 2019. *The Data-Centric Revolution: Restoring Sanity to Enterprise Systems*. Technics Publications.

Traditional Accounting System Architecture

At the most abstract level, an accounting system takes the events that occur in a business and converts them into the reports that can be used to satisfy the functions we described in the section, *Why People "Do" Accounting.*

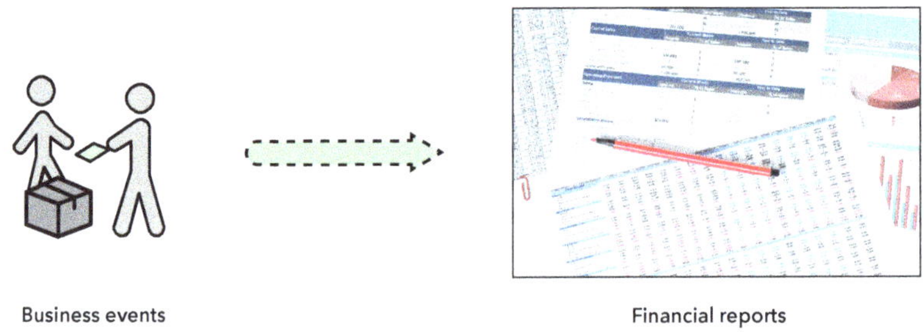

Figure 2.1: Accounting System Overview

This dotted arrow in Figure 2.1 glosses over the many twists and turns an event takes on its journey to its place in the financial reports. These financial reports, which we will detail below, are one of the prime deliverables from the accounting function.

Where do these financial reports come from? Most of them are created from something called the *General Ledger* or GL.
For hundreds of years, the GL was manually compiled and was known (and is still referred to) as "the books and records" of the organization, which is why we depict it as a pile of books here in Figure 2.2 (they aren't literally books anymore).

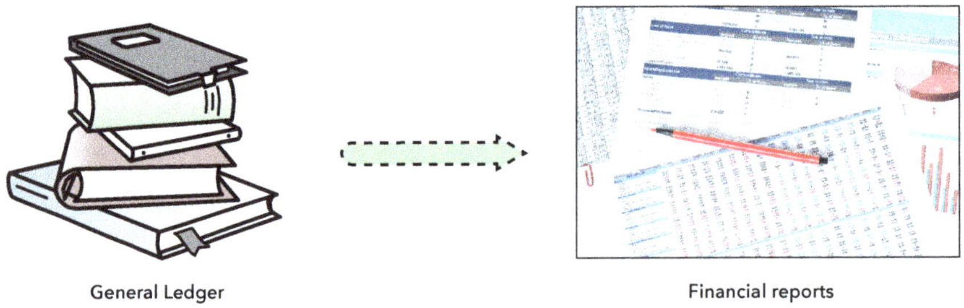

Figure 2.2: The Books and Records of the Organization

Financial reports are produced from the GL. Today, of course, the GL is compiled by software, but it still holds its position as the core of the accounting system.

The General Ledger (GL)

The general ledger is made up of *accounts*. Each account has a number (the general ledger account code) and a balance that reflects all the transactions that have been posted to this account.

You can think of each account as having a structure that is similar to a checking account transaction register (also known as a checkbook register). When you opened your checking account, your bank probably gave you one, even if you have never used it.

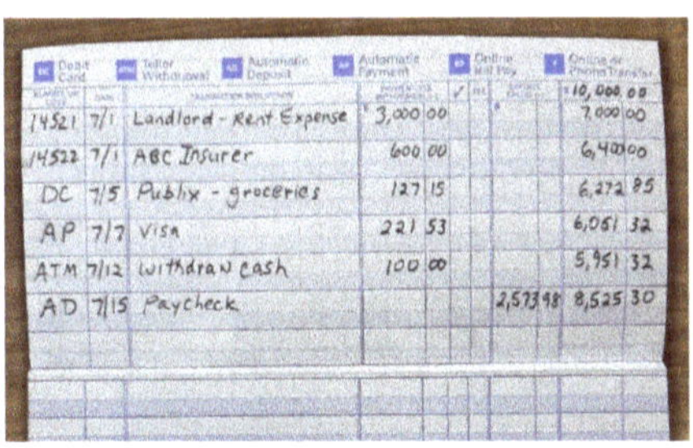

Figure 2.3: **A Checking Account Transaction Register, aka a Check Register**

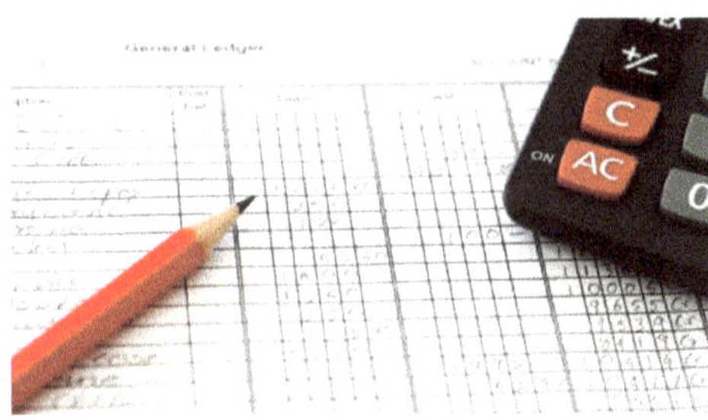

Figure 2.4: **Simple Ledger**

In a checking account transaction register, as shown in Figure 2.3, you record the initial deposit you make to open the account as the account's beginning balance. Then—usually in chronological order, though things occasionally get recorded out of sequence—you record every transaction that affects your checking account balance (increase or decrease) and keep a running balance of the account.

Similarly, each GL account has a beginning balance (initially zero), then transactions are posted to the account that increase and/or decrease its balance, and a running balance is kept for the account.

Accounts

An accounting system has a lot of these *accounts*. They are the bedrock of the traditional accounting system. It is admittedly a bit odd to think of accounting without accounts, but that is part of where we are going with data-centric accounting. If you know anything about accounting you may already be questioning the wisdom of this pursuit, but please stick with us as we make this case. We're not doing this lightly; we have decades of experience implementing and using traditional accounting systems, so this pivot did not come easily.

As we will elaborate in the data-centric chapters, there is a need for some *real accounts*. When you sell goods to one of your customers (customer A) and grant them credit (that is you allow them to pay you later), you need to set up an account for them. You need to keep track of how much they owe you. This is what we call a *real account*, there is a real need for this, it is essential.

But that account (customer A's account) is not in the General Ledger. It is in another system, or another module. The GL has just one account called *Accounts Receivable* that is (or should be) the total of all your customer accounts. Even without all these *real* accounts, the GL has a lot of accounts that it indexes in something called the *Chart of Accounts*. The Chart of Accounts essentially defines the level of granularity that you can report on, and as such, it can get quite voluminous and detailed.

The Chart of Accounts

A large organization will have thousands of accounts. Most of these are to make fine-grained distinctions in their financial reports. For instance, if one wished to distinguish between marketing expenses and advertising expenses (which the FASB provides for in its reference taxonomies), you must have two separate accounts for these types of expenses.

FASB is the Financial Accounting Standards Board, an organization that promotes standards for comparable financial reporting.

> **Marketing Expense** – "Expenditures for planning and executing the conception, pricing, promotion, and distribution of ideas, goods, and services. Costs of public relations and corporate promotions are typically considered to be marketing costs ."
>
> **Advertising Expense** – "Amount charged to advertising expense for the period, which are expenses incurred with the objective of increasing revenue for a specified brand, product or product line. " With this interesting disclosure example: "The Entity expenses the production costs of advertising the first time the advertising takes place. "

You can name (number) the two different accounts for the marketing and advertising expenditures whatever you want (although in a minute we will outline how almost everyone does it) and then you will map these accounts to line items as you'd like them to appear on your financial reports and assign the corresponding XBRL tags.

XBRL is the eXtensible Business Reporting Language, which is a standard that publicly traded firms in the US must use in their published financial reports.

The Chart of Accounts is the predefined set of accounts that are allowed. It is very much a controlled vocabulary; end users do not make up new accounts on the fly. In almost every case the Chart of Accounts is a taxonomy.

Taxonomy is a hierarchical arrangement of terms. Informal taxonomies, such as those used to find things on a website, have very few constraints. Formal taxonomies, including the Chart of Accounts, have a couple of important constraints. The first is that every lower-level term is a proper subset of the higher term. If our hierarchy starts with:

1000 Assets
1100 Cash | Then cash **is an** Asset.

The other constraint is that all terms are mutually exclusive and completely exhaustive, which prevents double counting and missing items at different levels of reporting.

The structure of the Chart of Accounts mirrors the structure of the key financial reports. The first level division is between balance or position accounts and flow accounts. The balance or position accounts represent the balances of the accounts at specific points in time. For instance, a specific bank checking account will have a meaningful balance as of a point in time. Flow accounts, by contrast, do not have meaningful balances in themselves; rather, their balances represent the total activity over a time duration. For instance, the marketing expense account is a flow account, showing how much was spent on marketing during a defined time frame—say, over the course of a year.

From these two broad categories of accounts emerges a second level of classification—one that is essential to understanding both financial reporting and the mechanics of debits and credits.

Balance Accounts

> **Assets** – each asset account will represent something of economic value that you own. It might be tangible, like inventory; intangible, like some intellectual property; or based on obligations owed to you – for example, accounts receivable. You may have accounts for individual assets—for example, many companies have an account for every bank account they own—or groups of assets, such as a single account for all their raw material.
>
> **Liabilities** – each liability account represents something you owe to someone else. If you have a mortgage, that is a liability – as is a credit card balance or an account called accounts payable, where your vendors have provided goods or services and allowed you to pay them later.
>
> **Equities** – these accounts represent the owners' interest in the organization. There will be capital accounts for all the investors' contributions. There are also accounts that represent the accumulated profit of the firm less any amounts distributed to owners (dividends or withdrawals). The undistributed profit of the firm ultimately accrues to the owners and is reflected here.

Flow Accounts

> **Revenue** – there will be accounts for all the distinctions you wish to make among the activity that generates income for the firm, for example, product sales and service revenues.
>
> **Expense** – there will be accounts for every distinction you wish to make on the expenditure side, such as the difference between marketing and advertising above.

There are many subtypes of these accounts, but these five are essential to understanding how debits and credits work, and how financial reports are constructed.

When the accounting department creates the organization's chart of accounts, they must decide how long the account numbers should be. By the way, there's no rule that says account codes must be numbers—but in almost every case we've seen, they are. And they follow a pattern very closely—all by convention, not by regulation. The pattern is this: the companies assign account numbers in a structured way that reflects account categories. A small company might use three-digit codes, while large firms use 6–8 (or more) digit codes. Once the length is set, the numbering usually follows this convention:

> **Assets →** typically start with "1." (e.g., bank accounts: 1101, 1102)
>
> **Liabilities →** typically start with "2." (e.g., Accounts Payable: 2101; Long-term Debt: 2501)
>
> **Equity →** typically start with "3." (e.g., Capital Contribution: 3101; Retained Earnings: 3201)
>
> **Revenue →** typically start with "4." (e.g., Product Revenue: 4101; Service Revenue: 4102)

> **Expenses →** usually start with "5" or higher. Many organizations use 5 for operational expenses (rent, labor, etc.) and 6-9 for non-operational expenses (financing costs, gains/losses, etc.).

The reason for numbers like 1101 and 1102 is that most accountants like to create their chart of accounts as an indented list, or tree. They also like the digits to line up, so 1100 is usually the parent of 1101 and 1102. *See Figure 2.5.*

```
        Chart of Accounts Excerpt
1000 Assets
      1100 Cash in Banks
            1101 Checking Account
            1102 Savings Account
2000 Liabilities
      2101 Accounts Payable
      2501 Long-term Debt
3000 Equity
      3100 Contributed Capital
            3101 Common Stock
            3102 Preferred Stock
      3301 Retained Earnings
4000 Revenues
      4101 Product Revenue
      4102 Service Revenue
5000 Operating Expenses
      5001 Rent Expense
      5002 Payroll Expense
6000 Non-Operating Expenses
      6001 Interest Expense
```

Figure 2.5: **Partial Indented Chart of Accounts**

The main motivation for this structure is to aid financial reporting, as we'll understand further in the following section.

The Coding Block

We introduced the numbering convention that most accountants use in the section called *The Chart of Accounts*. Accountants sometimes refer to these as the *natural accounts*, and depending on the size of the organization, they may range from three to eight digits long.

But that's just the starting point. Accountants typically tack on more numbers, resulting in what is often called the *coding block* with multiple fields to support other information needs. Any organization that is comprised of multiple legal entities (which includes all large organizations and most medium-sized ones) add a segment to represent which legal entity each account is associated with.

Government agencies and non-profit organizations have an additional consideration called *fund accounting*. Because their charters require that they segregate sources and uses of money into these fund categories, they usually add a fund field to their coding blocks.

There are usually fields for divisions and departments to support financial reporting along the lines of the organization. This is often supplemented with cost center fields. Sometimes companies put project or product information in their account coding blocks.

Here is an example with a 20-character coding block:

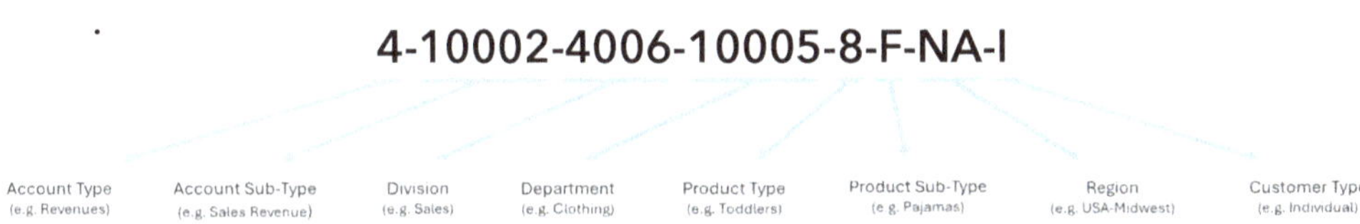

Figure 2.6: **A Large Coding Block**

The thus extended chart of accounts can get quite complex. And when you use the account code for these purposes, you end up needing to create additional transactions to move balances from one account to another to facilitate reporting.

We will employ several other techniques to get the same level of granularity without bloating the coding block. This is something a few more modern systems have already promoted, but we will be taking it much further.

Debits and Credits

Debits and Credits have been the bane of students in introductory accounting classes since the beginning of time (almost) – especially for those who are not accounting majors. Most accountants believe debits and credits are somewhere on the spectrum between necessary evil and essential components. They are neither. They are neither necessary nor essential in any fashion. We have postponed the full discussion of this to our implementation handbook (partly because there are some other implementation-related decisions that flavor the exact way you replace debits and credits) but suffice it to say, they are only needed to understand how traditional accounting works. We will try to make this brief.

In the internal implementation of all major accounting systems, there are actually no stored debits or credits. There is one column with an amount. If that amount is positive, it will typically be portrayed as a debit on reports and displays. If the number is negative, it will typically be multiplied by -1 (to make it positive) and portrayed as a credit on reports and displays.

We will explain the current use of debits and credits in the context of a report called the **Trial Balance**.

The Trial Balance

There is an accounting report which is rarely presented to anyone outside the accounting department called the *trial balance*. It is useful in this pedagogic context in that it can bridge us from the world of debits and credits into the world of financial reports.

The trial balance is simply a list of each account and its balance. If you have 1,000 accounts, this report will have 1,000 lines and therefore be more than 20 pages long. The only other thing the trial balance does is that it separates the account balances into debit and credit columns. Positive numbers are shown in the debit column, and negative numbers are multiplied by -1 and shown in the credit column.

If you look at the first part of a trial balance in figure 2.7, the balance sheet accounts (the assets, liabilities and equity) probably look reasonable to you. Assets normally have positive balances. Usually, your checking account is not overdrawn, and it is very hard to have negative inventory. Because assets are usually positive, they show up as debits.

Trial Balance
As of Jan-31

	Debit	Credit
1101 Unity Bank Checking	32,135	
1102 Worldwide Bank Savings	89,167	
1105 Accounts Receivable	63,128	
1501 Land	36,800	
1511 Buildings	1,572,830	
1512 Equipment	212,896	
2101 Accounts Payable		10,734
2104 Salaries Payable		27,319
2121 Deferred Revenue		43,125
2501 Long-term Debt		531,265
3101 Capital Contributions		1,180,390

Figure 2.7: **First Part of a Trial Balance**

The liabilities probably also make sense to you. You owe someone money. The amount owed is represented in the system as a negative amount and shows in this report as a credit. The equity accounts may look odd to you. The money you contributed to your company—that stock you bought—shows up as a negative number, and therefore a credit on the trial balance.

Keep in mind that the money invested was actually represented in the cash account as a debit, but it is mixed with all the other cash and is indistinguishable from the cash from other sources. The credit side of the transaction, contributed capital, shows as a credit balance because it represents the claim you have because of contributing the capital. Accountants like to think of the asset side of the balance sheet as the assets (of course), and the liabilities and equity side of the balance sheet as the claims against those assets. The liabilities represent claims creditors have because they sold goods or services to the company on credit or because they loaned money to the company. The equity accounts represent the claims owners have because of the investment they made in the company. To be clear, though, these are theoretical claims. Creditors' claims take precedence over owners' claims, and if a company's operations are discontinued and its assets are liquidated, nothing may be left for owners. In fact, even creditors' claims may not be fully satisfied if the company was bankrupt.

3201 Retained Earnings		111,133
4101 Product Revenue		198,301
4102 Service Revenue		1,402,938
5101 Salaries Expense	655,565	
5103 Cost of Goods Sold	108,521	
5104 Insurance Expense	118,306	
5105 Advertising Expense	23,158	
5111 Payroll Tax Expense	72,112	
5195 Depreciation Expense	446,432	
5201 Income Tax Expense	44,139	
6101 Interest Income		2,310
6102 Gains on Sales of Long-term Assets		7,986
7101 Interest Expense	37,189	
7102 Losses on Sales of Long-term Assets	3,123	
	3,515,501	3,515,501

Figure 2.8: **Rest of a Trial Balance**

The trial balance for the flow accounts is where it really gets weird. As you can see in figure 2.8, which completes the trial balance started in the previous figure, revenue is a negative number in the system and therefore shows up as a credit. Expenses are positive in the system and therefore show up as debits. That may seem counterintuitive to you—especially as profit is calculated by subtracting the expenses from the revenues. Mathematicians will note that subtracting positive numbers from negative numbers always results in numbers that are even more negative. This may dissuade mathematicians from ever going into business! Fear not! Revenues are not actually negative—they are simply stored that way because of the effect they have on the retained earnings equity account. Because revenues increase equity, they have credit balances like the equity accounts have. Similarly, expenses are not actually positive—they are simply stored as debits because they decrease equity (retained earnings) and thus must have the opposite kind of balance. In simple terms, profit is just revenues minus expenses, where both are treated as absolute values.

We must make one more point here. We have flow accounts with balances. In an earlier section, we said they couldn't have meaningful balances. They don't—and they won't—show up in any other reports like this. But again, the trial balance is an internal report used to make sure the books are in balance.

What actually happens—as we'll see in the financial reports section—is that reports on flow accounts subtract the difference between these "balances" over time, to get a flow.

Financial Reports – Balance Sheet

The balance sheet is a report, at a moment in time, of the balances in the balance accounts. It is derived from the accounts in the trial balance, but usually at a higher level (most people prefer balance sheets that fit on one or two pages.)

Balance Sheet
As of Jan-31

Assets	
Current Assets	
Cash	$830,000
Receivables	350,000
Total Current Assets	1,180,000
Non-Current Assets	
Equipment (net of Depreciation)	440,000
Total Non-Current Assets	440,000
Total Assets	$1,620,000
Liabilities	
Current Liabilities	
Credit Cards	$30,000
Accounts Payable	470,000
Total Current Liabilities	500,000
Long-Term Liabilities	
Loans	770,000
Total Long-Term Liabilities	770,000
Equity	
Common Stock	210,000
Retained Earnings	140,000
Equity	350,000
Total Liabilities + Equity	$1,620,000

Figure 2.9: Balance Sheet

This report summarizes, at a moment in time, the value of the organization's assets, liabilities, and equity. There may have been dozens or even hundreds of accounts that rolled up to the line item called *cash*.

At this point we get our first glimpse at the "Accounting Equation." The accounting equation states, and subsequent application of policy ensures, that Assets = Liabilities + Equity.

Financial Reports – Income Statement

The Income Statement financial statement, and thus the income statement accounts, are meant to communicate a company's profitability over a date range. Income statement accounts are called flow accounts because they do not really have meaningful balances. To create an income statement report, you first must supply the beginning and ending dates you are interested in, say January 1 – January 31. Perhaps you brought in $700,000 of revenue in January. That is not really a balance. Hopefully the $700,000 eventually made its way to your bank account, and when it hit there (say in February) it will have increased the bank account balance by that amount (perhaps from $800,000 to get to $1,500,000). If you sell nothing in February, your revenue for February will be $0, but your balance in the checking accounts will still be $1,500,000 (provided nothing else happened).

Income Statement
From Jan 1 - Jan 31

Revenue	
Sales Revenue	$650,000
Service Revenue	50,000
Total Revenue	700,000
Cost of Revenue	
Cost of Goods Sold	365,000
Cost of Services Provided	10,000
Total Cost of Revenue	375,000
Gross Margin	325,000
Operating Expenses	
Sales & Marketing	70,000
Depreciation	40,000
Occupancy	10,000
Insurance	15,000
Operating Expenses	135,000
Operating Income	190,000
Other Income (Expense)	
Interest Expense	(50,000)
Net Income	$140,000

Figure 2.10: **Income Statement**

Figure 2.10 shows a simple income statement. The numbers in this report represent the sum of activity that occurred over the period of time noted in the statement's heading (in this case, the month of January), and not the cumulative balances in the line items' accounts.

As we discussed earlier, the revenue is negative in the system and recorded as a credit in the trial balance, but because virtually no one wants to see it shown as a negative number, the report writer reverses these amounts for presentation purposes. There are conventions for how this is presented to minimize the appearance of negative numbers on these reports, though they do appear occasionally.

Financial Reports – Statement of Cash Flows

There are two other key financial reports that are required for publicly traded companies and encouraged for others. They are the statement of cash flows and the statement of changes in equity.

Statement of Cash Flows
From Jan 1 - Jan 31

Cash Flows from (for) Operating Activities	
Net Income	$140,000
Depreciation Expense	40,000
Increase in Receivables	(350,000)
Increase in Credit Cards and A/P	500,000
Total Cash from (for) Operating Activities	330,000
Cash Flows from (for) Investing Activities	
Purchase of Equipment	(480,000)
Total Cash from (for) Investing Activities	(480,000)
Cash Flows from (for) Financing Activities	
Issue Stock	210,000
Borrow from Bank	770,000
Total Cash from (for) Financing Activities	980,000
Net Increase (Decrease) in Cash	830,000
Cash Balance at Jan 1	-
Cash Balance at Jan 31	$830,000

Figure 2.11: Statement of Cash Flows

The statement of cash flows is less useful than it sounds and curiously hard for traditional systems to produce. All businesses need to track cash carefully—it is the life blood of any organization, profit or non-profit.

The reason we say this report isn't so useful is that it provides historical information produced long after the fact. It is a "just so" story about where the cash came from and where it went. If your operation is losing money on a cash basis, you need to explain where you got the cash to keep going. Was it from debt or investors?

To be more useful, cash reports should be forward-looking. Running any kind of organization is about predicting when and how much cash you will need in the future.

The reason we say traditional systems struggle to produce statements of cash flow is because they were not set up for this. Companies typically "back into" the statement of cash flows by analyzing changes in accrual accounts (explained below) and inferring from those changes what must have happened to cash. Such preparation is called the indirect method, and it is the most common approach. The direct method, on the other hand, reports separately each common operating activity source and use of cash—for example, cash received from customers, cash paid to employees, and so on. This often requires a duplicate set of transactions, stored separately from the GL-based system, to build up the cash positions directly.

Financial Reports – Statement of Changes in Equity

Depending on the business, some are very interested in changes in owners' equity.

Statement of Changes in Equity
From Jan 1 - Jan 31

	Contributed Capital	Retained Earnings	Total Equity
Balances at Jan 1	$0	$0	$0
Issuances of Common Stock	210,000	-	210,000
Net Income	-	140,000	140,000
Dividends	-	-	-
Treasury Stock Purchases	-	-	-
Balances at Jan 31	$210,000	$140,000	$350,000

Figure 2.12: **Statement of Changes in Equity**

Changes in owners' equity are a combination of economic activity (profit) and various capital account transactions (issuing of stock, stock buybacks, dividends, stock options, stock splits, etc.).

Journal Entries

We've covered the main financial reports and how they are derived from the account ledgers. Now the question is: how did the ledgers get updated?

Where do the GL Accounts get their balances?

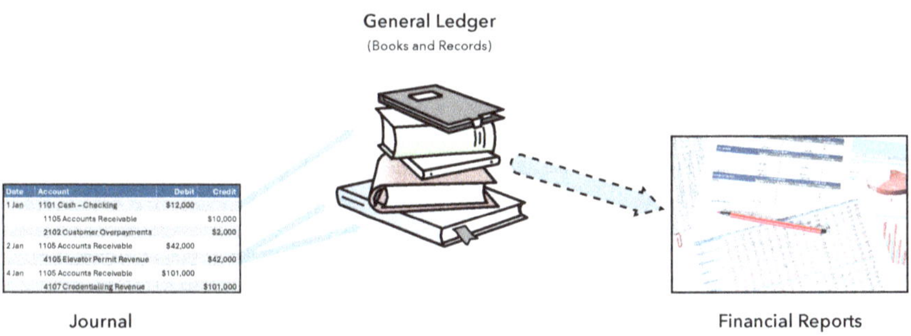

Figure 2.13: **Journal Entries to GL**

In the days of manual bookkeeping, there was a single chronological journal called the General Journal, where all activity entered the accounting department. Each entry in the journal was copied into a journal entry and later posted to the relevant ledger accounts. This process included what is called "double entry accounting." It is called double entry because each journal entry must have at least one debit and one credit line item (and they must balance). Today, the process is essentially the same. While there is usually no single chronological journal, transactions now flow in from source systems or are entered interactively by bookkeepers, the underlying mechanics remain unchanged.

Each atomic transaction is called a Journal Entry and consists of two or more line items, which we will refer to as the Journal Entry Line Items.

Each Journal Entry Line Item is applied to the balance of a separate General Ledger account, in a process called posting. When the journal posts, each account's balance has been updated.

Subsidiary Ledgers/Subledgers

Most accounting activity does not happen in the GL. The GL is often just the summary of activity recorded elsewhere. That "elsewhere" might be another accounting system, a module within an "integrated" system, or even a non-accounting system that generates financial side effects. We call this latter type source systems, and we'll cover them in the next section.

A subsidiary ledger (also called a subledger) is a detailed set of account balances that summarize to a single account on the GL. The larger companies get, the more they rely on subledgers and source systems to handle much of the actual accounting heavy lifting.

A company might nominate one GL account—say, account number 1200, to summarize all accounts receivable. That account's balance should be the sum of all unpaid customer invoices for which the company has earned revenue and expects payment. Most organizations create an accounts receivable subsidiary ledger (also called an AR subledger) in which they store the individual customer accounts. The subledger is a set of individual accounts that make up the balance of the "control" account in the GL. The subledger account numbers are typically customer IDs and have nothing to do with the account structure in the GL.

The distinction we want to make here is that these subsidiary ledger systems were conceived and implemented as accounting systems. They typically appear to have debits and credits and may be either tightly or loosely integrated with the GL.

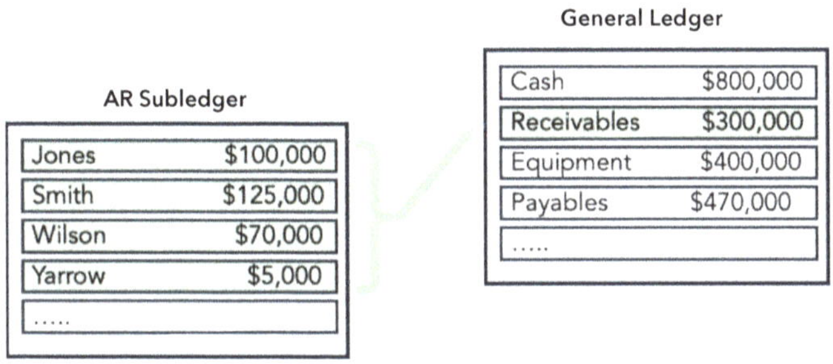

Figure 2.14: Subsidiary Ledgers

If all journal entries have been made and posted correctly, the sum of all individual account balances in a subledger should equal the corresponding "control" account in the GL. For example, the Accounts Receivable (AR) subledger should sum to the balance in the Accounts Receivable control account—GL account number 1200.

Other common subledgers include Accounts Payable (with an account summarizing unpaid bills for each supplier from whom the enterprise buys goods or services on credit), Inventory (with an account for each type of product), Equipment (with an account for each individual item), and Employees (with an account for each employee).

Source Systems

In today's modern systems, we don't typically see paper journals; instead, we see transaction files for which the totals are posted as journal entries into an electronic general journal. These transaction files often come from source systems. That is, the transactions and all their details are stored in the source systems and only the relevant totals are captured in a journal entry that is posted to the GL.

The difference between a source system and a subledger is that the subledger is typically part of an accounting system, under the purview of the accounting department. It understands debits and credits and is fairly easy to integrate. A source system, on the other hand, was usually built for non-accounting purposes but can generate transactions that, with a bit of systems-integration wizardry, turn out to have accounting implications.

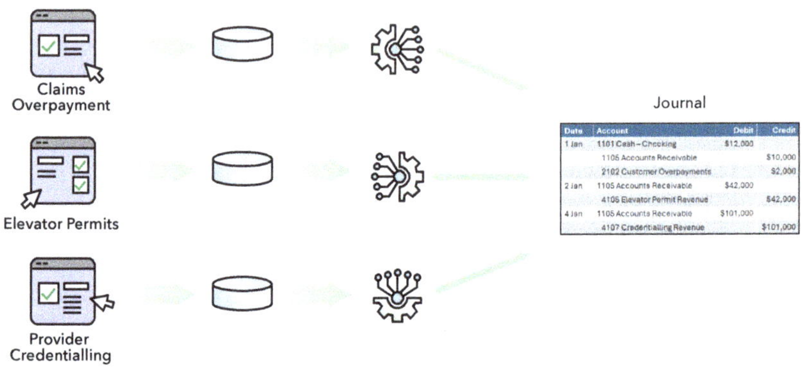

Figure 2.15: **Source Systems**

In this example, three source systems give off updates that are conformed and fed to the accounting system journal, from which they are posted to the GL.

This example is loosely based on a workers' compensation insurance client of ours who discovered, after some analysis, that they had 23 different systems that generated transactions functionally equivalent to invoices—though almost none of them called them invoices.
In one case it was claims overpayment, in another physician credentialling, in another elevator permits. Each system fed not only these invoice-like transactions but also related items such as cash receipts, and write-offs, into the accounting system as journal entries to be posted to the GL.

Financial Data Warehouse

Very often, companies also maintain a financial data warehouse. This warehouse is populated with an extract from the GL and organized in a way that makes ad hoc analysis simpler.

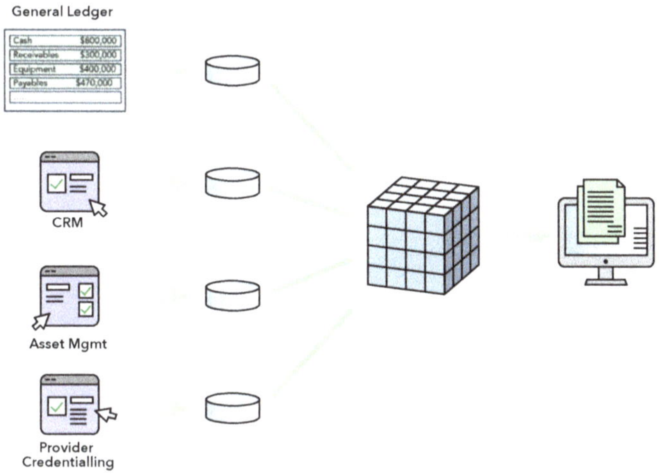

Figure 2.16: An ETL Process

Frequently, the financial data warehouse is combined with other operational systems and metrics databases, enabling more interesting Business Intelligence reporting and dashboards.

ETL (Extract Transform and Load) is the predominant technique for getting data from one application system to another.

The process of getting data from the GL (and other source systems) is called ETL—Extract, Transform, and Load. The data is extracted from where it is, converted (transformed) into a format suitable for the data warehouse, and then loaded into the data warehouse.

They often create *data cubes* which are *n-dimensional* structures which allow analysts to *slice and dice* information in many ways. Most of these reporting platforms include sophisticated graphics and interactive dashboards.

Many management accounting reports are generated from the data warehouse and rely on detailed transaction records rather than account balances, since managers often need to drill down into the details to explore the causes of exceptions.

Financial Reporting System

Some basic reporting can be done directly from the GL. As organizations get larger, they generally adopt more and more sophisticated financial reporting systems. Initially these are data warehouses that specialize in financial reporting, similar to the financial data warehouse described earlier.

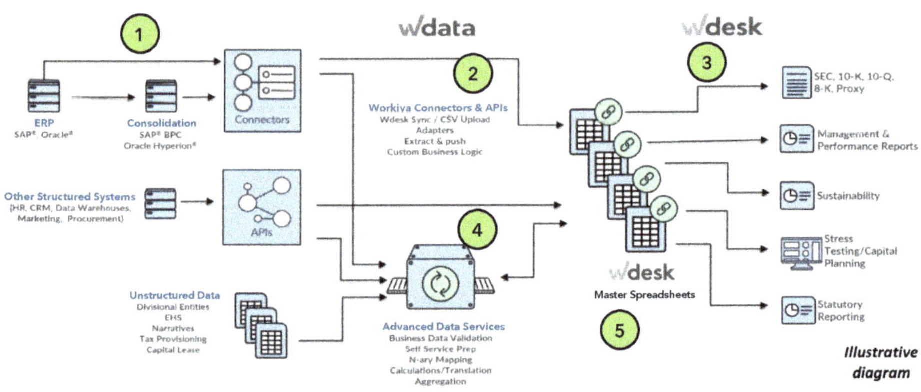

Figure 2.17: **A Financial Reporting System**[7]

Figure 2.17 is meant to hint at the complexity typical of large organizations. Dozens of systems and countless numbers of spreadsheets are orchestrated (using workflow software and a lot of manual intervention) to produce the published financial reports.

This graphic, from Deloitte, shows a workflow based on Workiva, a product many publicly traded companies use to organize the assembly of their financial reports. There are suites of tools to help with the many new requirements.

[7]Deloitte. Unlocking Potential: How Workiva Enhances an ERP Migration. 2024. PDF. https://www.deloitte.com/content/dam/assets-zone3/us/en/docs/services/risk-advisory/2024/us-advisory-unlocking-potential-how-workiva-enhances-an-erp-migration.pdf

Balancing the Books

In a paper-based system, it is essential to do a process called *balancing the books* to make sure there haven't been any clerical errors introduced in posting and transposing entries. Even early automated systems were prone to the occasional dropping or mis-posting of a transaction.

Modern systems have been designed to prevent these types of problems. Old habits die hard. Accountants still like to reassure themselves that the sum of all the debits in the organization is equal to the sum of all the credits. They do this by producing the trial balance report described earlier. This is a ritual. With modern systems, the books always balance.

Closing the Books

Closing the books is a monthly ritual for some companies, though many close their books only quarterly or annually.

The first part of the closing ritual involves rounding up and entering any outstanding transactions that might affect the period being closed. Classically, this includes hectoring employees to get their time reports and expense reports forwarded and entered. It also includes making sure that any last-minute vendor bills are entered into the system. This part of the process often involves summarizing and reconciling all the subledgers to the GL to ensure their balances agree and making sure all source system integration points have been run.

The second part is necessary because of a number of batch processes that depend on complete data. There are adjusting entries, reversing entries, depreciation calculations, and allocations that are more easily done once at the end of the month. These are often done with scripts and memorized journal entries.

The third part is the literal closing, which means closing the income statement to the balance sheet. There is a balance sheet account called *Retained Earnings* which represents the inception to date net income for the organization less dividends paid to date. Every year (and for some organizations, every quarter or every month), the accountants enter a journal entry to move the income and dividends for the period from the income statement and dividend accounts to the Retained Earnings account.

The fourth part involves extracting the data from the GL and loading it to the data warehouse or other reporting platform and doing some quick checks to make sure everything looks reasonable. Once the accountants approve the results, the mechanical procedures of transferring the temporary account balances to retained earnings closes the previous accounting period so that no subsequent transactions can change the published, or soon to be published data.

Some organizations add additional procedures to their monthly close, such as bank reconciliations or billing—if done monthly—to ensure bills are recorded in the correct period. Many also still prepare the aforementioned trial balance.

The closing process tends to take about 10-15 days in most organizations.

Organizations will launch projects to trim that number down a bit every few years, but it tends to creep back up.

Two major problems make this lengthy close particularly pernicious. First, it is a universally accepted evil. Everyone seems to think it must be this way. Second, managers are running portions of the company using data that is 10 to 70 days old. Even a fresh report produced immediately after the close reflects events from the previous month—beginning 40 days ago and ending 10 days ago. If a decision must be made on day 9 of the month, you will only have accounting reports for the month before, which will be 40 to 70 days old. The net result is a cottage industry of flash reports and shadow IT systems, giving managers access to more recent data for real-time decisions. The downside is that these reports are never fully aligned with the authorized books and records—they rely on guesses and approximations.

Sneak preview: in a data-centric enterprise, the closing process will be unnecessary. There will be no need for flash reports or shadow IT, because the official books will be as current as any ad hoc report.

Mechanics to Policy

The above has been a reasonably complete and representative description of the mechanics, the "how" of traditional accounting. Another layer involves the policies and decisions that go on in traditional accounting systems. From the outside, some of this appears mysterious, as if it involves some secret knowledge. But as we break it down, we'll see how much can be automated. It's not quite as obvious as the side bar with Nancy, but it is not impenetrable either.

Interviewer: So, Nancy, what is your role in the ordering process?

Nancy: I am the interface between Sales and the work center that delivers services.

Interviewer: As the interface, what do you do?

Nancy: I process the orders.

Interviewer: How do you process the orders?

Nancy: I get the order in my email, add the billing code, and forward the order to the work center.

Interviewer: Could someone else do that step?

Nancy: No.

Interviewer: Why is that?

Nancy: They wouldn't know what billing code to put on the order.

Interviewer: How do you know what billing code to use?

Nancy: It's always "001."

Collectively, everything that follows in this chapter falls under a broader topic of *policy*, though there are different aspects of policy that must be understood separately.

Revenue and Expense Recognition

Not everything that the organization buys is an immediate expense. When the organization buys raw material, it is posted to a raw material asset account on the balance sheet. As the material is used in a product, its cost becomes part of the product's cost, and at the time of sale, is recorded as the expense called *Cost of Goods Sold* on the income statement.

This idea of *recognition* is so central to accounting policy that we are going to repeat ourselves a bit here.

This determination as to whether and when a transaction affects the income statement is called recognition.

This has a profound effect on reported net profit. *Revenue recognition* (under what circumstances and at what time the organization posts sales on the income statement) and *expense recognition* (when expenses are charged to the income statement) play key roles.

There is a great deal of variety across industries and organizations, although all publicly traded companies must comply with the relevant accounting standard for their jurisdiction[8].

These standards attempt to provide greater uniformity in revenue recognition, to improve comparability across companies and industries. Greatly simplified, they require companies to recognize revenue once they have fulfilled all—or virtually all—of their obligations for earning it, regardless of whether the customers have fulfilled their corresponding obligations. For companies with especially long earnings cycles (such as construction), partial revenue may be recognized as they fulfill parts of their obligations. For most companies, the revenue recognition standard boils down to recognizing revenues when they ship goods or when they provide services.

Determining the internal rules for revenue and expense recognition is a key part of an organization's accounting policy.

[8]ASC 606 for those following US GAAP, IFRS 15 for those following International GAAP or similar standards in other countries' accounting principles.

Accounting Policy

An organization's accounting policy is the sum total of its own written policies—policies adapted from standards boards, guidelines, norms, and procedures that the organization has adopted in order to best and most consistently report on the financial activities of the organization. The policy is ultimately expressed in application software configuration, the organization of the chart of accounts, the mapping of accounts to financial statement line items, and the assignment of transactions to account numbers. The policy is executed by accountants using their judgement in the way they initially record transactions and also in the many adjustments and allocations they make later.

The most significant accounting policy area concerns the recognition of revenue and expense, as described in the previous section. Other key policy areas include:

> How **inventory** is costed to determine COGS (Cost of Goods Sold).
>
> How **direct labor** is applied to finished products, also for determining COGS.
>
> How **property**, **plant**, and **equipment** are depreciated (which is how capital expenditures are recognized as expense on the income statement over time).
>
> How **intangible assets** are amortized (another example of recognizing capital expenditures as expense on the income statement over time).
>
> How **subsidiaries** are consolidated when providing consolidated financial statements.

We've spent some time on accounting policy because, as you'll see later in this book, one of our intents is to automate the execution of these policies.

Cash-Basis Accounting versus Accrual Accounting

You may have heard the terms *cash-basis accounting* and *accrual accounting*. These are policy differences for the recognition of revenue and expense.

Cash-basis accounting essentially records revenue and expense on the income statement when cash is received or paid. This is simple. But it often delays profit, as many businesses incur expenses before they sell their goods and services, and sales made on credit can delay cash receipts by one to three months. For this reason, small- to medium-sized organizations may elect to calculate tax liability on a cash basis. Delayed profit recognition delays tax liability, which is consistent with IRS's (Internal Revenue Service, the US tax authority) goal for companies to have the wherewithal to pay the taxes they owe.

A downside of cash-basis accounting is that it makes it hard to evaluate an organization's economic activity, since revenue and expenses often show up in different periods—sometimes in different months, or even different years. To address this, accountants created accrual accounting, which attempts to align revenue and expense to the period they were earned and incurred, regardless of when the cash was received or paid.

Most companies use accrual accounting for their internal and investor reporting, and if permitted, cash accounting for tax reporting. This creates two interesting reconciliation problems that we will take up in the next sections, but let's dive in a bit on the mechanisms that enable accrual basis accounting.

Accrual Accounting Based on Different Events

Because they are no longer using cash-based events to post results on their income statements, companies must choose other events to trigger recognition, appropriate to their industry. For many industries, the event of shipping a product or delivering a service triggers revenue recognition, and, conversely, the event that signals the receipt of a product or service triggers expense recognition.

In many situations, organizations do not capture an explicit receipt event—this is especially true of services. A close proxy that most small- and medium-sized organizations use is the sending of an invoice to a customer, or the receiving of an invoice from a vendor. To avoid overloading the term *invoice*, for the rest of this book, we are going to refer to the receiving of an invoice from a vendor as receiving a *bill*. Usually, the invoice or bill is close enough in time to the actual delivery that it doesn't make much difference.

Recording the receipt of goods or services—or receiving a bill for them— doesn't create much extra work for accountants. We cover what happens when these events fall out of order in an upcoming section, *Timing Problems*.

Matching Principle

First, let's pick up one more accounting concern that comes up when you ship a product (and in some cases, when you deliver a service). When you sell, ship, and invoice a $1,000 widget (and let's assume you did all three on the same day, as sometimes happens), that is certainly $1,000 of revenue—but is it $1,000 of profit? No. You either bought or built that widget prior to making the sale, and that widget cost you something.

Let's go with the simplest possible case and assume that this is the only widget you have, and that you bought it last month for $700. You want to post a $700 expense in the same period as the revenue. This will show that you had $300 profit for the period. This aligning of the revenue and the cost of the corresponding goods is called the *matching principle*.

This is the essence of accrual accounting. It can get a lot more complicated, but this will be sufficient for the points we're about to make.

Accounting Standards

Investors and creditors rely on financial reports. For them to be comparable, they must be held to some common standards. There are many standards organizations and, of course, companies in different industries are subject to various regulatory guidelines and standards. In the US, the overarching guidelines are called GAAP (Generally Accepted Accounting Principles), which is published by the Financial Accounting Standards Board (FASB). Jurisdictions outside the US have either adopted local variations of GAAP or another standard called IFRS (International Financial Reporting Standards) from the International Accounting Standards Board (IASB).

GAAP and IFRS set the rules for classifying and reporting financial information on financial reports. External auditors perform the final quality assurance on the processes and results that produced these reports.

All organizations must develop their own accounting policy to comply with the accounting standards that govern their jurisdiction and industry.

US GAAP and IFRS

Corporations that offer shares of stock for sale to the public are subject to government regulations that require them to publish financial reports that comply with standards adopted by the country(ies) in which the corporations do business. Two of the most common are US GAAP and IFRS; however, other countries have their own versions of GAAP. Interestingly, these standards apply to the information to be reported to the public and do not require specific accounting system mechanics.

Simulating Flow

Your accounting policy will help determine whether a transaction should be recognized, and therefore, whether it should hit your income statement. Recall, the income statement is meant to represent activity over time. But there is an interesting problem in the middle of this. Traditional accounting systems are 100 percent based on transactions which occur at a point in time. More precisely, each transaction (each Journal Entry from above) has an *effective accounting date*. The effective accounting date posts the transaction as of that date. In the example earlier about marketing and advertising expenses, we saw that the standard permits booking the entire advertising campaign on the date of the first ad placement. While this might be advantageous, it is counter to the matching principle. If you put a year's worth of advertising expense in January, that month's P&L is going to look terrible, while the rest of the year is going to look better than it really is.

Effective Accounting Date: The date on a Journal Entry that determines in what accounting period that transaction will occur. You can enter a transaction on March 15 with an effective date of April 1 or February 1 (if appropriate and the books haven't been closed). It is this date that drives all reporting.

This is because traditional systems talk about flow in the income statement, but only in the broadest terms, with just a few very manual ways to simulate *flow*.

Many expenses are incurred over time but paid for at a moment in time. This can create a problem for the income statement. If you pay for a year's insurance—or even a year-long magazine subscription—on a single date, any report that includes that date will show the full year's expense. Reports that do not include that date, meanwhile, will not get any of that expense (understating profit in the first case, overstating it in the latter case).

For transactions that are *material*, there is an accounting procedure to correct for this.

In accounting, *material* means approximately—of sufficient magnitude to make a difference to anyone who is relying on accuracy of the reports.

In the above case, the magazine subscription is likely immaterial and will just land in whatever accounting period it was posted in. The insurance might be a material expense, in which case accountants will likely record the expenditure as prepaid insurance (an asset) and turn the one transaction into twelve separate transactions—one for each month in which one-twelfth of the prepaid insurance is transferred from the prepaid insurance asset to insurance expense.

This extra manual work helps the accounting system to better simulate flow, that is, to match the insurance expense with the correct month. Still, this method is somewhat coarse. If reports are prepared at shorter intervals (biweekly, weekly, or daily), the same problem shows up: the expense will only be in the period that contains the date of the transaction, making the results look lumpy.

We raise this point now because it's one of the many problems that a data-centric approach will solve automatically.

Timing Problems

A family of problems in financial reporting are caused by unusual sequences of events, which we call timing problems.

Typically, when an organization orders supplies, the sequence unfolds over time: first the supplies arrive, then the bill, and only later does payment follow.

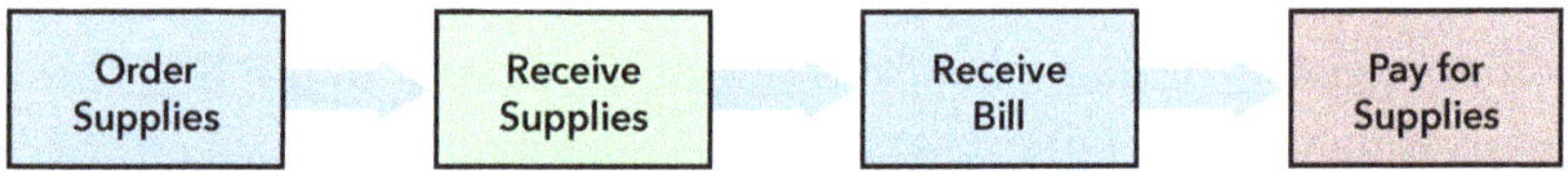

Figure 2.18: **A Normal Flow of Events**

This is the normal sequence of events. Depending on the organization's policy, the transaction is probably accrued either when they receive the supplies or when they receive the bill. That time period aligns with when the supplies were available and meets the matching criteria.

Alternative Event Sequences: Systems expect accounting events to occur in a typical order. When events occur out of sequence, accountants must invoke an exception process to record the transaction differently.

From the time the bill is received until it is paid, the organization has a liability on their balance sheet—accounts payable.

But sometimes these events occur in a different sequence.

Perhaps a vendor says they will give you a good deal or guarantee access to a scarce supply, but only if you prepay. In this case, the sequence becomes: bill, payment, then receipt.

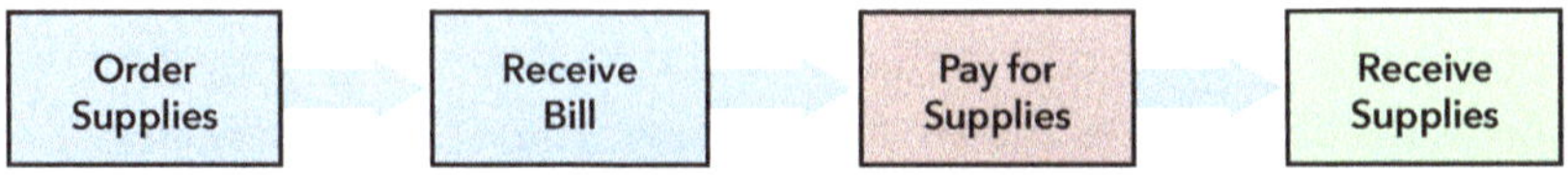

Figure 2.19: Alternative Sequence of Events

This situation creates accounting challenges if the system isn't flexible. After the payment, you don't have a payable and your cash is reduced, but you also don't yet have the goods—and you shouldn't recognize this expense at this stage.

The solution is, at the moment of paying, someone must notice that the goods haven't been received. This noticing is often manual or in some other source system as the accounting system typically doesn't have the context to make this connection. This triggers a different set of transactions from the typical scenario. The payment is accrued to an asset called *prepaid expense* or *prepaid inventory* depending on the nature of acquisition. When the goods arrive, someone must know not to book them to payables (which would be the norm) but instead to relieve the prepaid expense.

These kinds of situations occur a lot, require much manual intervention, and are prone to error. We describe how this will be addressed and automated in Chapter 5.

Accrual Accounting Adjustments

Some accounting transactions are not directly driven by events in the organization but are initiated by accountants to follow up on previous activities and adjust their amounts or status for newer information. These are generally worked out analytically, usually in spreadsheets, and then entered into the system through adjusting entries.

One such accounting adjustment is a bad debt write-off. After trying as hard as possible to collect on a customer receivable, an organization "writes off" the uncollected balance when they give up. The write-off removes the worthless asset from the balance sheet that had been recorded when the revenue was recognized earlier through the accrual accounting process.

In an industry where write-offs are common, you don't want to wait several months to find out which customers won't pay before you record the bad debt as an expense. To match bad debt expense against the related revenue, as the matching principle suggests, you estimate the expense based on analysis of receivables at the end of each accounting period and reflect only the amount you expect to be able to collect as Net Accounts Receivable on the balance sheet. Experience teaches us that the older a debt becomes, the less likely it is to be repaid. Accountants typically rely on a report called "Aged Accounts Receivable" that categorizes invoices based on how far past due they are. In a later period, when specific customers' bad debts are identified, they are removed from the net receivables without affecting that later period's expense.

Allocations are made in the accounting department to make managerial financial reporting for segments—such as divisions or product lines—more relevant. For instance, the "burden" (employer taxes, benefits, and vacation) might be spread over the direct labor cost to reflect the true total cost of labor. Similarly, overhead expenses such as rent or insurance may be spread over different departments so that departmental reports present a clearer picture.

Other adjustments include depreciation expense (which allocates part of the cost of fixed assets to the current accounting period), and interest that is either earned or incurred.

These and many other adjustments are typically made at the end of each accounting period, just before financial statements are prepared and the books are closed. Later in this book, and the subsequent implementation guide, we will explore ways of replicating such adjustments algorithmically.

Summary of How Companies Do Traditional Accounting

This was a lot, but we wanted to motivate you for the change.

Traditional accounting is complex, time-consuming, and resource intensive. Some of that complexity is essential—but a great deal of it is self-inflicted. We wanted you to wallow in this a bit. Partly to understand the nomenclature, which we need to use as we describe the solutions we propose, and partly to motivate for the change.

If we jumped straight into the data-centric approach, you might think it's unnecessarily complex. Armed with some information about how complex traditional accounting is, we hope we can motivate the change. Also, we've tried to provide enough detail so you don't feel we're glossing over important details. We've suffered through this complexity ourselves—in classrooms and in multinational accounting implementations.

We're not naïve about the complexity, but we are motivated to tackle it.

CHAPTER 3

It's Time for a Change

Why do we need a new approach to accounting? Because the current state of the art is badly broken, but only a few realize this. Dan Heath calls it *Problem Blindness*. In all walks of life, it is quite easy to accept the status quo as sufficient and not see egregious problems.

In Upstream[9], Dan explores areas such as the Chicago Public Schools, where teachers and administrators had become accustomed to a 52 percent high school graduation rate. "That's just the way it is," many thought. Real progress only began once the sources of the problem came into focus. They realized that waiting until juniors and seniors began dropping out was far too late to intervene.

By studying patterns, they discovered they could predict with 80 percent accuracy which freshmen would eventually drop out. They also realized some of their discipline policies essentially doomed students to not graduate. By fixing some of the discipline policies and creating freshmen success teams, and by shifting their mindset from resignation to advocacy, they increased graduation rates by 25 percent.

That's what we will attempt to do in this section: shine a light on the systemic inadequacies of the accounting status quo. This is not an indictment on any accountants, policy makers, or systems implementers. Everyone is working as hard as they can and providing extraordinary efforts to keep businesses and financial institutions functioning.

But until people are sufficiently dissatisfied with the status quo, little progress will be made.

Only Accountants are Privy

Traditional accounting is complex. There are a lot of policies to understand and apply consistently. There are thousands of account numbers to choose from. There is the opportunity for fraud. If you allow just anyone into your accounting system, you can imagine the mayhem that could result.

[9] www.amazon.com/dp/1982134720

The net result is a small number of highly trained individuals have access to the accounting system. They are the gatekeepers. Their timetable establishes when things get done. If you don't understand the financial statements, you may need their guidance.

Given that trained accountants are becoming a scarce commodity in recent years[10], we must find a way to provide more access to financial information without increasing risk.

Delay Is the Cruelest Form of Denial

Most managers in most businesses treat the financial records as the "official version" of their financial activity. These are the numbers that have been vetted and fretted over. They are often, eventually, audited. All this activity gives a great deal of credence to these figures.

As we mentioned in the section on closing the books, there are many delays built into the accounting process. Financial reports aren't available until after month-end, since numerous entries and adjustments must be made to ensure reports are accurate and comparable to prior months.

How Much It Costs to Know How Much It Costs

We've established that accounting is necessary. Accurate and timely accounting would be even more valuable.

But how much does it cost just to produce the out-of-date information with which most organizations run their businesses? Well, quite a bit.

It is difficult to get good across-the-board estimates of the total cost of accounting for an organization. Different organizations operate in different industries where different levels of precision and different sets of reports are needed.

That said, we can get a back-of-the-envelope guesstimate. The main factors that go into the total cost of accounting for an organization are:

[10] NPR, "The Indicator from Planet Money: What Happens When There Aren't Enough CPAs?," *The Indicator* (podcast), August 12, 2022, https://www.npr.org/2022/08/12/1117128403/the-indicator-from-planet-money-what-happens-when-there-arent-enough-cpas

Total burdened cost for everyone in the finance and accounting department.

Fees for outside accountants—including but not limited to—external auditors.

Costs for accounting systems, including a portion of the capital cost of implementation, licensing, and ongoing operational costs (such as support tickets and help desk tickets related to accounting).

A share of the maintenance costs for feeder systems whose transactions have become financial transactions. These may range from project management to time control to case management.

Activity-Based Costing (ABC) analysis of time the rest of the company spends on accounting support activities. ABC assigns the costs of activity to products and service according to their actual consumption. In this context, accounting support activities include tasks such as time that estimators spend looking up cost codes, time that drivers spend on their time reports or on validating customer numbers, time spent by customer support sorting out problems with client bills and payments, and so forth.

Penalties and fees related to financial noncompliance, late payments, and the like.

Accounting costs a lot of money. Typically, between one and four percent of a company's revenue goes directly or indirectly to the accounting department and to the systems that support accounting functionality.[11, 12, 13]

We've seen client organizations where the costs are likely far higher, though no formal studies exist to quantify them. Either way, it adds up to a significant expense—just to determine what everything else costs.

[11]Erik Parrish cites a range of two to six percent of gross revenue for accounting costs. See Parrish, "How Much Is Your Accounting Department Costing You?" *LinkedIn*, August 24, 2015. linkedin.com/pulse/how-much-your-accounting-department-costing-you-erik-parrish/

[12]Boost CPA suggests a somewhat lower range, one to four percent of gross revenue. See "How Much Should My Accounting Cost?" *Boost CPA*, accessed August 22, 2025. https://boostcpa.ca/how-much-should-my-accounting-cost/.

[13]David McCann reports an even smaller percentage, 0.6 to two percent, though this figure appears to only reflect the direct costs of the organization and not supporting systems. See McCann, "Metric of the Month: Total Cost of the Finance Function," *CFO*, June 1, 2017. https://www.cfo.com/news/metric-of-the-month-total-cost-of-the-finance-function-1/663997/

How Accounting Became the Leading Lagging Indicator

Managers want to know more than just what has already happened (as far as the accountants are concerned). To understand what else they need, we need to take a slight detour to the nature of leading and lagging indicators.

A lagging indicator tells how well you did at some point in the past. The further back, the longer the lag. Making decisions based on lagging information is like driving while looking only in the rear-view mirror: you can get a good sense of where you have been but have little sense of where you are now or what lies ahead.

For most businesses, their cash balance is the laggiest of indicators. Because customers may pay you 30 to 60 days after the time of a sale, and you, in turn, pay vendors 30 to 60 days after being invoiced, relying on your bank balance to tell how you are doing, is primarily telling you how you did two months ago.

Accrual accounting reduces the lag. We recognize revenue at the time we deliver goods or services to customers, and expenses when we are billed. Still, it remains a lagging indicator—and the delays from workflow and the closing process just exacerbate the delay.

Many business events allow us to predict what will happen in the future, and budgeting is the best known of these. There are several problems with budgeting as it is currently practiced, and we will take up some of them in the section on budgeting. The primary problem is that budgets, commitments, accruals, and actuals are usually only integrated in very ad hoc ways.

The business events that give us current information, and are more helpful for short-term financial predictions, are typically ignored by the accounting systems.

These include purchase orders and sales orders. As we will discuss in much greater detail later in the book, these two transactions often lay out very precisely what is going to happen, financially, within the organization.

Typical Enterprise Information System Ecosystem

The first thing to get to grips on is how many systems are likely to be in your enterprise's ecosystem. In our observations, enterprises tend to have about one order of magnitude fewer systems than employees. For example, one of our clients with nearly 100,000 employees operates just over 11,000 multi-user supported application systems. Another organization with only 3,000 employees has at least 600 applications. Sadly, the smaller the organization, the worse the ratios seem to go. Semantic Arts has 30 employees and before starting the data-centric transition had 20 multi-user applications. To start with, because we have employees in three countries, we had three copies of Quick Books, none of which were integrated with each other or with anything else. In addition to this, we had the usual litany of systems: CRM, Commission Management, Payroll, Benefit Enrollment, Expense Management, Time Control, Vacation Tracking, Project Management, Staff Planning, Cash Management, eCommerce, Calendaring, Service Ticket management, email, messaging, and several variations of Content Management.

> Enterprise Application: There is no uniform definition of what an enterprise application is, and therefore how to count them, but the consensus from our clients seems to include any system that is being centrally maintained, as well as any "End User Computing" (usually spreadsheets) that are essential to some key workflow. Most spreadsheets don't make the count but for instance those that contribute to the production of the annual report should.

Not all of an organization's application systems contribute to the books and records of the organization, but it is surprising how many do.

The trend toward more applications is getting worse over time.

> The advent of Software as a Service (SaaS) means that any mid-level manager with a credit card can add another application system to the company's portfolio of systems.

What's the problem with this plethora of applications, you might ask? After all, I have over a hundred apps on my phone. What's the problem?

SaaS: Software as a Service became popular along with the migration of applications to the cloud. SaaS allows organizations to pay for software on a subscription model. This has moved much application implementation from the capital budget (because previously you needed large one-time payments for the license or development of the system) to monthly operational expenses.

Your phone apps have little or no need to integrate with each other. Your Uber app doesn't care about your average sudoku score, how many miles you logged on Strava, or what's on your Spotify playlist. The enterprise is very different.

Each application holds a piece of the organization's information datascape. Think of it like a jigsaw puzzle: every system contributes a piece or two that, in theory, should come together to form a coherent picture. In practice, though, it's like trying to assemble a puzzle made of cardboard, wood, steel and Jello—some pieces flat, some three-dimensional, with each piece having different scale and patterns, and many of them overlapping.

Each enterprise application has its own data model—its own way of seeing and structuring its world. Each model is arbitrarily different. Put together ten inventory control systems and you'll likely come up with ten different ways to structure their data and ten different ways to name every table and column in the model.

If that weren't bad enough, most of the application systems we've examined (and we've examined plenty) are anywhere from ten to one hundred times more complex than necessary to solve the problem they were designed to solve.

You likely have hundreds—if not thousands—of application systems, each of which is 10 to 100 times more complex than the problem it needs to solve. Many of these systems were not sponsored by IT. They are *shadow systems* because they lurk in the dark. No wonder your information systems budget disappears into systems integration efforts, without really making much progress on it.

Traditional Accounting Systems

Accounting systems are a subset of Enterprise Information Systems. Turns out, if you look hard enough, you'll see that they make up a surprisingly large share of the enterprise's overall systems.

If you work in a small business, you might think that Quick Books is your accounting system. It is probably just one of them. As we'll explore later in this section, an accounting system is any system that contributes to the recognition of changes to the value of the organization. So that expense reporting system is part of your accounting ecosystem. So is your web-based ordering system. And your online banking. If you do project management and time control separately, those transactions also contribute to your accounting results. Maybe you allow salespeople to place orders from your CRM system—that is more accounting. Possibly the only systems that don't have an accounting piece are content management and email.

CRM (Customer Relationship Management): These are systems that sales and marketing people use to keep track of their prospects and customers. They generally keep track of all the interactions with prospects and often also capture sales orders.

And of course, as you scale up, many more systems contribute to accounting, and from there to the books and records of the organization. At first, each type of account (accounts receivable, accounts payable, inventory, etc.) becomes its own system, and with further growth and acquisitions, these multiply.

Handing off data from system to system becomes like the children's "telephone game": each whisper changes the message a little, and by the time it reaches the end, it barely resembles the original. With each handoff, the signal degrades.

We take this for granted. This is all we've ever known. We've all grown up with this. But it isn't the only way. Accepting this status quo is like settling for a 52 percent high school graduation rate—as in the case of Chicago schools—when we know we can do better.

What we have gotten used to is a simple structure (ledgers and journals) with a very complex implementation (a legion of systems integrators taking clues out of source systems to convert them to accounting transactions and an army of bookkeepers interpreting, encoding, and posting all the transactions that the systems integrators didn't get). Then, of course, comes the cumbersome adjusting and closing process we described in earlier sections.

Why Do Shadow Systems Exist?

A *shadow system* isn't sanctioned by corporate IT management. People don't build shadow systems and rogue IT just for the fun of it. People build shadow systems because they are responsible for their area's economic results, yet the official accounting systems provide information too late or in formats that don't fit their needs.

People intercept the events they are interested in, apply some sort of heuristics to them to come up with costs or revenue, and then dump information into personal databases and Excel spreadsheets. They apply categories to the events to suit their own needs. Sometimes these shadow systems are so useful they eventually become part of the official record.

Sarbanes-Oxley as a Window Into the Complexity

In the wake of Enron and other accounting mishaps of 2002, Congress implemented legislation called the *Sarbanes-Oxley Act*[14] (SOX for short). The law required all publicly traded companies to be able to prove where all the numbers in their financial statements came from. They further stipulated that the CEO and CFO would have to attest to the accuracy of the information and its source, subject to severe fines and jail time if they were later found to be inaccurate.

> **SOX** provided a very high level of accountability for executives at publicly traded companies.

[14]Sarbanes-Oxley Act of 2002, Pub. L. No. 107–204, 116 Stat. 745 (2002), https://sarbanes-oxley-act.com

You might think: the financial statements come from the financial data warehouse—isn't that good enough? But where did that come from? From the General Ledger. And where did each of those entries come from?

In most large organizations, the path from transactions to financial statements gets very complex. Most organizations launched very large projects to map out every source and flow. The results were usually huge flow charts that filled the walls of large *war rooms*. Sadly, many boxes in the many flow charts included steps that were executed in Excel spreadsheets. The real truth? There were far too many routes a given transaction could take on its way to its final resting place on the published financial statements. Organizations invested millions of dollars on these projects and, if they were honest, they would say they have a reasonable idea where the numbers come from—but they really don't know for sure.

Fixed Ideas

In many areas of life, we have *fixed ideas* (*idées fixes*, as the French like to say). Thought patterns need to be changed to make progress. Thomas Kuhn[15] called these *paradigms*. People change paradigms very reluctantly.

> "Science progresses one funeral at a time."
>
> — *Max Planck*

[15]Kuhn, Thomas S. 2012. *The Structure of Scientific Revolutions*. 50th ed. Chicago: University of Chicago Press.

Here is a 1915 newspaper ad urging people to reconsider their decision to give up on horseback riding in favor of the new-fangled automobile.

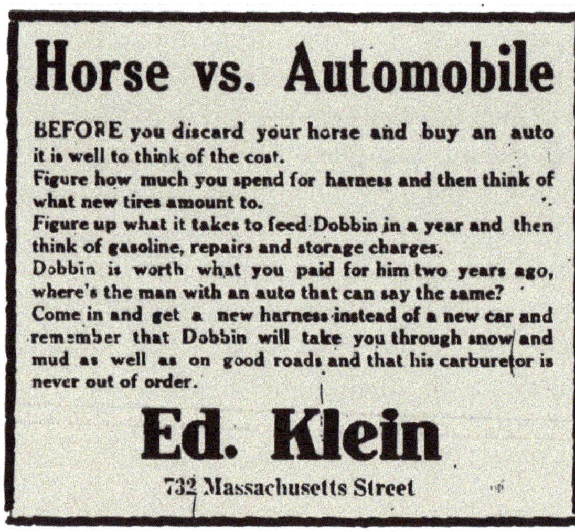
Horse vs. Automobile

BEFORE you discard your horse and buy an auto it is well to think of the cost.
Figure how much you spend for harness and then think of what new tires amount to.
Figure up what it takes to feed Dobbin in a year and then think of gasoline, repairs and storage charges.
Dobbin is worth what you paid for him two years ago, where's the man with an auto that can say the same?
Come in and get a new harness instead of a new car and remember that Dobbin will take you through snow and mud as well as on good roads and that his carburetor is never out of order.

Ed. Klein

732 Massachusetts Street

Figure 3.1: A Final Appeal to the Status Quo

Keepers and Discards

Hopefully, we now share a vocabulary and common understanding of the key building blocks of the traditional accounting information system circa 2026. We also have covered some of our motivation for changing this.

Some of our suggestions may have sounded radical—perhaps like we're throwing the baby out with the bathwater. That is not our intent. There is a great deal of accounting orthodoxy that we subscribe to and think is essential. But we also see a lot of accumulated cruft (unnecessarily complicated, badly designed, or unwanted code or software) that needs to be cleared away.

The following page contains a brief list of the concepts, practices, and norms that we plan to retain from traditional accounting systems, and those we plan to discard.

Keepers

Key concepts in traditional accounting systems that will remain integral to data-centric accounting include the following:

> **Accounting standards** such as the US GAAP, IFRS, and other country-specific GAAPs.
>
> **Income statements.**
>
> **Balance sheets.**
>
> **Statements of cash flows**, with an emphasis on direct method presentation.
>
> **Accrual accounting**, including revenue and expense recognition criteria.
>
> **Cash basis accounting.**
>
> **Accounting policy.**
>
> **Counterparty accounts** such as accounts payable and accounts receivable (existing accounts will be retained, with new ones as needed).
>
> **Resource accounts** such as inventory, equipment, and real estate (albeit at a more detailed level than those in traditional accounting systems).
>
> **Inventory valuation methods.**

Discards

As for the outdated parts of the current accounting orthodoxy, here's what we plan to leave behind:

> **Debits and credits as the organizing principle.** We will support debits and credits when ingesting data from source systems and when exporting them to downstream systems that require them.
>
> **Ledgers.** We'll have something analogous for tracking the balances of counterparty and resource accounts, but it won't be a ledger.
>
> **Journal entries.** Fully data-centric accounting systems will not have journal entries. Companies that choose a phased transitional approach may have financial transactions as rough equivalents to journal entries, as we will describe in the implementation guidebook.

Account numbers. We leave behind the idea that every General Ledger account has a number and that those numbers are digitally significant. Although we will have accounts and they will have some sort of identifiers, the identifiers will not be tied to the account's financial reporting location. Location in financial reports will be driven by types and categories attached to accounts or commitments.

The Chart of Accounts. In a data-centric accounting system, the traditional chart of accounts is unnecessary and even distracting—especially for the income statement. Transactions that affect the income statement will be included not by their account number, but by categories attached to the transactions and/or the commitments.

Reporting Taxonomies. Although we anticipate being able to support XBRL[16] (Extensible Business Reporting Language), we will do so with a simple set of orthogonal categories that will provide much greater fidelity with less complexity than the current large, complex taxonomy that tags financial statement line items.

Adjusting Entries. The need for most adjusting entries will be eliminated by the way in which transactions will be captured and processed in the data-centric accounting system. We will retain two categories of transactions that look like adjusting entries for cost allocation to time periods (e.g. depreciation and amortization) and allocation of shared expenses to projects and departments.

Manual determination of accruals and deferrals such as prepaid expense. These determinations are automated and will not require materiality judgments or human monitoring. This is manual work subject to much error that will be completely automated in fully data-centric accounting systems.

Manual classification of expense after the fact. Expenses will be classified at the moment when some employee commits the company to a course of action, as that is when the company has the most context for classifying the eventual expense.

[16]XBRL is a standard that the SEC requires publicly traded firms to adhere to. It provides a set of tags that are used to define the meaning of various line items and disclosures in financial reports. More detail at https://www.xbrl.org.

> **Manual entry of transactions by bookkeepers.** We expect data-centric accounting systems to require far fewer bookkeepers than traditional systems. Tasks that once relied on a bookkeeper's judgment—recording past business events and determining how to enter them into the accounting system—will be automated.
>
> **Closing Process.** The data-centric organization will always be closed. There will be no adjustments, accruals, last-minute revenue recognition, allocations, tax-inspired transactions, intercompany postings, or other closing transactions.

Following are a handful of areas where the existing paradigm is holding us back. In this section, we will hint at what will change, but it won't be until after we describe how data-centric works that the real changes will be evident.

Some deeply held beliefs will need to change before we can make the necessary shifts from:

- Application-Centric to Data-Centric
- Data Flow to Data at Rest
- Structured Data to Meaning
- Convenience Accounts to Real Accounts
- Ledger Accounts to Big Data

From Application-Centric to Data-Centric

The data-centric approach changes the system boundaries. The boundary is at the edge of the enterprise. There is only one data model. The organization's data may be co-located, or it may not. For a long transition period, most firms will source transactions in legacy systems, but gradually we believe they will migrate functionality to their core model.

Accounting will become a fully integrated function and a by-product of the activity of the enterprise. Because it is so integral with the practices and events of a given industry, we believe that systems of the future will be vertical. That is, they will contain the combination of functions for a given industry. In the last section of the book, we will outline how the systems of the future will differ from industry to industry.

> Enterprise Resource Planning (ERP) systems evolved from a prior generation of integrated systems, MRP I and MRP II. MRP I (Material Requirements Planning) was centered on managing the materials that went into the manufacturing process. MRP II (Manufacturing Resource Planning) broadened this to include closed loop planning and financials. ERP was the eventual end product of this evolution.

Some readers may remind us that this was the goal of ERP systems. Even in the early days of enterprise application building, the cost of integration became an obvious sore spot. "If we could just get all the functionality of the firm on a single integrated database, there would be no integration." The goal was valid. The technology of the day was not up to the challenge. Instead of a single simple model, the customer was faced with unfathomably complex data models. SAP, the leading ERP vendor, deploys a system with 90,000 tables. It has nearly one million attributes (fields) that have mysterious interactions. Even if someone could get all their functionality on such a system, the complexity of maintaining it is far greater than what is now possible. But for most clients the real tragedy is that they have 20 to 40 percent of the data and functionality of their firm in their ERP system, and the cost to integrate the remaining 60 to 80 percent is far higher than if they didn't have the ERP system.

Most ERP systems were forged in the days of COBOL and relational databases. Modern architectures and methodologies are now up to the task. The follow-on implementation guide will cover in much greater detail the key technologies and approaches that take most of the cost and risk out of endeavors such as this.

> A Data-Centric enterprise is one where all application functionality is based on a single, simple, extensible data model.[17]
>
> — *Dave McComb*

Rather than an application with 90,000 tables connected to hundreds or thousands of other applications with collectively as much complexity, the data-centric firm will have a core enterprise model (an ontology) with 400-600 key concepts that are structural and a few thousand taxonomic tags that make the remaining distinctions that are needed to manage a complex enterprise.

> An ontology is a data model that emphasizes the meaning of data— its semantics—as opposed to just its structure.

From Data Flow to Data at Rest

Most enterprise information system practitioners, and by extension most accounting system practitioners, think in terms of flow. Many projects start with a business workflow. The business workflow is a series of boxes, that describe how work (data) flows from systems to system, department to department.

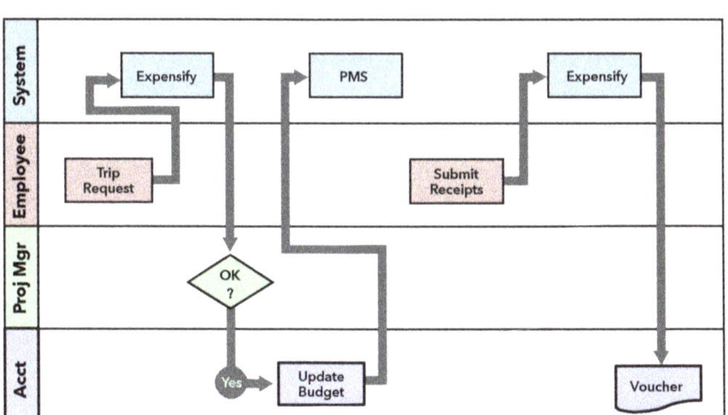

Figure 3.2: **A (tiny portion of a) Typical Business Workflow**

[17]McComb, Dave. 2019. *The Data-Centric Revolution: Restoring Sanity to Enterprise Systems*. Technics Publishing.

Time generally flows from left to right. The horizontal bands (called *swim lanes*) depict departments and sometimes systems. The idea is to capture the *as-is* and by rationalizing and removing boxes, the *to-be* can be more efficient.

Functional Programming: Many difficult-to-debug errors in systems come when two code modules access the same (in memory) data structure, sometimes in different sequences. Functional programming addresses this by ensuring that all processing is done on local copies of data structures and then returns them to other modules for further processing.

If you have some of these workflows lying around, go round them up and see if this characterization is generally true.

Many of the boxes in a workflow represent data integration, usually manual data integration. If there were fewer applications, there would be fewer swim lanes and usually far fewer boxes in the workflow. There will be a few boxes for authorization and a few for decisions. Try to imagine the workflow if all the data were integrated. The number of boxes in the various workflows drops precipitously.

The same is true of *data pipelines*. These days, many companies that ingest a lot of data have *pipelines* for the ingest.

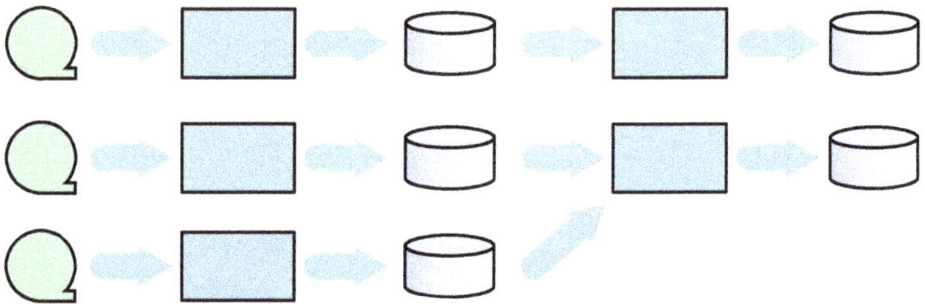

Figure 3.3: **A Typical Data Pipeline**

A dataset enters on the left, and every step reads a dataset in from the left and writes a new one on the right, sometimes augmenting it with data from above or below. Each step does something to the data. One step removes duplicates, another step *normalizes* some of the data (getting names in the same case for easier comparison or splitting addresses into a common format), another step augments the data with additional information that is known about the entity. Another step merges the data with other data. Each step copies and transforms the data from its previous form.

This is a modern architecture. A style of software development called *functional programming* sets out all the principles for doing this sort of "copy on write" architecture. It turns out this is efficient and greatly reduces certain types of programming errors. This method underpins much of the "big data" movement. However, despite its benefits, we advocate for its removal from the accounting data stream, as the cost is loss of data traceability. In accounting, a key requirement is the ability to trace back from financial statements or reports to the original events and data that produced them.

In order to make progress we need to realize that almost none of the dataflow is necessary and most of it gets in the way.

Data can be captured and just sit there. As we learn new information about it, we can just add it. But it takes a while for people to overturn a long-held habit like data flow by default.

From Structured Data to Meaning

Traditional database systems are more concerned with data structure than they are with meaning. Traditional database and application designers draw their models and focus on which fields are required, and which are optional, but assume that people know, from a brief label, what each of the boxes mean. Experience has taught us that it

---

Semantics is the study of meaning. When applied to information systems, it results in data structures that are far less ambiguous, and done well, simpler and more understandable to non-computer users, as the terms and labels are closer to their real world understanding.

---

is rare that two interpretations of a model are congruent. There is a belief that consumers of the data know what it means. This is rarely the case. What little meaning exists is maintained in application code and by manually enforced conventions that are often undocumented. Anyone who has worked with large enterprise information systems knows the sorry state of documentation. And even in rare cases where data is well documented, the sheer volume and variety make it nearly impossible to comprehend.

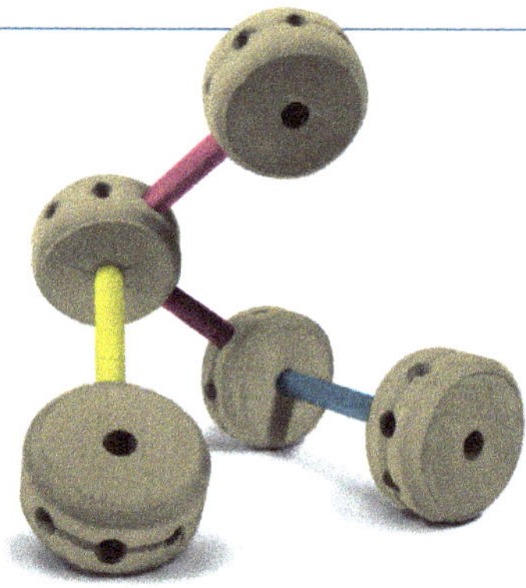

Graph database: Relational technology stores data in tables. Document databases (XML and JSON primarily) store data in small structured "documents." The storage mechanism of Knowledge Graphs is the di-graph (directed graph) which is a node, with an arrow pointing at another node. We call this atomic structure a triple because it has three parts (node, edge, and node). Think of Tinker Toys, where each node is a wooden disk, and the edges are the connecting dowels.

In semantic-based systems, designers obsess over meaning—that's what semantics is all about. Clear meaning provides reusable, and rarely misunderstood building blocks. The flexibility of graph databases allows us to delay the focus on structure. We can bring constraints into the system, but this can be done much later in the implementation process. In the companion implementation book, we will describe a graph-based implementation of these concepts in detail. We believe this approach to be a vastly superior approach to the requirements in this book, though we understand that many practitioners may prefer to continue using the tools they know.

The current state of the art in enterprise information systems, including accounting systems, includes an excessive amount of schema complexity. **Accounting systems are often hundreds to thousands of times more complex than the complexity of the problem they are trying to solve.**

The small business accounting software QuickBooks contains 10 million lines of code. The average software product has between 15 and 50 latent defects per 1,000 lines of code[18]. This means that QuickBooks has between 150,000 and 500,000 latent defects. This is not an isolated case; it is just a very common one. The sad thing is that, with good design and modern practice, this functionality could be implemented in a tiny fraction of this code base.

We arrived at this state because application developers interview users and ask what data they need to solve a problem. That data is then superficially described and converted to database table designs. Code and forms are eventually created, and the system comes to life. As problems arise during execution or use, more tables and columns are added—along with even more code. By then, the documentation of what the data actually meant is usually outdated or irrelevant.

When documentation existed at all, it was often shallow. When we deeply focus on the meaning, we uncover hidden patterns that end up being the key to deeper simplicity. Most of what we have learned and will describe in the next sections is a direct result of peering deeply into the meaning of concepts that we all thought were well understood but weren't.

From Convenience Accounts to Real Accounts

There are a lot of accounts in a typical accounting system. What is weird is how few are "real" accounts. Our contention—developed in the next section—is that an accounting system requires two fundamental types of accounts. The first is a counterparty account. When someone owes you money, or you owe them, you need to keep track of this separately. The best way to do this is by maintaining an account for each counterparty—for example, a customer account or a vendor account.

Real Accounts. Our distinction here is based on this: in some cases, there is a business requirement to maintain what we have historically called an account, one that posts activity and maintains a running balance. The only clear examples where this is a requirement are with counterparty accounts and accounts for inventoriable resources.

[18]https://axify.io

The second essential account is a resource account. An account is needed for each type of resource that must be tracked separately. For example, you need an account for each bank account you maintain, as well as for each item of inventory, since costing and tracking is done at that level.

All other General Ledger accounts are there for the convenience of financial reporting. Accountants move balances back and forth between these accounts as if they were moving money from one bank account to another, but nothing of the sort is actually happening in the real world. The monetary amounts are being moved, just so the balances can be combined differently on financial reports. This is a tremendous amount of non-value-added work to solve a problem that can be solved far more easily through other means.

From Ledger Accounts to Big Data

Each account has its own storage structure, resembling the paper check registers we used to get with our checking accounts—or the registers that Ebeneezer Scrooge and his clerk, Bob Cratchit used to balance their accounts in Charles Dickens' *A Christmas Carol*.

Despite being at the heart of all accounting systems, ledger accounts for storage are not strictly necessary. Yes, this is also going to freak a lot of people out, but it's true. As we know from a decade of working with big data, there are other ways to sum up large amounts of data for aggregate reporting.

There will be many cases where we cache aggregates for performance or convenience, but before we can make those trade-offs, we must give up on the idea that the ledger accounts are essential.

Summary of Changes Needed

The process of accounting, as currently practiced, has become quite complex. It takes a four-year degree to really be competent. A lot of the complexity is mastering the topics in the previous sections, many of which we have simplified greatly for brevity and readability. The sad thing is that many of them are not really necessary in the 21st century.

The modern accounting system is a barely cobbled together collection of dozens to hundreds of application systems built by different people for different purposes, held together by the systems integrators duct tape and baling wire.

We believe that for those that embark on this journey, change will not come by merely tweaking the systems that are in place. Instead, we will extract data out of the existing systems and re-express it in a simpler, more flexible format. This will give us a platform to begin to implement the functionality we describe in the next four chapters. Eventually, we will be replacing most of what exists. While the transformation is not incremental, it can be modular—meaning the change can be done in manageable chunks, but not by simply upgrading existing components.

CHAPTER 4

Basics of Data-Centric Accounting

We hope we've shown that accounting, as currently practiced, is far from optimal. Maybe we've also teased you a bit with the possibility and suggested, if not a technical solution, at least a technical turbo charge. There is even a place for GenAI and LLMs, though not as a magic bullet, just a few places where it will be helpful.

Now it's time to dive deeper into data-centric accounting. Doing so requires a new way of thinking—about both the problem and the solution. And thinking differently is never easy.

If data-centric accounting described in these next chapters feels overwhelming and or too much to implement all at once—***don't panic!*** In our follow-on implementation guidebook, we outline a three-phase approach based on our own experience. You can pause—or even stop—after Phase 1, at which point you will realize many (though not all) of the benefits of data-centric accounting. Likewise, you may choose to pause or even stop after Phase 2, by which point you will have realized the full benefits of data-centric accounting for single-business entities.

If your business functions as part of a greater whole—whether part of a multi-organizational conglomerate, a tightly woven supply chain, or a collaborative coalition—you may want to proceed with Phase 3. This stage will take you and your business partners into a realm of unprecedented information sharing and interoperability. Of course, you will need to convince your business partners to implement Phases 1 and 2. Convincing them should not be difficult once you begin realizing the benefits of data-centric accounting and can share your success story with them.

Some of the new concepts and features of data-centric accounting include:

- Financial activity directly driven by business events
- Immutable data at rest
- Machine-executable accounting policies
- Elimination of journals, journal entries and postings
- Closing redefined from a process to a state change

- Model-driven financial reporting
- Financial reports that contain their own lineage and provenance

Before we explain each of these, let's dive into what it means to be event-driven and consider the kinds of events that are common across all organizations.

Event-Driven

Anything that happens at a point in time can be considered to be an event. With that definition, a solar eclipse is an event, as is the robbery of a bank in a nearby town. Most organizations build their information systems around events that are of interest to them. We will call those *business events*.

Not all business events affect an organization's books and records. For example, scheduling or conducting a meeting is a business event, but only in very rare cases does it warrant financial recognition. We create a subtype of business event called the *financial business event*, to represent those activities that do lead to a posting to the financial statements.

In traditional accounting, all financial business events are converted into financial transactions, each tied to specific points in time. Each such transaction has a *posting time*—a very precise timestamp that represents the moment the transaction became known to the system. Each transaction also has an *effective accounting date* that is also a point in time, but a less precise point in time. To our knowledge, no one specifies the exact minute an invoice is submitted or due—we care about the date but not the exact time it occurs.

However, in business—and in data-centric accounting—we recognize that many business events, including financial business events, occur over time. We will take up the significance of this difference in the next chapter. For now, however, let's concentrate on events that occur at single points in time.

One of the organization's first jobs is to determine which business events rise to the level of financial business events, and to document exactly what they are and how they will be treated.

The simplest set of financial business events would be:

- Order goods or services
- Pay for goods or services
- Receive goods or services
- Sell goods or services
- Deliver goods or services
- Receive payment for goods or services

While not highly sophisticated, even this small set of events can go a long way. You can imagine capturing each event, and (if you read ahead) you could imagine how **each of these events could be converted into a financial transaction. These transactions can then post to our financial reporting model** and be rendered immediately as a set of financial reports.

Before moving to a more sophisticated view, we want to plant this idea: different industries have different financial business events, and within limits, each company can treat them differently. But rather than just arbitrarily adding new event types as we think of them, let's put some structure to the process of defining new events.

When we do this, we're pleased to find there are relatively few primitive components from which all the events can be built.

As we begin identifying and defining activities in our business that may give rise to new financial business events, it is useful to think of these in terms of four pairs of options. Each candidate event can be decomposed along these lines to see what kind of event it is. Some events deal with more than one obligation. For instance, when you pay for something at a retail store with a credit card, that event includes multiple components: the merchant fulfills their obligation by delivering the goods, you discharge your responsibility to pay the merchant, and at the same time you create a new obligation to pay the credit card company.

This sounds like a lot, but breaking down each event into its constituent parts allows us to treat things consistently. In doing so, we find events that are similar that we hadn't expected to be. To guide this process, we consider four aspects—or choices—when understanding the primitive event types.

Singular or Composite

The example in the paragraph above (buying something with a credit card) is creating multiple events from one. We will start with singular events, but later, we'll introduce some composite events.

Obligation or Right

Most counterparty transactions involve an obligation and a right. This pair sets up the directionality of the commitment. If you owe someone money, you have an obligation to pay them. If someone owes you money, you have a right to receive payment from them. Many events deal with one or the other of these two aspects.

Goods and Services or Money

This pair distinguishes money versus goods (or services). Most accounting systems focus on the payment side and only on an ad hoc basis do they deal with the goods and services side.

We will always consider both. If you have an obligation to pay someone $1,000, we will record that, usually as an account payable. If you have an obligation to deliver $1,000 worth of goods or services, we will record that as well, under a liability account we call *due out* which tracks the total amount of obligations to deliver that have been entered into.

Commitment or Fulfillment

This final pair deals with the degree of commitment. Generally, when a sales order or purchase order is signed, there is a commitment to deliver. That is what contracts are all about. The degree of commitment is really about how hard it would be to reverse the transaction. If you've ever booked a flight, a hotel, and a rental car, you can appreciate the difference. Cancelling the flight, depending on the airline, might only get you a credit, which is not a full reversal. Many hotel reservations are cancellable up to the day before, which is easy but still requires action. If you don't show up for your car reservation, it often just goes away.

The degree of commitment often goes up as time progresses. For instance, it may be easier to cancel an order before it is shipped. It is easier to cancel a custom order before it is made. In Chapter 5, we distinguish between events that originate commitments and those that modify them, but for now, the system doesn't contain enough context to make that distinction.

Finally, fulfillment is the other side of commitment. The normal way that commitments get satisfied is through fulfillment. If you have a commitment to pay someone, it is the payment that fulfills it. If you have a commitment to deliver goods or services, it is the delivery that fulfills it.

Semantic Similarity

People often give different names to things that are semantically similar. For instance, when an employee submits a time report, we think of that as a time report and as pretty much distinct from any other event. But semantically, a time report is a bill. It is a bill from a particular type of vendor that we call employee, but nonetheless, it is a bill. It behaves like a bill.

If we need to report on employee payables (accrued payroll) separately, we can do that easily enough by just looking at the type of vendor that the payable is for.

Many other events are semantically similar, even if, in everyday language, we don't usually think of them that way. Hiring an employee is a direct analog to placing a purchase order. In each case you are committing to future payments in exchange for the right to receive a resource. Even obtaining a loan has its analog in purchasing. You commit to making payments in the longer-term future for resources you will receive in the short term. In this case the resource you receive is the principal portion of the loan.

Goods and services are similarly alike. The economics are the same even though we use different verbs—*ship* for goods and *deliver* for services. In some cases, such as rent, subscriptions, or insurance, we don't even explicitly speak of delivery; it is simply assumed.

Core Events

We will organize our discussion around the core events that give rise to changes in organizations' financial statements. Three common long-running business workflows are:

> **P2P or Procure-to-Pay:** Tracks activity from the beginning of requirements through the receipt of goods and services and their payment.
>
> **O2C or Order-to-Cash:** Covers activities from marketing and sales through order fulfillment, invoicing, and receiving payment (which we will refer to as *remittance,* to avoid confusion with our payments).
>
> **Make:** Encompasses the events involved in making something, including production orders in manufacturing and projects in many other types of work.

Let's expand on the list we began earlier in this section, creating a more complete starting point. We will also apply the distinctions from above to show how the events are each different.

For each business workflow, we illustrate the events in diagram and table form. In the P2P and O2C workflow diagrams, our organization is shown above the line and our counterparty is below the line. In Make, our organization is both above and below the line, as we are essentially our own counterparty. The tables express events in the singular. In these tables, when we say *Updated Commitment*, we are referring to what is accomplished by events such as sending or receiving invoices and bills. These documents are often thought of as establishing the commitments, but in reality, the commitments were established previously—a point we will discuss in the next chapter. What we mean by updating a commitment refers to most business practice: the date on the invoice typically starts the clock for payment terms, and in some cases, the final number of units and unit cost aren't known precisely until invoice time.

Similarly, some events such as receiving acknowledgements of goods receipts or cash receipts don't change the state of the commitment but simply confirm fulfillment. We use the term *Fulfillment Confirmation* in such cases.

The P2P Core Events

Figure 4.1 illustrates the core events of the P2P workflow. The events don't always happen in this order; this is just an example.

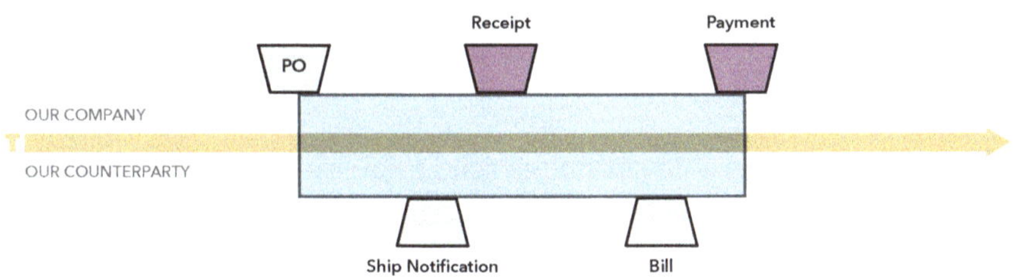

Figure 4.1: The Procure to Pay (P2P) Core Events

In figure 4.1 and subsequent figures we illustrate event workflows using the following symbols:

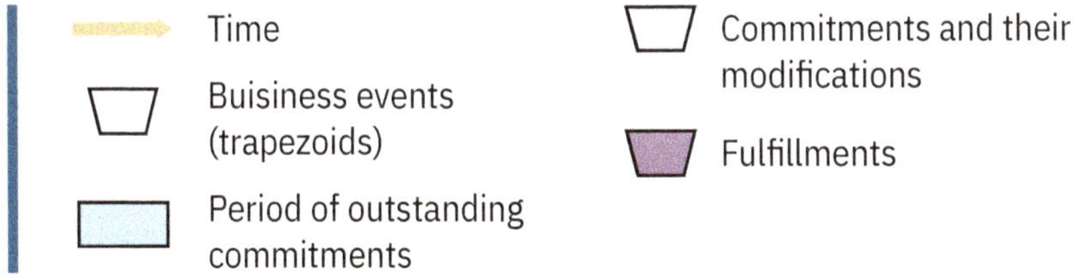

Figure 4.2 further describes the effects of the P2P events.

P2P Events	Enterprise has Obligation/Right	Event involves Goods-Service / Money	Event is a Commitment / Fulfillment
Purchase Order (PO)	Both	Both	Commitment
Ship Notification	Right	Goods / Service	Updated Commitment
Receipt (receive goods or service)	Right	Goods/Service	Fulfillment
Bill (receive request to pay)	Obligation	Money	Updated Commitment
Payment (send payment)	Obligation	Money	Fulfillment

Figure 4.2: **P2P Core Financial Business Event Details**

Let's use the table in Figure 4.2 to construct more formal definitions of each of these events and explore common variations.

Purchase Order – Committing to the purchase order (signing or its equivalent) sets up our right to receive the goods or services and our obligation to pay. We will defer full treatment of purchase orders until the next chapter.

Ship Notification – Vendors often send a notification of a shipment. Most companies ignore this from an accounting standpoint, preferring to recognize the transaction on receipt or billing. However, depending on the industry—and especially if the terms are FOB (Free on Board) Origin—it means that the buyer takes official ownership of the goods at the time of shipping and it would make sense to involve the shipping notification in the accounting policy.

Receipt – A receipt of goods or services fulfills your right to receive them. For goods, this is the physical act of warehouse staff receiving delivery. For services, it may be less tangible—for example, when your ad is placed on a billboard, you complete an airplane trip, or you receive another month of rent. In practice, many receipts are set up to be implied, with explicit recognition only if something interferes with delivery. If you squint really hard, you can imagine the receipt you get at a retail store to be the documentation of receipt of the goods or service. We usually think of it as the vendor's receipt of payment, which it also is—it's one of those events doing double duty.

Bill – To keep our terminology consistent, when a vendor sends you an invoice, we will call that a *bill*. Otherwise, each time we use the term *invoice*, we need a qualifier (sent versus received). In practice, a bill formalizes your obligation to pay, even though that obligation almost always existed beforehand (if it didn't, you'd be saying, "Wait—what is this for?"). Most contracts tie the actual payment due date to the *invoice (bill)* date, not the date of delivery or to any other date. Also often bills clarify some of the specifics (the unit cost, the quantity actually delivered, or adjustments from the original order). As alluded to above, we treat any demand for payment as a bill. When your employee turns in an expense report, that is equivalent to a bill, just of a different type. So is the monthly coupon to pay your mortgage (whether they actually send you a coupon or not). Even a fine from a regulatory agency is a bill, however it is distinct from other bills in that you never ordered it and presumably didn't get anything in return.

Payment – This is where we fulfill our obligation to pay money. Payment may take the form of cash, check, or an electronic method such as ACH (Automated Clearing House, a US bank-to-bank transfer system) or SWIFT (an international interbank settlement system).

O2C Core Events

Figure 4.3 illustrates the events in the O2C workflow. The events don't always happen in this order; this is just an example.

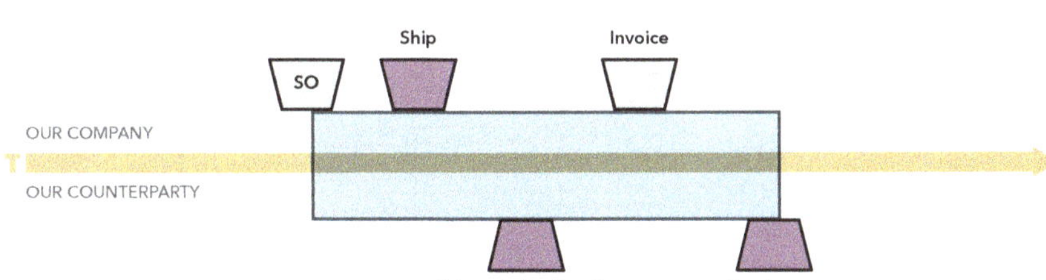

Figure 4.3: **The Order to Cash (O2C) Core Events**

Figure 4.4 summarizes the effects of the O2C events.

O2C Events	Enterprise has Obligation/Right	Event involves Goods-Service / Money	Event is a Commitment / Fulfillment
Sales Order (SO)	Both	Both	Commitment
Shipment (send goods or deliver services)	Obligation	Goods/Service	Fulfillment
Receipt Acknowledgement	Obligation	Goods/Service	Fulfillment Confirmation
Invoice (send a request to be paid)	Right	Money	Updated Commitment
Remittance (receive payment)	Right	Money	Fulfillment

Figure 4.4: **O2C Core Financial Business Event Details**

Sales Order (SO) – The sales order sets up our obligations to deliver and the customer's obligation to pay. We'll re-examine this in more detail in Chapter 5.

Shipment – We use term broadly to cover physical goods as well as services (and even bundles of the two). A delivered part, for example, is the bundle of the good itself and the service of delivery. Any delivery of service is considered a shipment, even when the delivery is implied, as with providing insurance coverage. In Chapter 6, we'll look more closely at services that are delivered over time.

Receipt Acknowledgement – In many industries, receipt acknowledgement is only recorded in the case of exceptions (such as rejections).

Invoice – This is when we invoice a client or customer. Functionally, it is the formalization of our right to receive money and thus updates the commitment.

Remittance – Again, to keep language consistent, we distinguish the act of paying others (payment) from receiving payment from others (remittance). Remittance is the fulfilment of our right to be paid.

Make

In the *make* scenarios, we are our own counterparties, at least initially. When we launch a production order, we make commitments to ourselves (about labor and inventory), but we may also be initiating P2P processes to buy parts or services that will be needed to satisfy the orders.

The top half of Figure 4.5 represents the originating portion of the organization who will ultimately be receiving the results of the project or production order.

Xfer (Transfer) is a standalone one-step workflow for moving resources —for instance, moving funds from one bank account to another.

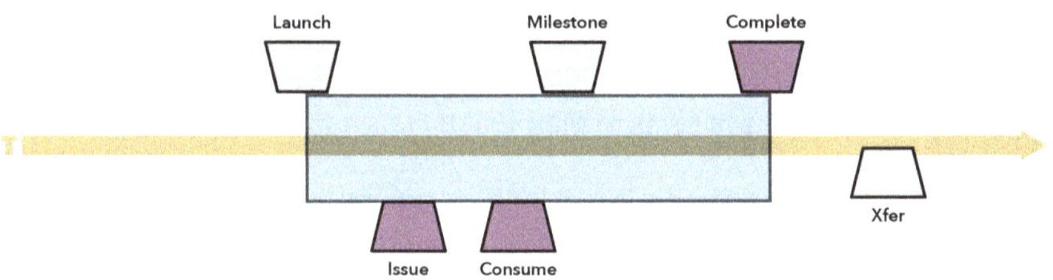

Figure 4.5: The Make Process Core Events

Figure 4.6 summarizes the effects of each of the Make events.

Make Events	Enterprise has Obligation/Right	Event involves Goods-Service / Money	Event is a Commitment /Fulfillment
Launch production or project	Both	Goods / Service	Commitment
Issue (send goods to WIP or project)	Obligation	Goods	Fulfillment
Resource Consumption (use resource)	Obligation	Service	Fulfillment
Milestone	Right	Service	Updated Commitment
Complete production or project	Right	Goods / Service	Fulfillment
Transfer (send money between accounts you own)	Right	Money	Fulfillment

Figure 4.6: Make Process Core Financial Business Event Details

Launch – A launch is the start of a production order or project. For example, when you launch a production order to build 100 bicycles, you are setting up some obligations and rights—although in this case the obligations are initially internal. Supplies, equipment, and labor are committed, and the finished goods warehouse is granted the right to eventually receive the output. Most organizations set up a "Work in Progress" (WIP) object to collect all the costs involved with the production order. Launch also applies to projects, though projects usually deliver services. If the project is to build a product (as in "make-to-order" manufacturing), it is really more like a production order, even if people still label it a project.

Issue – An issue is the act of releasing parts or materials to a production order or a project. In this case, the project or WIP holds the right to receive the part, and that right is fulfilled when the part is issued. Companies with complex manufacturing processes set up obligations for the issue of these parts in their Bill of Materials processing.

Resource Consumption – When labor or equipment is used on a project or WIP, we record a resource consumption event. Labor is straightforward, equipment more subtle. While equipment itself is an asset, the *use* of equipment is a service. The distinction is like buying a car (purchasing an asset) versus renting a car (acquiring the use of asset over time). Using a production machine is similarly the fulfilment of the WIP or project's right to receive services.

Milestone – In some industries, partial completion can be considered an economic event.

Complete – Completion often signifies the fulfillment of a production order or project. This often has economic significance: the finished good is inspected and received into inventory, much like a receiving report from an external vendor There may be the equivalent of a receiving report when the warehouse inspects and receives the completed good. While the activity resembles an external receipt, the accounting is quite different, which is why most manufacturing companies define "completion" as a separate event.

Transfer – Unlike most events, a transfer does not involve a change in ownership or obligation. Instead, it reflects the movement of resources under the same owner's control. For instance, moving money from a savings account to a checking account changes *where* the money resides, not *who* owns it. The bank serves as custodian in these cases, not as counterparty to an obligation. One common variation of transfer is *deposit*, where cash or checks on hand are transferred to a bank account. Similarly, moving money into an investment account is also a transfer. But if in that account you buy stocks, that will involve the usual buy, pay, and receive events. If you're familiar with financial services, this is what is known collectively as *settlement*. All our examples involve the transfer of money, which is a (short-lived) obligation from one account and is a right for the other account. This is more obvious if there are two banks involved. Organizations rarely record in their books a transfer of goods (say, from one warehouse to another), as it generally does not affect the overall financial position of the organization. The exception would be if moving to a different jurisdiction affects valuation or property tax obligation, you should consider physical movement a financial business event.

Recap on the Core Events

Our discussion did not include an exhaustive list of core events. Different industries will have additional events, and as described below, some events will be composites of the aforementioned events. But don't be too quick to add additional event types. Our list covers a great many cases. You might be better off creating an alias for some of these events if you would like to use different terms but try to keep with the core concepts.

We will introduce a few additional events in the next chapter.

Most companies have several frequently occurring events that are combinations of the above. For instance, paying cash to buy an item at a store is the combination of ordering and receiving the goods, being billed for them, and paying all in one. Companies may create combo events for convenience, but in accounting, each underlying step is still treated as if it occurred independently. We call the process of creating additional events from initial events *spawning*—for example, event X spawned event Y.

We also expect many implementations to use spawning rules that are more complex than just copying. For instance, a retail sales event may spawn a sales tax event. In this case, the original event (the customer purchase) spawns another set of events, each at the prevailing jurisdiction's tax rate. One is the right to receive payment from the customer for the amount of the tax (recognized immediately at the point of sale), while the other records the obligation to pay to the tax authority the amount levied, which will be paid later.

Intention

In data-centric accounting, the main driver of policy is the event type. The event type, together with attributes attached to the event—such as unit cost and resource type—provides most of what's needed drive the automation, though not entirely.

Sometimes the treatment of an event isn't clear-cut. Take, for example, the purchase of chocolate. If you run a cookie company, the chocolate might be raw material for cookie production, in which case it should be charged to the raw materials account (an Asset). But if it's for the tour room or the executive lounge, the chocolate's cost should instead be recognized as a general operating expense.

We believe the person best equipped to make that determination is the one who placed the order. Presumably, they know why the chocolate was purchased. Instead of requiring them to assign an account number or make a *recognition* determination, we propose introducing a simpler classification we call *intention*.

For our purposes, intention is simply shorthand for why someone initiated a transaction—for example, the purchase of some chocolate. Most companies will only need a small set of intentions to handle these distinctions—and the fewer you define, the less training is required, and the fewer errors will be introduced.

Some of the intentions you will likely want to consider are:

- Material for production (raw materials inventory)
- Material for resale (merchandise inventory)

- Operating expense
- Sale in normal course of business
- Sale of fixed asset (not revenue, but may have gain or loss)

Depending on the nature of the business, you will want a different set of intentions. For instance, if you are not manufacturing, you do not need an intention to distinguish raw material from directly expensed material.

Armed with this, most of the accounting policy decisions can be resolved by a simple table evaluated at run time by the system.

Policy-Driven Recognition

Here is a small sample of an accounting policy. This policy is not fully data-centric, as it still uses general ledger accounts to help accountants see how policy-driven recognition can work. In the follow-on implementation guidebook, we recommend a transition phase to data-centric that includes this type of policy.

Intention	Event Type	Affects Income Statement?	Account to Increase	Account to Decrease	Timing	Valuation
Operating Exp	Receive Bill	Yes	540 (Op Ex)	210 (AP)	Bill Date	Bill Amount
Material for Resale	Receive Bill	No	120 (Inventory)	210 (AP)	Bill Date	Bill Amount
Operating Exp	Payment	No	210 (AP)	101 (Checking Acct)	Check Date	Check Amount

Figure 4.7: **A Policy Excerpt**

The first two columns drive the rest of the results. If we know the intention and the event type, we know whether to recognize the event, and further what account to charge it to. The last two columns help us with the timing and valuation issues of policy. In some cases, the policy will be delegated.

This represents only a small subset of a full policy, but with a bit of imagination, you can see the total scope is, at most, the product (multiplication) of the number of intentions and the number of event types. By keeping both sets limited, the policy table remains manageable.

This raises another question: if our policy table only contains a few dozen—or at most a few hundred—rows, how do we get to the number of accounts typical in traditional systems? The simple answer is: we don't. We don't need them. We can use other attributes on the transactions to make finer-grained and more consistent distinctions in our financial reports.

Now that we've described the event-driven foundation of data-centric accounting, we return to the concepts introduced at the beginning of this chapter.

Financial Activity Directly Driven by Business Events

Traditional financial accounting requires a human in the loop, directly or indirectly.

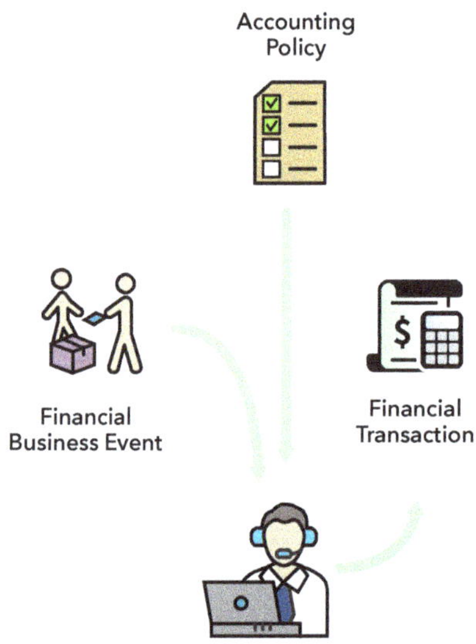

Figure 4.8: How Financial Transactions are Currently Created

In the bookkeeper model, the bookkeeper considers the event that has just occurred, determines how it is to be valued and classified, decides what accounting period it applies to, and so forth.

The bookkeeper considers the organization's accounting policy and accounting standards in making these decisions.

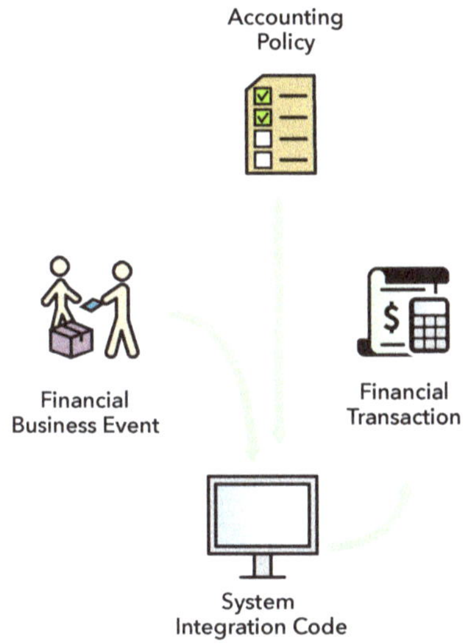

Figure 4.9: How Some Current Systems Automate Creation of Financial Transactions

In Figure 4.9, the systems integrator is making these same determinations for a set of transactions from a given source, based on their understanding of accounting policy and standards.

This process is straightforward to automate. Doing so not only improves speed and reduces labor, but it also ensures that the policies are always consistently applied.

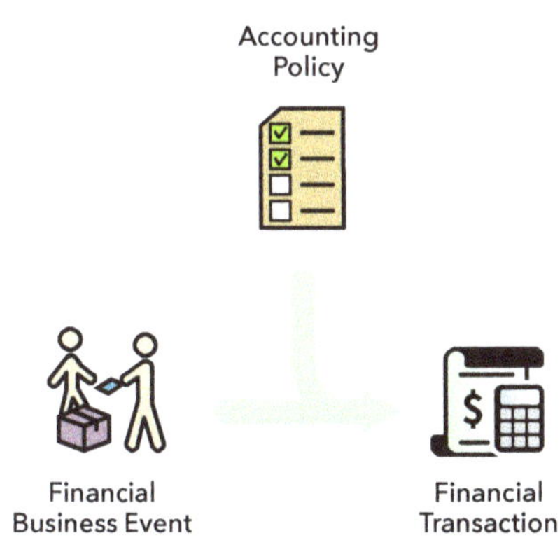

Figure 4.10: Automating the Creation of Financial Transactions

We could imagine GenAI making these determinations. Or perhaps a simple, previous generation AI rules engine. It turns out we don't need anything nearly that complicated. A simple table is all you need. In fact, a table that is stored as a graph. This approach is far more verifiable and easier to implement than what will no doubt become next years' fad: trying to get LLMs to understand your accounting policy without hallucinating.

We will show a simple version of this. You might say, "That's too simple—we have much more complex scenarios." Of course, you do. But in every case we've seen, this principle can be employed to derive the information needed for financial processing and reporting. Even if you only get 98 percent of your workload automated, that is still a big win.

The two things you need to know are:

> Very few business event types give rise to most of the financial transaction instances.
>
> A simple secondary bit of information that we are introducing, we call *intention*, can make the remaining distinctions that cannot be made based solely on the event type.

Immutable Data at Rest

Earlier, we discussed the need to shift from data flow to data at rest. Let's now get more specific about what that means in data-centric accounting.

In a data flow—or data pipeline as they are often called—each process has one or more data inputs and one or more data outputs. The process transforms the data in some way.

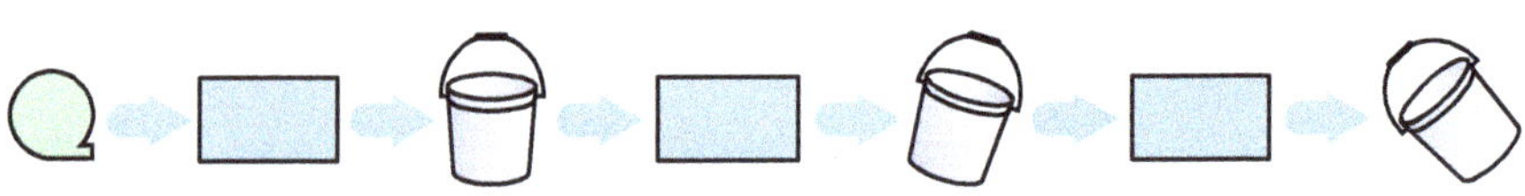

Figure 4.11: **The Typical Data Workflow**

We see it as a bucket brigade except, at each step, water is being combined from other sources, aggregated, and otherwise cleansed. By the time you get to the end, you've lost any hope of direct traceability.

In Chapter 3, we discussed Sarbanes-Oxley audits as a symptom of a problem. This is the problem: we have financial reports, but their origins are murky. When we trace them back, we find out that the data came from hundreds of bucket brigades. So we go out and document hundreds of bucket brigades and believe we have an idea of where our financial data comes from. By the way, these are bucket brigades that change on a monthly basis. They combine and split data—and many of the buckets are literally just Excel sheets[19].

In contrast to the bucket brigade, in a data-centric system, the data isn't copied, and this makes it easier to trace it to the source. It is possible to know exactly where your data comes from, down to the individual contributing transactions, events, and evidence.

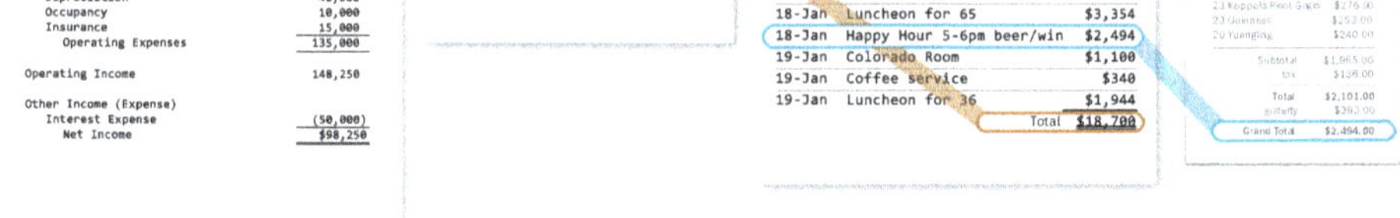

Figure 4.12: **Tracing a Financial Report Line Item**

[19]Panko reports that 88 percent of Excel spreadsheets have errors in at least one percent of their formulas. See Panko, Raymond R. What We Know About Spreadsheet Errors. Honolulu: University of Hawaii, 1998. https://www.researchgate.net/publication/228662532_What_We_Know_About_Spreadsheet_Errors

This illustration shows drilling down from a financial report to its supporting detail. For example, the Training Venues expense of $37,400 on the January income statement can be drilled down to see the breakdown of January workshops whose costs made up that total. From there, the $18,700 workshop at the Marriott can be further drilled down to show its individual cost components. Finally, the January 18 happy hour within the Marriott portfolio can be opened to display the actual receipt from that event.

Not shown in the illustration is that this drill-down capability applies to all other income statement line items as well. Many existing accounting systems do this, but only up to a point. That point typically is to the edge of the accounting system. If the accounting system got its input from another system—say, an expense reporting application, a CRM system, or a benefits election system—its ability to follow the flow pretty much stops at the application boundary.

What we are suggesting here is that the boundary is coterminous with the boundary of the organization, not the accounting department.

As soon as the event occurs anywhere in the organization, it is captured, and every aspect of that capture is now available as part of its audit trail.

Machine-Executable Accounting Policies

Recall that when we first introduced the concept of accounting policy, we said it can get quite complex—especially when you consider all the possible situations and variation across industries. Our contention is you do a lot of that heavy thinking once and reduce your company's policy to a few simple tables that can be executed by the system. ***When you do so, the policy becomes machine executable.***

The first policy question to be addressed is this: *what does this policy apply to, and therefore, what should it be attached to?* Policies always have context—they are attached to something.

Let's begin with simple ones that are usually already automated (although often this automation is hard coded in the application system or its configuration). We will look at the basis of each policy and think through where, in your data-centric database, the policy and its options should be attached. From there, we will work our way up to more difficult examples. As we'll see shortly, these policies are organized around different types of resources, specifically:

- Inventory
- Equipment
- Labor
- Receivables

Inventory Costing

When you sell your finished goods inventory (or on-hand inventory, if you are a retailer or wholesaler) or issue raw material to a production order, you must assign a cost to the inventory sold or used. In the case of the sale, this cost becomes the Cost of Goods Sold. For raw material issues, it goes into the work-in-process cost, which will eventually become part of the finished goods cost.

There are several methods for assigning a cost to the next item taken from inventory. For now, our point is simply that there are different methods, and we need a way to assign the methods to different inventory items. Each method determines the value of the next item you take from inventory based on:

> **Average Cost** – The issued part value is based on the average cost of the items on hand.
>
> **FIFO** (First In, First Out) – The issued part value is that of the oldest item on hand.
>
> **LIFO** (Last In, First Out) – The issued part value is that of the newest item on hand.
>
> **Specific Item / Specific Lot** – The issuer specifies which cost lot to use for cost determination (commonly used in investment accounts).
>
> **Market or Replacement Cost** – The value is based on market.

Each of these decisions will have major impacts on costs, and therefore, profit. They will also affect taxes. There will be a great deal of thought and analysis that goes into the choice of method. Once the method is selected, it merely needs to be implemented consistently. Many accounting systems allow only one method, because the methods require storing different information (for example, FIFO and LIFO require keeping the receipt records with their costs at least until those quantities have been issued, where Average Cost does not). Accounting policy, however, allows a company to select different methods for different items, as long as they are consistent.

Theoretically you could assign a different method to each SKU[20] (Stock Keeping Unit), but we have never encountered this. More common is to assign a method to a class of resources. The policy ends up being a table.

Inventory Class	Financial Reporting Method	Tax Reporting Method
Produce	FIFO	Average
Canned Goods	LIFO	LIFO
Investments	Average cost	Specific Tax Lot
All Other Inventory	Average	Average

Here, "produce" is being used as a noun (as in lettuce), not as the verb meaning "to make."

Figure 4.13: **Inventory Costing Options**

Note: For instance, if you choose LIFO for tax purposes, you must also use LIFO for financial reporting for that class of inventory.

[20]SKU stands for Stock Keeping Unit. It is the level of detail at which parts are interchangeable, making it the correct level for detailed inventory accounting records.

The implementation then must do three things:

> Ensure that every resource is assigned to exactly one class.
>
> Upon receipt of new goods, maintain separate costs by shipment or lot.
>
> Use the specified algorithm at time of issue to cost the items, depending on the method chosen.

Depreciating Fixed Assets

Fixed assets—such as property, plant, equipment, and vehicles—are purchased and used over time. The economic value associated with their usage is called *depreciation*. It is not tied to the reduction in value of the asset. You might buy an apartment complex for $5,000,000 and sell it 10 years later for $7,000,000. Each year you owned the asset, you are allowed to depreciate (expense) part of your investment, even if it is going up in value.

Similar to inventory, the depreciation method you choose has a profound impact on profit and taxes. Tax law allows a company to use different methods and schedules for financial reports versus tax reporting, so a depreciation policy will often show both:

Fixed Asset Class	Estimated Useful Life	Financial Report Method	Tax Method
Buildings	40 years	Straight Line	MACRS
Production Machinery	1,000,000 units	Units of Activity	Section 179
Vehicles	200,000 miles	Units of Activity	MACRS
Office Machinery	5 years	Double Declining	Section 179
Furniture	7 years	Straight Line	Section 179

Figure 4.14: **Depreciation Options**

We won't go into the details of each depreciation—they can easily be looked up. The purpose here is to show how to organize your depreciation policy. The method you choose will determine what additional information you need to retain. To implement this, you need to make sure:

> Every fixed asset must belong to exactly one class.
>
> The depreciation method associated with each asset class will determine what additional information needs to be maintained (for instance, some methods require an estimated salvage value).
>
> Record when the asset is "put into service," meaning the date when it was installed and ready to be used for its intended purpose.

At disposition time, you need to know the actual value you received (if any) for the asset.

We advocate generating the entire depreciation schedule for the expected life of the asset at the time it is put into service. In this way, any future-oriented reports (such as commitment reports and budgets) will have this information available, and it eliminates the need to run periodic batch processes. When the asset is disposed, the book value (original cost less depreciation to that point) can be determined and future depreciation cancelled.

Labor Costing

There are several policies around costing labor. The key question is: what should be included in the calculation of an hour of labor? Should you include the employer costs that vary directly with time spent (such as payroll taxes or vacation accruals?) Should you include employer period costs for employees (like health insurance or office space)? And should you apportion a share of department overhead—such as HR or Accounting—onto labor costs?)

There is also a consideration on the mechanics of applying labor cost to projects or products. One option is the *actual* method, where employees complete time reports and record, hour by hour, what they were working on. The other main option is *standard*, which is used when the volume or indirect nature of work makes it impractical for employees to track specific products or orders. In a production line, there may be hundreds of orders being processed at a time, and employees may simply charge their time to the line as a whole. Engineers then estimate the "standard" hours per product and reconcile periodically.

These are policy decisions. They can be applied to different labor groups. While these methods are less standard, they are still amenable to automation. Below is an example of a labor costing policy:

Category	Burden Includes	Burden Allocated via	Applied via
Direct (Manufacturing) Labor	Employer taxes and benefits + overtime premium	Hour	Standard Cost Unit
Indirect Labor	Employer taxes and benefits	Hour	Actual Cost
Individual subcontractors	Occupancy allocation	Hour	Actual Cost
Salaried	Employer taxes and benefits + Pension + Occupancy	Month	Actual Cost

Figure 4.15: **Labor Costing Options**

To implement this, you need to ensure:

> All labor (employees and hourly subcontractors) is assigned to a category.
>
> Indirect costs (such as employer taxes, vacation, rent, etc.) are grouped into defined cost pools.
>
> Hours or other allocation metrics are aggregated per pool to determine a burden rate.
>
> The burden cost is then added to direct labor cost and applied to projects, products, or departments according to the chosen method.

Allowing for Bad Debt

Sometimes, customers don't pay for goods they've already received. Since the revenue and related expenses have already been recognized, this creates a need for an adjustment. How an organization handles this is another policy.

The two main mechanisms are to wait until the event occurs and declare it to be "bad debt," or to provide for it ahead of time, "allowance for bad debt." The former is based on an event the organization declares (occasionally, there is an external event such as bankruptcy or turning the account over to an outside collection agency, but often it is just an internal declaration) the other a periodic evaluation of experience with bad debt.

As with other accounting policies, the bad debt reporting policy could be linked to Geographic Region or Product Line.

Recognition and Classification

The revenue recognition policy determines when revenue (and its attendant cost of goods sold) should be reported on the income statement. There are similar criteria for non-cost of goods expenses. Standards for recognition are stipulated by GAAP and IFRS and vary across industries.

In traditional accounting, classification is implemented by assigning the proper account number, as this is the primary mechanism for getting financial amounts onto specific line items in the financial report. Therefore, at the highest level, classification is recognition. If your classification process assigns a transaction to an income statement account (typically starting with 4 or higher), you are recognizing that transaction.

We will keep the two concepts separate (recognition and classification) as we will have many other mechanisms for both. The trick to automating the policy is providing appropriate parameters at the time a financial business event is originated to ensure that the recognition and classification are done consistently. Most financial business events are initiated by non-accountants, so this mechanism must not rely on information only available to accountants (including even the term *recognition*).

The core driver is the type of financial business event, but additional context is needed to make a final determination. We'll explore this in more detail in the next chapter.

Elimination of Journals, Journal Entries, and Posting

Traditionally, a journal served as the chronological record of all activities entering the accounting department. Entries were first captured and later posted to the affected account ledgers.

The journal is primarily an artefact of accounting being a system separate from all other systems. And it is a product of the fact that often accounting was at the end of a long series of input and output transactions. The accounting system needed a single consistent representation to begin its process.

In the data-centric approach, events are captured at the point where they occur within the organization—not in a traditional journal. However, the system knows which events lead to financial activity, so it can add financial information (such as valuation, recognition, and classification) to the event.

Closing Redefined from a Process to a State Change

Two factors led to and reinforced the closing process. The first was the inevitable delay between the occurrence of an event and its capture in the books. The second was the number of entries that were based on analytic calculations that could only be done after one was sure that all the transactions of the previous period were closed.

These characteristics will no longer be true. The financial impact will be posted within a fraction of a second after the event is first registered in the organization. Allowances, allocations, and similar adjustments will be performed algorithmically, eliminating the need to wait for an arbitrary batch process.

For instance, if we determine that our bad debt allowance should be two-tenths of one percent of sales, the system will post two-tenths of one percent of every invoice to bad debt allowance, immediately, as the invoice is posted. Actual bad debts will then be written off against the allowance when they occur.

Model-Driven Financial Reporting

In traditional accounting, financial reports are driven from the ledger balances of the account ledgers in the chart of accounts. This is the generalized model of where financial reports come from.

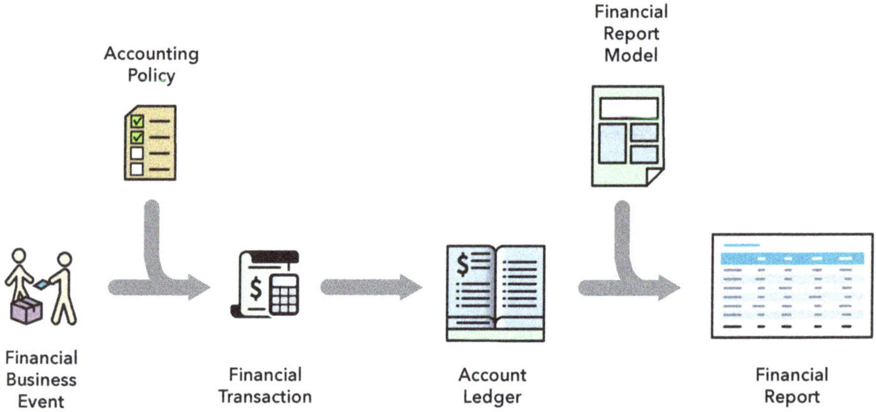

Figure 4.16: Traditional Model-Driven Financial Reporting

We will explore the mechanics of future report generation in the follow-on implementation guidebook, but here we outline at a high level how the process will change. Traditionally, financial reports come from the ledger. Management accounting reports often come from a warehouse that stores the transactions posted to the ledgers. Because of this, they can make some distinctions that are not available at the ledger level.

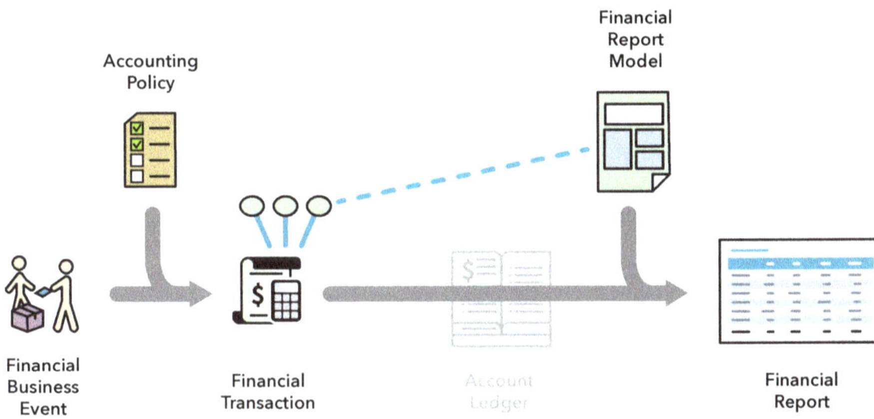

Figure 4.17: **Model-Driven Financial Reporting Without Ledgers**

Big Data refers to techniques for dealing with large volumes of information. Massively parallel, cloud-based techniques have made developers comfortable with transaction volumes that previously were unthinkable.

Data-centric financial reports as described thus far will draw directly from the financial transactions. Fifty years ago, we would have thought the volumes prohibitive. In today's processing environments, these often wouldn't even qualify as *big data*.

In the next chapter, we will take data-centric accounting a step further by processing directly from commitments (not shown in this illustration), which are directly modified by business events.

Equity Accounts as Counterparty Accounts

One final thought to close this out. As we have mentioned and will elaborate more, we are convinced that the only accounts that we need to have in an accounting system are resource accounts and counterparty accounts.

This includes the equity portion of the balance sheet. The counterparties are the investors. For a closely held company, these consist of a limited number of people and organizations. Each has a capital account, and each gets a proportional share of distributions or dividends as of their date of record.

There may be multiple categories of ownership (preferred stock versus common stock for instance), and companies may repurchase their own shares (treasury stock). In substance, however, this still represents ownership, with the company itself as the owner.

Summary of Data-Centric Accounting So Far

Data-centric accounting deals directly with the business events that give rise to economic activity of the organization.

> Data is captured immutably at its source. It is not transformed, transmitted, or transmuted in any way.
>
> Each source event is automatically augmented with valuation and classification information based on machine-readable accounting policy.
>
> New financial business events are immediately posted to the financial report model.
>
> A rigorous model defines every financial report the organization provides to outsiders.
>
> Real-time financial results are available, containing everything that has happened in the organization.
>
> Every reported value can be traced back to its source, with the full history of every human and computer process that was involved preserved along with the data.

It's hard to imagine how it can get better than this: most events end up on the financial reports within a second of being captured. ***What's not to like?***

Well, nothing, really. This is great, and most companies would be ecstatic with this. "But wait there's more!"

In the next chapter, we explain how a fully data-centric accounting system can go further: enabling temporal slicing of expenses and revenue so that weekly—or even daily—P&Ls make sense, while also providing more complete visibility into an organization's commitments.

CHAPTER 5

Data-Centric Accounting Directly from Commitments

As we've seen, data-centric accounting provides a baseline of instantaneous financial reporting. Work with this for a while, and we believe you'll soon want more.

Instantaneous reporting naturally creates the desire for shorter financial reporting time-intervals. Why not weekly, or even daily, income statements? The challenge lies in the nature of temporal resources and services. To make meaningful short-interval financial reports, we need to address this first.

The manual work that remains in areas such as determining prepaid expenses and unearned income will challenge us to think through what gives rise to these situations—and how might we automate them. It turns out there is a deeper relationship between many events, and once we uncover these connections, we will find a way to automate this concern.

Getting to the bottom of that issue opens up a series of new possibilities. The main one being the ability to fully integrate commitment management. Once commitments are integrated with actual results, the ability to control spending steps up a level.

By capturing the relationship among events, we can reduce the amount of information needed to capture with each event. Not only is this labor saving, but it also sets us up for an additional level of automation. Depending on the industry, a high percentage of all financial business events can even be anticipated. This shifts us forward to something much closer to the way human perception works and even puts us on the precipice of cross-organization accounting.

Deeper Dive Into the Semantics of Accounting

The concepts in this section need a bit of introduction. We take some common terms and make sure we have a shared deeper understanding of what they mean, as these are important building blocks. We use terms that are familiar to everyone but perhaps for which their full ramifications haven't been fully considered. We hope you enjoy this bit of the journey; we've found that, in a relatively brief space, it ties together some previously diverse ideas.

Asset

In its latest Conceptual Framework for Financial Reporting, the FASB defined an asset as

---

"An asset is a present right of an entity to an economic benefit.[21]"

We're going to break down what rights and obligations are, where they come from, and how they are rooted in forms of ownership. We're going to look at what economic benefit means and when it is appropriate to place a value on it.

Ownership Rights

Most of our ideas about ownership start with possession—as in "possession is nine-tenths of the law." But, in reality, possession is only one aspect of ownership. Ownership is a bundle of rights. The exact set of rights determines the nature of ownership and by extension our accounting treatment. Each industry tends to use different terms and bundles these rights differently, but if you carefully dissect what is being described, we think you will find some combination of these ownership primitives.

These are the primary rights that contribute to ownership (full ownership means possessing all these rights):

> **Possession** – In most contexts, possession refers to the right to move something. If we possess a lamp, a car, or a book, possession gives us the right to physically move it. When we refer to possessing a house, we are really referring to the right of access rather than the narrower definition of possession. For physical items, possession is exclusive—only one entity can possess them at a time. For digital items, possession is having a copy that you can move. It's important to note that one can possess something without holding many of the other rights associated with ownership.

[21]FASB. 2021. Statement of Financial Accounting Concepts No. 8: Conceptual Framework for Financial Reporting, as amended December 2021.

Right to use or access – One of the most central ownership concepts is the right to use the thing owned. This is sometimes called *usufructuary* rights, which are rights to use and benefit from someone else's property without owning it. When you rent a building, you have the right to use or to sublet it, but you won't have the right to destroy it or sell it.

Right to economic benefit – Some assets have streams of economic benefit that accrue to the owners of this right. The separation of these rights made mortgage-backed securities possible. The right to receive the economic benefit (the mortgage payments) was separated from the underlying mortgage itself. It was bundles of these rights that became MBSs (Mortgage-Backed Securities). Note that sometimes the economic benefit is contingent, as in the case of being a beneficiary of a life insurance policy.

Exclusivity (right to prevent others from using) – A patent or a copyright is an ownership right that is the right to prevent others from using the asset. This right is necessary for non-physical things—like inventions, written works, trademarks, or songs—because they are easily copied, potentially undermining exclusivity of possession. For physical goods, having control of the item usually prevents others from using it. A patent provides some of that protection for assets that are harder to prevent others from using.

Right to transfer (sell) – You may possess a copy of a movie but not have the right to sell it. Your right to sell may be impinged—for instance, if you own shares in a privately held organization, you may be prevented from transferring them.

Right to modify – Leasing an office space does not, generally, give you the right to make structural changes, such as knocking out walls, without prior approval of the building's owner.

Right to consume or destroy – Perhaps the strongest level of ownership includes the right to consume the asset (as in a raw material) or destroy it (as in the leveling of a house on a property to make room for another building). If you "own" a historical building, you know that you do not have the right to knock it down. This idea of consumption also brings up some edge cases. You can't really "own" human resources, but you do have the right to consume them (that is, to utilize their labor during their normal working hours in the normal course of their work).

Control – The ability to control a resource can be independent of its beneficial ownership or its possession. Control also involves the right to make decisions about a resource. For example, in a managed IRA (Individual Retirement Account—a US form of self-managed pension), you have beneficial ownership, but not possession (which lies with the custodian) nor do you have control (which lies with the asset manager).

Right to pledge – Pledging means offering your ownership rights in exchange for something else, usually a loan. For example, when you get a mortgage, you pledge your ownership rights in the house against the risk of nonpayment. Pledging is also called putting up collateral or securing a loan. If you pledge your right to receive the economic benefit of your accounts receivable, that is called *factoring*. Margin accounts are loans to buy additional securities or options, where other assets in your portfolio are pledged. The financial services industry calls putting up one asset to secure credit or a loan the act of *hypothecating*. The key point to note is that pledging reduces your ownership rights—and that same asset should not be pledged multiple times.

We will return to many of these distinctions later, as we explore how different forms of ownership determine whether something shows up on our financial statements.

Rights and Obligations

Generally, rights are permissions. Many rights, such as the right to free speech or even the right to transit on public lands, are nice to have and nice to reflect on, but don't have any bearing on accounting valuation. In accounting, the rights that matter are those that are based on obligations—specifically, someone else's obligation to us. However, these obligations only become economic rights when we have a beneficial ownership right in them.

It is the obligation that creates the right.

For example, a mortgagee's obligation to make loan payments creates the mortgage holder's right to receive them. That right, together with the creditworthiness of the mortgagee, is what makes the asset valuable. Similarly, if you own a bond, you have the right to receive interest and principal repayments on a corporate or government loan, and you treat it as an asset. Unlike a car or a warehouse full of inventory, however, this asset's value is entirely contingent on the borrower's repayment.

Debt is an obligation (for the company or individual who has committed to its repayment). While the right to receive the payments is relatively easy to transfer, the obligation to make those payments is much harder to transfer.

Granting Credit

Speaking of debt, it may be worthwhile to explore where it actually comes from. While we typically think of debt coming from a bank or the government, it is a much broader concept than that.

> Anytime you sell something and allow the buyer to pay you later, you have granted credit. This is the equivalent of loaning them money, except you arrived at it by offering goods or services first and allowing them to pay later.

We now turn to another form of granting credit. When you commit to buying something but allow the seller to deliver later, we say you have granted a form of credit. The seller owes you the goods or services just as a customer who pays later owes you cash.

In both cases, credit arises when one party agrees to receive cash, goods, or services in the future.

Value

Part of the FASB's definition of assets involves economic benefit. Yet many things have economic benefit without being assigned an accounting value. For instance, a company's brand or reputation may carry a great deal of economic benefit but is rarely reflected in financial statements. The rare case of monetizing some of these less tangible assets will be taken up under the section, *Goodwill*.

This creates situations where we may have an asset—a right that provides economic benefit—that carries no value and therefore does not show up on the balance sheet. We will explore other ways an asset's value may go to zero.

A major task of accounting is assigning value to an organization's resources and transactions. Accountants call the value recorded in the books the *book value*. These book values are conservative, usually based on what was historically paid in an arm's length transaction. They are often adjusted through procedures such as depreciation, which can reduce an asset's value on the books to zero.

Fully depreciated assets effectively vanish from the balance sheet even if the company is still using them. But they aren't gone. They still have *economic benefit* even though they financially are no longer assets. We keep records for such assets for two reasons. First, if the asset is sold (and our ownership rights allow the sale), we will recognize a *gain* on the difference between the sales price and the updated depreciated cost. Second, historical cost and depreciation are just two ways to value an asset. Other ways are allowed in some scenarios, including market value, replacement cost, or other measures.

For this reason, accounting keeps track of all resources that provide *economic benefit*. For GAAP reporting, historical cost is typically used, but for other purposes, we may employ an alternative.

Resource

The term *resources* gets thrown around pretty casually. We refer to "Human Resources" and "Natural Resources," but in accounting we need to narrow down the scope and be precise.

It is tempting to consider any asset on the balance sheet as a resource, as many of them are. I don't think we'd get any pushback suggesting that inventory or cash on hand are resources. They can be employed in carrying out the mission of the organization.

> A resource is a thing you own that you can consume.

In fact, these are what we call *storable resources*, a category we'll contrast with *temporal resources* shortly.

But we need to draw the line with items like *accounts receivable.* The true resource here is cash, but we don't yet have it, so it is not our resource. Accounts Receivable is a *right*, as discussed above, to receive cash in the future, not cash itself. Only when you collect (or sell the receivable to a collection agency) do you actually have a resource you can spend.

There are other things that *look* like resources but don't meet our definition. Take *prepaid expenses*, for example. If you've paid for something that you haven't yet received, it shows on the balance sheet as an asset. It is meant to reflect the economic value of a good or service you haven't yet received. In reality, that's just a right to receive a future good or resource—it isn't a consumable resource today.

Storable Resource: A resource is storable if it can be accumulated for later consumption. Temporal resources, like labor can be consumed, but only at the same rate they are acquired and therefore are not storable. Storable resources include cash, inventory, and equipment.

Human resources—and many types of services—fall into a different category. They are consumed at the same time they are acquired, making them *temporal resources*. You can't stockpile labor hours or keep them in inventory. All you have is a *rate* of consumption: one hour per hour, or forty hours per week. Once that time has passed, the resource is gone.

Equipment (often lumped in the heading *Property, Plant and Equipment* in most financial reports), by contrast, is interesting. You acquire it all at once, but you typically consume it over time.

Consumption

The word *consumption* comes from the root *consume*, which originally meant "to eat." In a broader sense, it refers to using up a resource. Eating certainly fits that bill: once eaten, food can't be used again.

Consuming a resource makes it unavailable for other uses. When we consume raw materials by putting them into our finished products, they are no longer available for any other product. When we consume an hour of someone's time, that hour cannot be reclaimed or used for another task.

But not everything we acquire is consumed in this way. Some things—like recipes, data, programs, or manuals—can be used repeatedly without being used up. These are resources that don't diminish with use, which makes them distinct from consumables like raw materials or labor hours.

Account

Early in the book, we suggested that *account* is a very loose term. Most of the "accounts" in a modern accounting system are just mechanisms for categorizing financial information on reports. But this doesn't mean there aren't any true accounts.

Counterparty Accounts

We need an account for every counterparty that has granted us credit, and for every counterparty to whom we have granted credit. This allows us to track their standing with us—their balance—after multiple transactions. For example, if we make several sales to one entity and they make a payment to us, we need to know what they still owe. This is the basis for *accounts payable* (when a vendor extends credit to us) and *accounts receivable* (when we extend credit to a customer).

In the same way, we also need to track goods and services that are ordered but not yet received, as well as those that our customers have ordered but not yet received.

Resource Accounts

We also need accounts for inventory. For each part type, we must track both its quantity on hand and its value. More generally, we need accounts for all resources such as bank accounts and equipment accounts.

This brings us back to the distinction between *real* and *convenience* accounts. The only real accounts we need are those that (1) maintain the values of our relationships with counterparties, and (2) track the quantity and value of our storable resources. All other accounts exist to aid report writing, and as such we call them *convenience accounts*, especially as we have other ways of providing the same level of reporting granularity.

Goodwill

Goodwill is occasionally a line item on an organization's balance sheet. It shows up in the aftermath of an acquisition. You are not allowed to book transactions that would recognize goodwill in the normal course of business.

Goodwill is excess value of an acquisition of another company. When you acquire a company, all their assets and liabilities become yours (though there are asset-only acquisitions, we'll go with the default case). The net fair market value of their assets and liabilities is called their *book value.* If the acquired company had $1 million in inventory and a $400,000 note payable, its book value would be $600,000.

Most companies are not purchased based solely on the value of their assets; they are typically purchased on their ability to generate future income. As industries become less capital-intensive, these values drift further and further apart.

Let's explore the example of the organization we just mentioned with a $600,000 book value. If the company had been making a $120,000 profit per year, a buyer might pay five times earnings to buy that company. Multiplying $120,000 by five gives a selling price of $600,000. In that scenario, the purchase price equals the book value, and there is no goodwill.

But the company could have been making $240,000 profit per year—or even $2 million. The amount of inventory does not limit revenue or profit if it can be turned over rapidly enough. In strategic industries, a buyer might pay far more than five times earnings. Any purchase price over $600,000 generates *goodwill.*

For example, if the company earns $240,000 per year and a buyer pays ten times earnings, the purchase price would be $2.4 million. The difference between the purchase price ($2.4 million) and the book value ($600,000) is $1.8 million—this is recorded *goodwill* on the balance sheet as an intangible asset.

Under GAAP, public companies cannot amortize goodwill. Instead, they must test the goodwill asset for *impairment*, an analysis meant to determine if the intangible asset is still worth what the company originally paid for. If it is not, the difference between the current value and the book value is a markdown called *impairment*. The process does not allow for a markup based on this analysis. Private companies, however, may choose to amortize goodwill—typically over ten years—thereby avoiding the need for impairment testing.

Intangible Assets

In a few cases companies are allowed—and even encouraged—to record intangible assets (besides goodwill) on their books. The most common case is when an organization buys a patent or a trademark. GAAP does not permit companies to book internal expenditures to intangible assets. For instance, if your scientists and lawyers spent $1 million on inventing and filing a patent, only the filing fee (a few thousand dollars) could be booked. However, if you bought that same patent from another organization, you may book the full amount you paid for it to Intangible Assets on your balance sheet and amortize it accordingly.

One important accounting distinction for intangible assets is that they can be transferred (sold) separately.

Internally developed intellectual property is often a key reason why companies are acquired for far more than their book value. For example, imagine acquiring an organization whose only real asset is an internally developed patent. Because the filing fee was immaterial, the company's book value is essentially zero. If you purchase that company for $1 million, the difference is not recorded as a patent in your books, but as goodwill—even though, in substance, you are really paying for the patent.

Assets

As defined by the FASB, an asset is ***"a present right of an entity to an economic benefit."***

Now, let's further define what this means. Assets are cash and storable resources (such as inventory and equipment), along with our committed rights to receive them from others. These committed rights include accounts receivable as well as prepaid inventory, prepaid expense, and goods, supplies and services ***"due in."***
A reportable asset is any asset (as defined above) that has a non-zero value, plus the value of intangible assets and goodwill, whether or not they provide an economic benefit.

It's hard to believe, when you look at the dozens of accounts on many balance sheets, that they are all directly derivable from the resources, rights, and goodwill. But they are.

Liabilities

All the liabilities on the balance sheet are just obligations to third parties. There is no such thing as a *negative resource*. What we call *liabilities*—loans, taxes payable, accrued salaries, unearned income, and goods, supplies and services ***"due out"***—are all just obligations to third parties.

Contingent Obligations

Up to this point, we've only discussed obligations that are extant—commitments that have been made but not yet fulfilled.

There is a whole category of obligations that are contingent on future action. Depending on the industry, some of these will be factored into the balance sheet.

The simplest form of contingent obligation is an offer.

An offer is essentially half of a contract—a contract in search of a counterparty. Depending on how it is expressed, an offer may become binding without any further negotiation. Until recently, airlines had to honor "mistake fares" where they inadvertently offered international trips for a fraction of their typical prices.

Once again, in the department of "*same word, different meaning,*" we find an interesting twist in the Financial Services industry around the term *order*.

In most businesses, the term *order*—whether a purchase order, sales order, or even a production order—refers to a mutually agreed commitment.

In financial services, however, an *order* is an offer. If you place an order to buy a stock at $90 a share while the market price is $100, that order will likely sit idle. Your order is just an offer. If something happens (say, the market crashes) and someone accepts your "order" at $90, the order becomes a *trade* (which is what most other industries would have called an order in the first place).

Another form of contingent obligation is insurance. When you buy insurance, you have an immediate and certain obligation to pay the premium.

An insurance carrier's core obligation is to provide *indemnity*. What indemnity really represents is an obligation contingent on some future, unknowable occurrence. For example, if you purchase fire insurance on your house, the insurer has a contingent obligation for the period of indemnity.

As long as nothing happens, the obligation is dormant—the premium you paid (say, $5,000) reflects the economic value of the indemnity. But the moment the contingent event occurs—the house burns down—the contingent obligation kicks in for $500,000 (or whatever is the value of the house).

The Illusion of Event Independence

In the accounting department, financial business events often feel like they come raining down on us. We deal with them one at a time. We call these events *atomic*—meaning each event can be processed to completion on its own. This is a good characteristic of events, and we're not going to remove it.

What we are going to do, however, is make explicit the connections that have been mostly implicit, manual, or ad hoc.

Suppose a bill arrives—say, for a new printer. The bill gets sent to someone to approve it. That person reviews it, considers their budget, asks who actually ordered it, maybe adds the account number for where it should be charged, and decides whose budget will absorb the cost. Once satisfied, they send it to Nancy, who adds the billing code "001." After that, they finally approve the bill and send it back for processing.

At this point, the processors ask a natural question: *have we received this printer yet?* They ask around and find out the answer is no. Still, because the purchase was made with a prepay discount, they approve it for payment. The bookkeepers, however, are astute enough to realize there is a relationship between this bill and the eventual receipt of the printer. They book the bill as a *prepaid expense* and create a note to ask the department to notify them when it arrives, so they can move the charge from prepaid to the expense account or asset account (depending on the value and your accounting policy) that the original requester indicated.

In this scenario, people rely on general knowledge, research, and asking around to piece things together, and make the right decision. But beneath the surface, there are a series of connections between things that could easily have been explicit, which are currently implicit.

For major purchases, such as raw material, there is typically something called the *three-way match*. This means that before paying an invoice (part 1), they check that the item was actually ordered (part 2) and that it was received (part 3). This creates some connection between events, but the process is either done manually or by source systems other than the financial accounting system itself. The financial accounting system typically does not have all three parts of the three-way match, and often only is notified when the match is complete.

Interestingly, a precursor to this line of thinking—the REA model of accounting (Resource, Events, Agents)[22,23,]—had a provision for part of this problem. REA introduced a relationship called *duality* to connect causally related events. For instance, duality was meant to link the payment for something directly to the receipt of the thing paid for. However, implementation of duality is difficult. In practice, accounting systems typically link invoices to payments rather than linking the payments directly to the related shipping documents.

We dug deeper and found that the real foundation for most of these connections—and more—comes down to longer-term commitments.

Long-Running Business Transactions

So far, we have raised the idea of commitments and relied on a shared, mostly informal sense of what they are and where they come from. Now it's time to go deeper to explore not only the different layers of commitments, but also how fundamental they are to business.

At one point, Semantic Arts introduced the idea of what we then called Long Duration Business Transactions (LDBTs). We are all accustomed to transactions that take seconds to complete. With the advent of high-speed automated trading, the timeframe has gone from milliseconds to microseconds for some transactions. On the other end of the spectrum are LDBTs. Unlike a quick, one-off transaction, an LDBT might take years—or even decades—to complete. A mortgage, for instance, may take 30 years before it is finally complete. Employment is another example of a long-running transaction, as are operating a bridge or recovering an ore body. As we examined businesses and government entities, we found that most of the organization's activity was in the context of a handful of LDBTs (which, of course, vary widely from one industry to another).

[22]McCarthy, William E. 1982. "The REA Accounting Model: A Generalized Framework for Accounting Systems in a Shared Data Environment." *The Accounting Review*, 554-578.

[23]Dunn, Cheryl, Gerard, G. J., & Grabski, S. V. (2016). "Resources-Events-Agents Design Theory: A Revolutionary Approach to Enterprise System Design." *Communications of the Association for Information Systems*, 38(1)29.

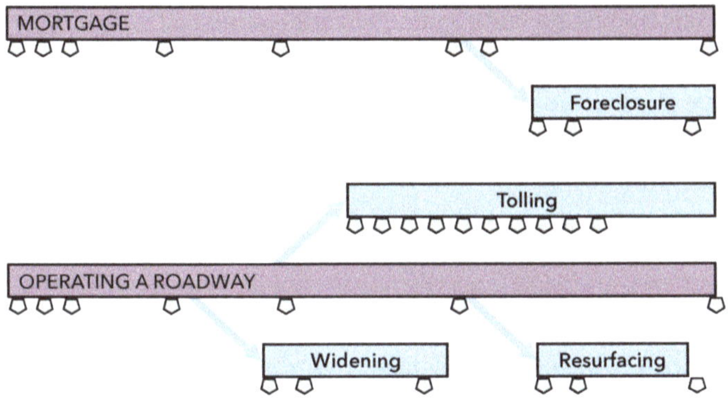

Figure 5.1: Some Long-Running Transactions

Think of all those reminders, payments, penalties, rate adjustments, and foreclosure warnings as events in the life of a mortgage. Or the painting, guardrail repair, toll collection, and resurfacing as part of the life of a bridge. Recognizing the importance of mortgages and bridges to their respective industries was not the profound insight. The real breakthrough was seeing the value that could be obtained by more explicitly linking the day-to-day activity to these long-running pillars of the organization's economy.

Long-Running Commitments

As our gaze shifted to accounting, we became more interested in the commitment aspect of these *long-duration business transactions*. Most of the organizing principles that affect the organization's finances are commitments to third parties and commitments regarding resources.

If you look closely, you will see that most business activity affecting the organization's finances comes down to one of a few things: creating, modifying or fulfilling commitments—or producing, maintaining, or consuming resources. In each case, the day-to-day, minute-to-minute events are simply the execution of a longer-running commitment (with very few exceptions).

Resources generally appear on financial statements as Assets, but commitments only show up partially. Historically, accounting systems recorded sales orders or purchase orders in the books and records only occasionally, and only in certain industries. Accounting principles are generally conservative, and for this reason, there has been a reluctance to include orders in the organization's books and records. Yet in practice, most managers in most industries treat their contracts as firm commitments. We believe commitments are the key to getting a complete picture of an organization's economic situation.

This reluctance to book commitments results in a great deal of information important to running the business being excluding from financial reports. We propose a method for including this information while maintaining clean separation from traditional financial information.

Surprisingly, including this information also solves some other problems that historically have relied on diligent manual processes. As we will see later in this section, we will see how accounting patterns, such as *prepaid expenses* and *unearned income,* are automatically captured and reported based on information we have on long-running commitments.

The Nature of Commitments

We're going to take a slightly deeper grounding in the semantic meaning of commitments to give us some basis for the rest of the discussion.

Informally, we can probably all agree that a bill represents a commitment to pay someone money. But that raises deeper questions: what is the basis for this commitment? How do we know when it is real? How should we value it? And how should we think about unwinding it?

Commitments behave differently from tangible assets. If we own a piece of equipment, we don't spend much time questioning its "realness" or how to unwind it. The equipment exists in the real, physical world; our concerns are mostly about ownership and valuation.

But commitments—where do they actually come from? For this, the work of philosopher John Searle[24] is helpful. Searle believes that

[24]Searle, John R. 1969. *Speech Acts: An Essay in the Philosophy of Language.* Cambridge University. http://dx.doi.org/10.1017/CBO9781139173438

language is related to the world through what he calls *speech acts*. Speech acts come in two flavors: ***"world to word"*** and ***"word to world."***

Speech acts: something expressed by an individual that not only presents information but performs an action.

World to word is about describing the world as it already is. When we talk about the azure sky or the height of a desk, we proceed from the world to words. Many domains have a great deal of "world to word" content—including science, medicine, land surveying, journalism, and surveillance. When we assay a sample, measure a blood pressure, triangulate a benchmark, report a natural disaster, or record an intrusion, we are proceeding from world to word.

World to word: a speech act that records the state of some aspect of the world.

Word to world: a speech act that creates something that didn't exist before, such as a commitment.

Word to world is where language brings something into existence that wasn't there before the utterance. A promise brings something into the world that wasn't there before. Contracts are promises. Contracts contain commitments, which are specific and enforceable promises.

These commitments may be intangible—meaning they don't take up space or weigh anything—but they are real. Consider your commitment to make timely payments on your mortgage or property taxes. You might ignore the intangibility for a while but eventually you will find your tangible self on the very tangible street, with your very tangible possessions out on the very tangible yard. The mortgage is every bit as real as your stuff.

Following this thread highlights something important: the exact *moment* commitments come into existence. That moment is not the moment you receive a bill. The bill simply documents a new state of the obligation—it doesn't create it. Nor is it when you begin a procurement process. There are many procurement activities that never lead to any commitment.

Commitments come into existence at the moment of mutual agreement.

Mutual Agreement

Commitments generally come into existence when two parties agree to something that will affect their futures. If two people agree who won the Princeton-Harvard football game, that's simply consensus—it doesn't bind either of them to a future action.

In business, the most common ways to manifest mutual agreement are:

> **Countersigning contracts** – The classic source of commitment is a signed contract. Most significant business transactions involve signed contracts. Both parties know each other when they enter into the contracting process. These contracts are often negotiated, modified, and rehashed until both parties agree and both parties sign. Until both parties sign, there is no commitment.
>
> **Offer plus acceptance** – An offer begins as a one-sided contract, where only the offeror is identified. The commitment arises when a second party accepts the preconditions of that offer. A common example is online shopping: displaying the items on the website with selling prices constitutes the offer, while clicking the "buy" button is the acceptance. The timing becomes obvious when you realize you can put things in your shopping cart all day long, but until you click "buy," no commitment exists. Clicking "buy" constitutes mutual agreement (read the End User Legal Agreements if you are in doubt).

Commitments in Contracts

Contracts are full of commitments, many of which are too difficult to monetize. For instance, you may have committed not to disclose trade secrets or to refrain from publicizing the contract. These are valid commitments, so you need to keep track of them, but there's no meaningful way to value them. Even broader agreements—like master services agreement or blanket purchase orders—may set billing rates and payment terms, but in the absence of a commitment to a specified quantity, there is still no way to turn this into a financial commitment.

This difficulty may be one reason accountants have historically been reluctant to capture and monetize contracts or even orders.

Exemplar Financial Commitments

The classic form of commitment is when you agree to buy something that will be delivered in the future and paid for in the future. In this case, there are two commitments: a commitment to deliver and a commitment to pay.

As the buyer, you have the commitment to pay, which we will call an obligation. The counterparty's commitment to deliver is a right to you—the right to receive delivery.

The difference between this scenario, as it was handled in Chapter 4 and in traditional accounting, is the timing of capture and valuation. In fully data-centric accounting systems (as described in this chapter), commitments are captured at the moment they are made. And importantly, we capture both sides of each commitment: the obligation and the right.

Degree of Commitment

One argument against recording contracts such as sales orders and purchase orders in the General Ledger is the possibility of them changing or being cancelled. While this is possible, it is not an argument for ignoring them.

First, most commitments are fulfilled. Companies enter into commitments with the intention of carrying them out, and in the vast majority of cases they do. Failure to do so is the exception, not the rule.

Second, it takes an explicit action to cancel or reverse a commitment.

Finally, visibility into all outstanding commitments is a very valuable capability.

That said, we want to recognize that contracts can be cancelled, and commitments can be undone. We think the best way to handle this is to capture the commitments you've entered into, value those that are appropriate, and indicate the difficulty and process for reversing.

Sometimes, canceling a commitment is as simple as clicking a link on a website. Wouldn't it be nice to have all your subscriptions (commitments to pay, coupled with the right to receive whatever the subscription provides) linked to the unsubscribe button? In addition to capturing the process of ending a commitment, we think you should record the cost of cancelling. Occasionally you can put an actual number on the cost of cancelling, sometimes only an estimate, and often just a category.

For instance, when you hire someone (a commitment), you might want to record the estimated cost of canceling this commitment. For executives with golden parachutes, the cost could be very high. It could be higher in some countries that have very high severance penalties. In other cases, it might just be the norm in your industry or company. Any estimate is better than having none—and better than the financial surprises that seem to accompany every company that announces a layoff with its attendant severance costs.

Accountants who cringe at the thought of recognizing uncertain events should remember: you already do this when you recognize credit sales as revenue, even though collectability is not guaranteed. How do you handle that? By creating an estimated allowance for uncollectible accounts receivable and recording bad debt expense to reflect the uncertainty of collection.

In the same way, we could create an allowance for potential decommitments and adjust the financial statements accordingly.

In the absence of quantifiable estimates, it is still useful to go with categorical estimates. Think in terms of low, medium, and high to categorize the cost of unwinding a commitment. This way, an executive facing the need to do cost cutting might get a list of commitments (complete with outstanding payment amounts) sorted by categorical cost to cancel.

Originating/Committing Events

In most industries, there are a small number of events that kick off these long-running commitments and create the context for most of the events that follow. These are also composite events, in that each of these events generates at least two primitive events.

The most common originating events are:

- **Committing to a purchase order**
- **Signing a sales order**
- **Launching a production order or project**

Here is a table that summarizes each:

Event	Right	Obligation	Other Notes
Purchase Order	To receive goods or services	To pay	Many services have implied receipts, and are temporal
Sales Order	To receive payment	To deliver goods and services	The right to receive payment is at a different unit price than the obligation to deliver (which is at the unit cost) and therefore the right and obligations are equal at the unit level but unequal at the financial level (this is the basis of profit)
Launch Project / Production Order	To receive completed finished goods or project results	To supply required materials, labor, and equipment	Many of these obligations are internal (or cross departmental) but they often spawn additional external commitments

Figure 5.2: **Originating Events**

The rights and obligations above will be implemented as their own primitive events. We first thought these might not warrant being standalone events, but then we began considering the impact of *laterality*.

Laterality

Most financial commitments in business are bilateral. That is, there are two parties, typically a buyer and a seller. We suggest that even internal projects and production orders can be viewed the same way. In these cases, there is both a commitment to provide resources and a commitment to deliver something (whether that be a finished good, a constructed building, or a completed service project). In the internal case, the two parties are simply different parts of the same enterprise.

Bilateral

One nice thing about bilateral commitments is that there is usually a close symmetry in accounting for those commitments. In a purchase commitment, the financial value of the *Right to Receive Delivery* (goods or services) is exactly equal to the financial value of the *Obligation to Pay*. This is also true in internal bilateral commitments: the *Cost of the Obligated Input Resources* (materials, labor, equipment usage, utilities, etc.) is equal to the cost value of the finished goods. Only the sales commitment has a slightly unequal commitment. The *Commitment to Deliver the Goods or Services* is calculated at cost, while the *Right to Receive Payment* is calculated at the sale price.

But now let's take up the cases that are not bilateral.

Unilateral Commitments

Unilateral commitments show up when there is not a reciprocal quid pro quo. A classic case is a non-profit or charitable donation. The pledger commits to paying a donation but gets nothing of equal value in return. They might get a "gift" such as a mug or a calendar, but the whole point is that it is not of equal value. This looks similar to our bilateral commitments but with either only one half, or very unequal halves. The donor records it as an *Obligation to Pay* with little or no corresponding *Right to Receive*. Usually the "gift" is so de minimis that it isn't recorded. The receiver also books a very unbalanced commitment, but in this case, there is a *Right to Receive Payment* with a very meager *Obligation to Deliver*. In this case, they will record the *Obligation to Deliver*, because they need to track the swag inventory.

The second type of unilateral commitment concerns fines and most fees. When you are fined by a counterparty or by a governmental organization, there rarely is a quid pro quo. In a few rare cases there is premeditated behavior that looks a lot like an intentional purchase. When you decide to park illegally, you may consider the parking ticket as the equivalent of paying to park. But most fines are not like that. They range from an overdraft fee (penalty for not paying closer attention) to massive regulatory fines such as the hundred-million-dollar MRAs (Matters Requiring Attention) levied on major banks.

These, then, are not commitments entered into intentionally or with the expectation of getting something in return. The accounting in these cases involves recording the *Obligation to Pay* without any corresponding *Right to Receive* anything. The fining party does the opposite, records a *Right to Receive Payment* without having to do anything directly in return.

Small "n" Multilateral Commitments

There are also obligations that involve three or four counterparties. A common example is insurance. Here, the provider (the underwriter) and the premium payer (often the insured party) are the primary parties. But the insurance may be bought on behalf of a third party. Also, in many cases, there is a named beneficiary.

In these cases, we end up with contingent obligations and therefore contingent rights to receive payment (on the part of the beneficiaries). We don't know of any case where the beneficiaries' contingent rights are recorded financially, even though, in principle, they could. Similarly, cases where one party procures indemnity on behalf of another are complex situations and are usually attached to some other arrangement the two parties have.

Large "n" Multilateral Commitments

From an accounting standpoint, perhaps the most interesting—and from a business standpoint, often the most lucrative—situation is where a delivery satisfies multiple rights to receive delivery.

Consider putting on a concert. The moment a concert goer buys a ticket, they establish a bilateral commitment with the concert organizer. The attendee has a $100 obligation to pay (which they likely fulfilled immediately with a credit card) in exchange for the right to receive $100 worth of entertainment.

Each should keep track of these obligations. For the attendee, the obligation to pay (and the organizer's reciprocal right to receive payment) is usually satisfied at the time of ticket purchase. What remains outstanding, however, are the attendee's *right to receive entertainment* and the organizer's reciprocal *obligation to deliver it.* The concert organizer, having sold 1,000 tickets, has collectively $100,000 worth of obligations to deliver entertainment.

The organizer has the obligation to deliver the concert, but the cost recorded as the obligation on the books has little to do with the sum of the tickets they have sold. Because they haven't yet delivered, all the income is unearned income. The obligation to deliver should already have been estimated and recorded at the time they originally committed to put on the concert.

This pattern shows up anywhere a single delivery can satisfy multiple rights to receive. This includes data providers, broadcasters, various forms of entertainment (including sports), training programs where individuals pay separately for their own attendance, mass transit, non-bulk transport, and most subscription-based businesses.

Counterparties

Commitments have parties. The parties that aren't "you" are counterparties. We're accustomed to thinking about parties with terms like *customers* or *suppliers*. Most systems create a different entity every time a company shows up in a different context in their accounting systems. If you buy something from a company, they will create a record in their customer database and give you a customer ID. If you subsequently sell something to them, they will set you up in a vendor database and give you a vendor ID. Most of the time, they don't even realize the two different IDs refer to the same company.

One solution to this problem in traditional systems is to create a *role* table that sits between you and your orders. In some cases, this is a great step and enhances the overall capability of the system. If you have a frequent flyer program or rewards program, you will want to attach sales orders to this role (but probably not purchase orders). However, this approach also creates some problems, as you need to have an ID associated with the role and must decide when to use it—not everyone will have a frequent flyer account).

In this diagram below, we describe conceptually what is going on.

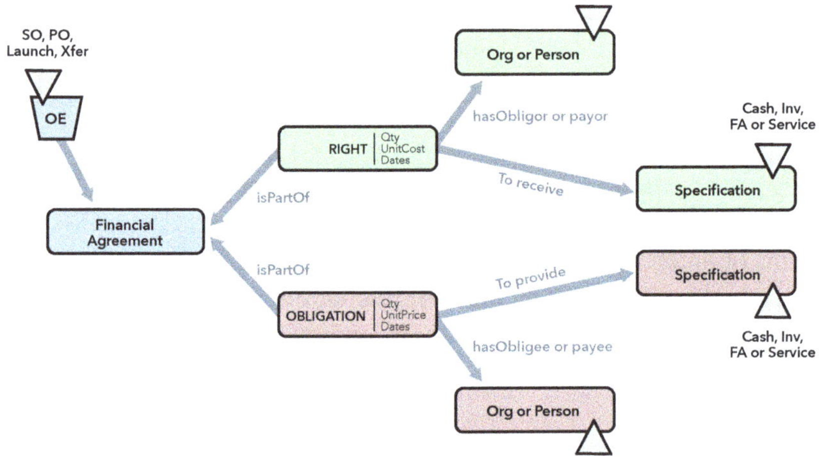

Figure 5.3: **Key Financial Agreement Relationships**

The Financial Agreement on the left was created from the Originating Event (OE—let's say, a Purchase Order (PO), or more precisely, the Purchase Order Event. The Financial Agreement is essentially the Purchase Order. It contains both our right to receive the product and our obligation to pay for it.

The specifications describe the resource involved. On the receipt side, this is a description of the item you ordered. If you ordered a 4x6-foot whiteboard and you get a 2x3-foot whiteboard instead, it is the specification that tells you (and the vendor) that this is not what you ordered. On the payment side, the specification is usually just *cash*, but it might be a *cashier's check* in some cases.

It is the relationship of the right or obligation to the counterparty that defines the nature of the obligation or right. There are four main cases:

> **hasPayee** – The payee is the person or organization you ultimately will—or did—pay. On your check, the payee is the company or person you wrote it to. On a purchase order, the payee is the entity that you will be paying. On your mortgage, the payee is often not the company that holds your mortgage, but rather the mortgage servicing firm delegated

to receive payments. Many accounting systems conflate the payee with the vendor. While they are often the same, there are important exceptions. For instance, when you buy something online, the vendor is not the payee—your credit-issuing company is. Note that the payee is not Visa or Mastercard; you pay the bank that issued your card. It is the bank that determined and granted your credit. The card is a mechanism, not a payee.

hasPayor – The payor is the party you expect to receive payment from—the one to whom you send your invoices to. For example, if you subcontract through a partner, the partner will likely be your payor, even if they are not involved in receiving or approving the goods or services.

hasObligee – The obligee is the party to whom you have promised to deliver goods or services. They are the ones who inspect and approve your goods or services. In subcontracting agreements, the obligee might be the contracting organization or the ultimate customer. It's essential to know which situation you're in.

hasObligor – The obligor is the party who owes you the goods and services. For example, if you order something from Amazon, Amazon is the obligor. Until you receive the goods, they remain responsible for fulfilling that obligation.

The Future-ness of Commitments

Commitments are about the future—but only the future that was committed to in the past.

Normally, in business, the future is in the realm of prediction: we use external data and models to predict what might happen. This is still important in some aspects of the business. But once commitments exist, there isn't much need for prediction. You already know what is going to happen.

Take Semantic Arts, a professional services firm. Most of their contracts have three-month to nine-month durations. Once a client contract is signed (a commitment) and staff (hiring is a commitment) are assigned (another commitment, though internal), the financial impact is known. A future financial statement (based on known commitments) can be produced. It won't be perfect—an employee assigned for 40 hours on a project may call in sick—but it will be far more accurate than budgets and predictions, and easier to produce, since the data is already there.

Types of Financial Commitment

Just as we analyzed the three primary types of business processes to discuss the events for which organizations need to account, we analyze those same processes as the sources of commitments. To refresh your memory, those three main end-to-end workflows are:

> **Buying** – the classic procure-to-pay (P2P) workflow, covering all activities related to obtaining and paying for goods and services.
>
> **Selling** – the order-to-cash (O2C) workflow, which includes acquiring a customer, delivering goods or services, and receiving payment.
>
> **Making** – the processes of production or project management that convert acquired resources into more valuable resources.

Commitments within these workflows come into existence from the originating events we introduced earlier: the Purchase Order, Sales Order, and Launch Project or Production Order.

As discussed in the previous chapter, many procurement situations sound different because they use different terms. Hiring, renting, leasing, and borrowing may sound different, but semantically they are all variations of procuring something.

These commitments differ from their business process counterparts in two ways. The first is scope. The scope of the procure-to-pay business process includes such things as requirements definition, sourcing (evaluating vendors), preparing RFPs (requests for proposal), and negotiating.

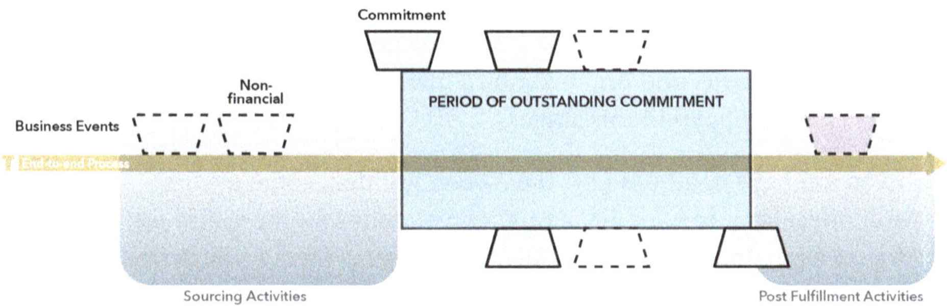

Figure 5.4: **Business Events and Financial Business Events**

Imagine Figure 5.4 as an end-to-end process for acquiring a raw material. In real life, the process isn't a single straight line—there are branches and loops—but for now, imagine the simple case.

We will expand upon the diagrams in this chapter with additional colors and shape definitions, so let's explain those first.

Originating Event. There is always a financial business event that creates the mutual commitments, and we show that perched on the left edge of the commitments it created.

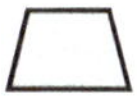

Completion Event. Likewise there is an event that resolves the outstanding commitments. We will show it on the edge of the outstanding commitments box. Often the completion is a final fulfilment, but occassionally commitments are closed out by a commitment modification such as a deobligation.

Financial Business Events. (solid trapezoids)

Non-financial Business Events. (dotted trapezoids)

Other important time intervals. Occassionally we will draw to your attention another key time period. In this case it is pre-commit activity, in other cases it is the effect of reporting intervals on the inclusion of certain events or commitments.

During the period of outstanding commitment (the activities inside the rectangle), many financial business events affect both the commitments and organization's finances. Non-financial business events also happen in this stage.

Even after the commitments have been fulfilled, some events still affect your vendor. For example, you may call them and ask for an assay for the last lot of material or send them a Christmas card. While these activities involve the vendor, they do not affect your accounting.

Another important distinction is how processes are managed. Business process management tends to treat different vendors or products differently, because often they involve different steps in the business process. In contrast, when it comes to commitments, we treat them more uniformly: a commitment is a commitment.

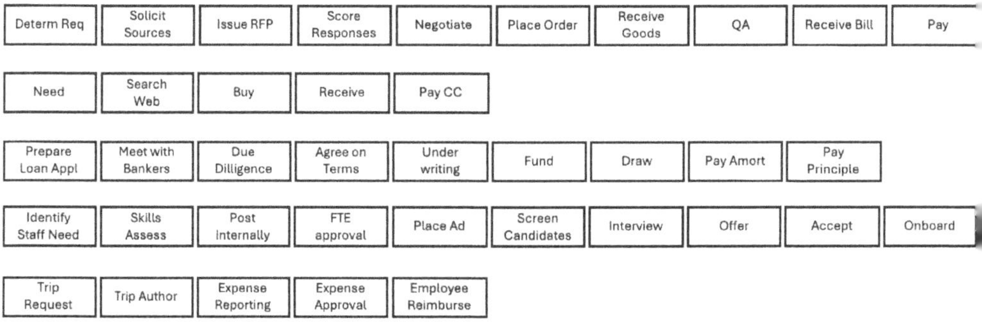

Figure 5.5: **Different Workflows, Similar Commitments**

In this figure, we see five simplified business processes, shown from top to bottom: procuring a major raw material, buying an MRO (Maintenance, Repair, and Operations) spare, borrowing money, hiring a new employee, and processing an employee's out-of-town expense report.

From a business process engineering standpoint, each of these P2P commitments has a very different workflow with unique steps. However, when viewed through a commitment lens, their similarities become clearer. By aligning them in this way, we can see that while the steps differ, the underlying pattern of commitment and fulfillment is much the same.

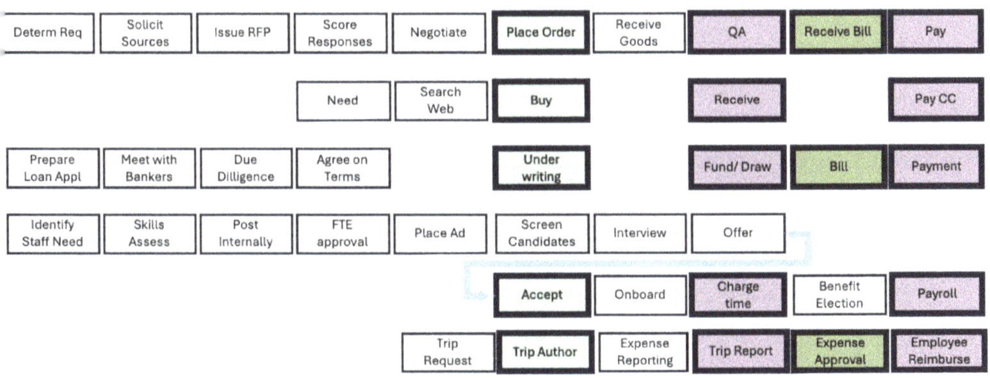

Figure 5.6: **Different Workflows Aligned by Similar Commitments**

From our standpoint, placing the final order, buying an online product, committing to a loan underwriting, having an applicant accept our offer, and authorizing a trip are more alike than different. Each one establishes our right to receive what we acquired and our obligation to pay for it. The dark-bordered boxes represent a sample of the other analogues across these procurement processes.

Commitment Accounts

We are familiar with accounts that track our obligation to pay and our right to receive payment—we call them *payables and receivables.* However, only a few industries keep track of the obligation to deliver or the right to receive delivery when no advance payment is made. And as such, there isn't a standard term for this.

To avoid confusing this with similar traditional accounting terms, we'll make a distinction. First, we will refer to commitments initially as being *committed*. When we place a purchase order, our obligation to pay for it will be a *committed liability*, and our right to receive the goods or services will be a *committed asset*. As the events unfold in the life of a commitment, various subsequent events firm up these commitments. For example, our committed payable liability firms up to become an Accounts Payable liability in the act of the vendor delivering. If the delivery is partial, we record a firm Accounts Payable for the delivered amount, while the undelivered amount remains a committed payable.

These new commitment accounts function much like their financial cousins—Accounts Payable, Prepaid Expenses, Accounts Receivable, and Unearned Revenue. Just as with those, it is not sufficient to track these accounts only at the GL account level. You must also track the outstanding balances for all four types of commitments, broken down by counterparty.

In fully data-centric accounting systems, a committed payable and an accounts payable aren't separate accounts—they are the same account tied to the same counterparty. It is just the *state* of the obligation that changed. However, as we discuss in the follow-on implementation guidebook, a transitional approach may include a phase in which the system doesn't have the longer running commitment tying these reciprocal obligations together. In that case, if committed payables are maintained at all, they would need to be managed as separate counterparty accounts.

Resource Accounts

We now need to consider another type of account: what we call *resource accounts*. In a traditional accounting system, summary accounts exist for items like inventory and equipment. For simplicity, we'll group these into the broad category of *resources*. You may be tempted to call these *assets*—and they are assets—but some accounts that are considered assets are not resources, such as Accounts Receivable.

In a traditional system, the details of these resources are kept in subsidiary ledgers or source systems. As we are migrating toward a future without either of those, we need to consider how we'll handle the accounting for resources.

Typically, little thought is given to how many detailed resource accounts are required. For inventory accounts, we often assume there will be one SKU (stock keeping unit) without really considering what an SKU represents. While an SKU is often thought of as being a part number (which it is), it is not necessarily synonymous with part number. Two manufacturers may produce interchangeable parts, yet each will use a different part number. These are sometimes referred to as manufacturers' part numbers. And if you buy two identical parts (even from the same manufacturer) from two different wholesalers, you will likely have two different part numbers.

The question is: how many account numbers or how many SKUs should you have? To get to the bottom of this question, we need to review the ***item of supply concept***. The *item of supply* concept concerns which parts are fungible—that is, which items can be freely substituted for one another.

> An Item of Supply is the level of product specification at which an organization defines individual instances of the product as interchangeable. It is subjective, that is, it can vary from one organization to another.

The *item of supply* concept says that if two parts are interchangeable for your purposes, then you can mix them in the same SKU account. For example, if you require a given specification of bearing that can be sourced from either SKF or Timkin, and your internal or external users are indifferent between the two, you can store them in the same bin and combine their accounting into the same resource account. If, however, your users of the bearings are not indifferent (perhaps there are issues with the latter's equipment's warranty) then the bearings need to be physically separated and accounted for separately. In that case, they would require different SKUs and different resource accounts.

When it comes to equipment, vehicles, and buildings, each item should have its own account. You can group a bunch of similar assets into one account (say, all the chairs in the conference room) but it doesn't buy you that much. Most companies affix a numbered tag to each chair, making them easier to track individually when one breaks, is sold, or moved to another location.

A bank account is both a resource account and a counterparty account. It is a counterparty account because the bank is acting as a custodian: they record your balance as a liability on their books, because they are obliged to provide the funds whenever you request them. At the same time, it is a resource because you can spend it freely by merely writing a check. In essence, your bank balance represents the amount of resources you have to work with.

That said, not everything that sounds like a resource actually is. For example, despite the popular executive phrase that "people are our most important asset," the only time Human Resources make it to the balance sheet is when you accrue unpaid salaries. At year-end, you may have already run payroll and therefore owe your employees and the IRS, but if you legitimately can wait to pay them until January, the cash remains in your books until then. That means at the end of year you have "accrued payroll." It sounds like a resource, but it's just the opposite: it's a commitment—a liability—that reflects money you owe but haven't paid yet.

Resource Account Types

Resource accounts come in two major types, with a few key subtypes.

Storable Resources

Cash – Includes all cash on hand, bank accounts, and money market accounts. Each account, as well as each location holding cash, should have its own resource account.

Inventory – Covers raw materials, work in process, work in progress (for projects), and finished goods. A separate resource account is maintained for each interchangeable type of part.

Investments – Refers to investments in other organizations' stock, exchange-traded fixed income, or derivative investments. Investments in credit or loans will be covered under counterparties.

Fixed Assets – Encompasses equipment, real estate, buildings, vehicles, and the like. Generally, there will be one account for each separate asset.

Intangible Asset – For completeness, intangible assets are treated as storable resources, although generally it is very difficult to consume them.

Non-Storable Resources

Services Consumed – These are transient resources, such as human resources or leased equipment. We never have them on hand, but we consume them over time almost as if they were. When we directly expense goods (e.g., maintenance spares, office supplies, etc.), we are treating them as services that are being consumed rather than inventoried.

Services Provided – When the organization sells services (such as renting a space, providing insurance, or supplying labor), we will categorize this as services provided.

We will look at how each of these appear on traditional financial statements and on data-centric accounting financial statements. But first, we need to consider how they are committed and fulfilled.

Events in the Context of Commitments

The events that we introduced in Chapter 4—such as Receipt, Bill, and Payment—all exist in the context of commitments.

This is a typical sequence of events:

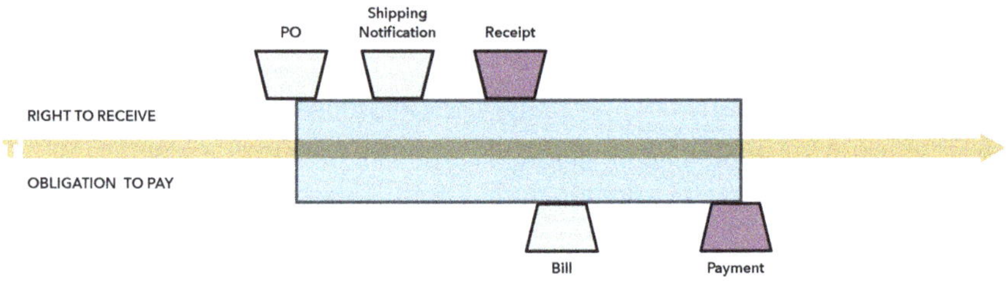

Figure 5.7: **Some Key Financial Business Events in Context**

In this case, the PO (purchase order) creates two obligations—though one of them, to us is a right. The vendor is obligated to ship (our right to receive), and we are obligated to pay for the goods or services. These commitments exist as soon as the PO is signed.

FOB (Free on Board) is a term that defines when ownership of a procured item changes hands. Under FOB source, ownership changes hands as soon as it is put in a truck, train, or airplane. At that point, the buyer must insure it. Although the buyer can record it as an asset on their Balance Sheet, they cannot consume it yet because it is not physically in their possession.

These commitments are easily valued since the PO specifies quantities and unit prices. While these are "softer" commitments than most people would expect to see on their balance sheets, they are nonetheless real, and we will take care to keep them separate.

When dealing with physical goods, the most common sequence of events begins with the vendor sending a shipping notification. You would want to record this, as it may have more accurate dates or adjustments to quantities or unit prices—updates that affect the value of your commitments. In fact, if goods were shipped FOB source, your records need to reflect the fact that you now own them, even if they haven't arrived. Typically, the goods arrive shortly thereafter, and many companies wait until delivery to update their records to reflect the fact that they now own them. And if the goods were shipped FOB destination—meaning ownership transfers at receipt—then the correct time to update records is upon receipt. In either case, once title transfers, the goods become a resource on your books, and your right to receive them has been fulfilled.

On the payment side, the obligation begins as soon as the PO is signed, but again, this is a slightly softer obligation than a typical account payable. We might call this a *PO payable*. At some point, you firm up the payable. In most contracts, it is the billing date that sets up the payment due date. Once you receive the goods or services, you have an actual account payable. Whether you recognize the commitment payable at the time of receipt (the ideal) or when you receive the bill (how many companies do it) is up to your accounting policy.

When the payment is made, the obligation to pay is complete. All commitments have been satisfied. There may be a resource if it was a goods purchase. If it was a service, then once the service is fully delivered and paid for, the commitments are complete.

We refer to these two commitments—the right and the obligation—as *reciprocal*, as they are tied to each other, such that changes to either one also affects the other.

Fulfilling Commitments

We're going to dive into this very deep. This is a lot to follow, and for most people accustomed to reports based on transactions posting to ledgers, this will be uncomfortable. But we think that the level of automation and transparency will be worth the effort. We will build this up one step at a time. Hopefully, the graphics can help you stay grounded. Once we have all our new concepts in place, we will describe how reporting will change.

Committing Events

There are a small number of events that create new commitments. They include accepting a purchase order, signing a sales contract, and launching a project or a production order.

Our visuals depict events as trapezoids and the component rights and obligations as rectangles. As noted earlier, light green shapes involve commitments and berry shapes involve fulfillments.

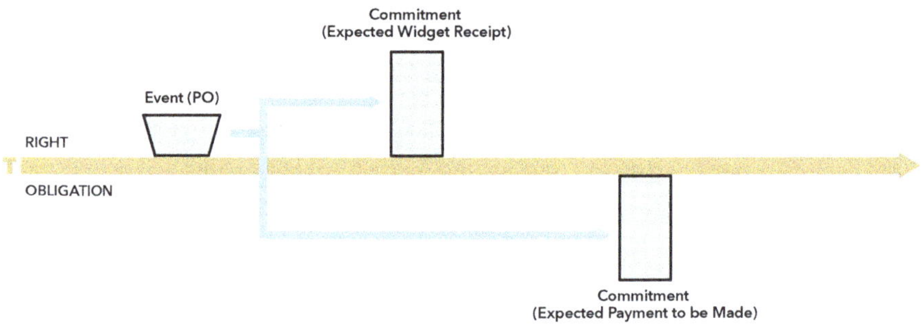

Figure 5.8: Making Commitments

The center line represents the agreement itself— the element that ties the commitments together. In this example, it might be a purchase order to buy some widgets. The event of placing and accepting the order sits on the order itself (the horizontal line). It is the moment that brings the two commitments into existence. The commitment on the top is the company's right to receive the ordered widgets, and the one on the bottom the obligation to pay for them. For the rest of this chapter, we will put rights on the top and obligations on the bottom.

The line also serves as a timeline. The commitments are almost always in the future. In this case, we expect to receive the goods before making payment—a common sequence in practice.

Changing Commitments

There are many financial business events that change the nature of our commitments. Any agreed change to a contract, such as a change order or a price change, is a financial business event that changes the commitments.

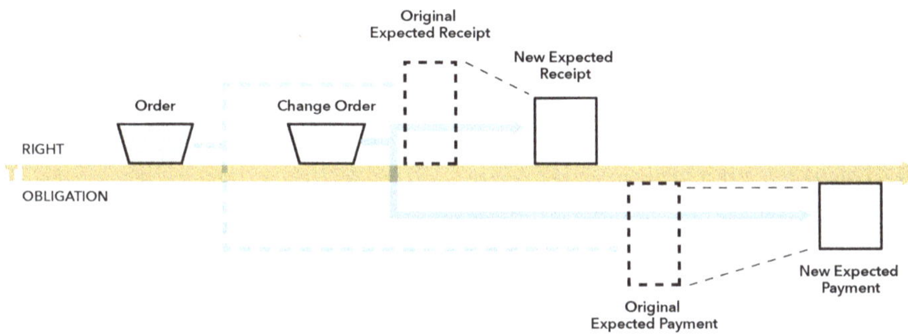

Figure 5.9: **Changing Commitments**

The second trapezoid represents a change to the original commitment. We place it directly on the agreement line, because any change affects the rights and the obligations. In this illustration, we're showing the date being changed (pushed to the right) and representing that the price and the quantities may have changed as well (the height and width of the commitment rectangles).

Although most people don't think of it this way, a vendor's bill is almost always a change to the commitments. The commitment itself existed prior to the bill arriving. In most companies, the bill is often the first visibility the accounting system has of the commitment. We recommend that the commitment should be entered at the time of order capture. If the commitment was entered, the bill should trigger an update, as most contracts stipulate that the payment terms (and therefore the due date of the obligation to pay) are based on the invoice (bill) date.

If a vendor had 60-day payment terms and you ordered a product to arrive on April 1, you probably would book the obligation to pay on June 1. If the vendor ships on April 1 but does not bill until April 30, you can legitimately change the due date of the payment by the 29-day difference to June 30.

Another major category of mutually agreed changes to commitments is what one of our clients calls "deobligation." Many contracts include provisions to reduce commitments at a milestone or upon completion. For instance, you had a time and materials contract with a "not to exceed" clause of $1 million. If the vendor only delivers $900,000 worth of services and both parties agree that this closes out the contract, then the right to receive and the obligation to pay are both reduced accordingly. In addition, this adjustment is independent of where the fulfillment of the commitments stands.

Unbalanced Time

One thing that might stand out in these graphics is that the timing doesn't line up. Accounting standards include the *matching principle*, and there is a desire to have values line up in the same time periods. At first glance, this looks like it might violate that principle, but we're going to take a closer look.

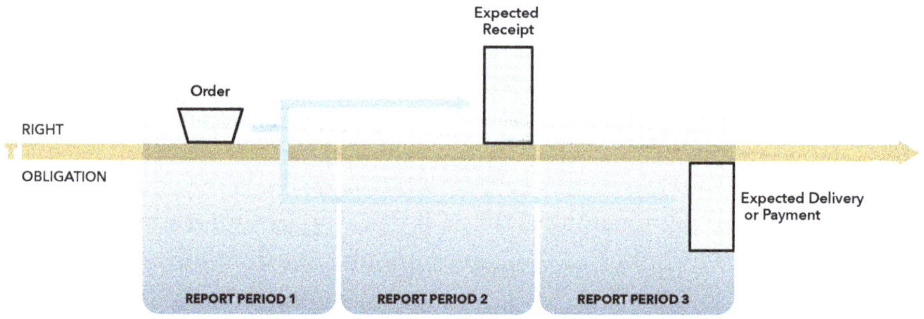

Figure 5.10: Unbalanced Commitments

It looks like the rights are in the second period and the obligations in the third. But that's not actually what is happening—nor is it the case in traditional accounting. Both commitments come into existence the moment the agreement is made (period 1). They exist as commitments in that current period. This is also true in traditional accounting, but people don't think of it this way. For example, when you issue an invoice at the end of the year, payment may not be due until the following year. Still, the right to receive that payment is recorded in the period the invoice was issued. The thought process here is identical—only applied more broadly.

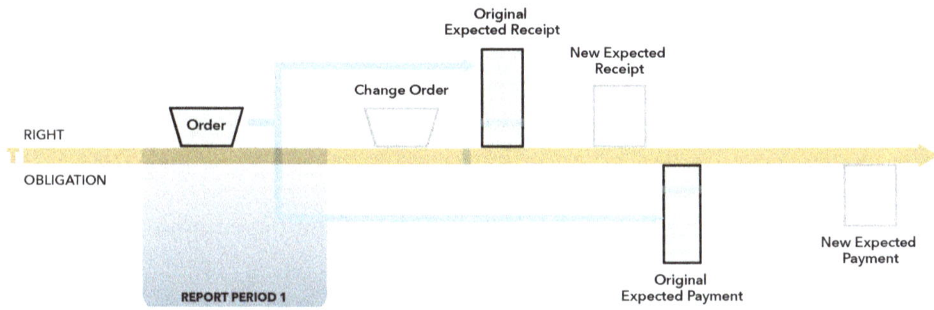

Figure 5.11: **Future Events**

Imagine we had the change order in the system, but we were reporting on a period that was prior to the change order's acceptance date. In this case, the report should ignore the change order and its side effects.

The key insight here is this: it is the event date that drives reporting, not the commitment dates. Commitment dates still matter—we'll see their role later in the reporting section—but they don't affect whether a commitment appears in a report. Instead, they determine where in the report the commitment belongs once it is in scope.

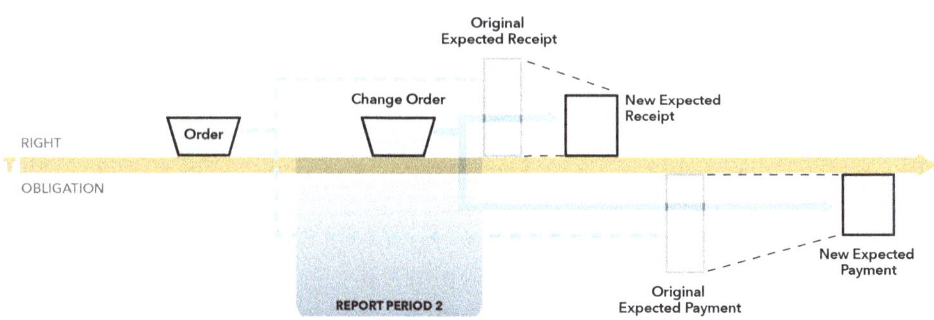

Figure 5.12: **The Modified Commitments**

In these diagrams, whenever a subsequent event modifies commitments, we will show the original commitment in a lighter green shape with a light gray border. This indicates that the original still exists and can be traced if needed, but it also signals that we should not double count them.

Current and Long-Term Liabilities

This perspective offers a fresh way to think about current versus long-term assets or liabilities. Traditional accounting nominates certain accounts to be *current* or *long-term* and then adjusts account balances to achieve the correct allocation of current and long term.

When you look at a loan through the lens of mutual commitment, you can see it a bit differently.

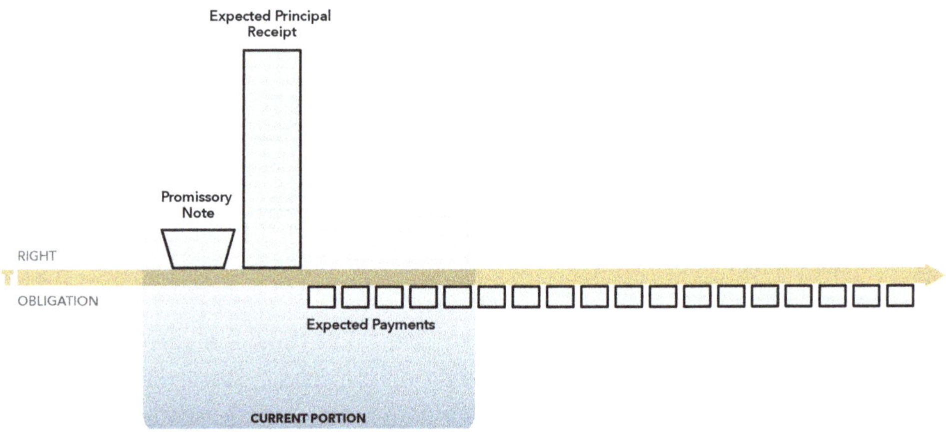

Figure 5.13: **A Loan**

When you enter into a loan, two commitments are created: the banks' commitment to fund the loan and your commitment to repay it. You see the funding as your right to receive the funds (in the near future) and your obligation to repay may span a long time period.

Our reporting system could look at the stream of committed obligations to pay and determine—algorithmically—which ones should be considered *current*. Standard accounting practice generally defines *current* as within a year, which could certainly be done here. But for many cash planning reporting scenarios, a year might be too long a period to be considered *current*.

Fulfilling a Commitment

We've dealt with setting up and modifying commitments. The final piece is fulfilling them.

Your right to receive materials is fulfilled by the vendor's delivery, and your obligation to pay is fulfilled by your payment. Unlike setting up and modifying commitments, fulfillment is not concomitant. Each side happens in its own time, and not always when originally planned.

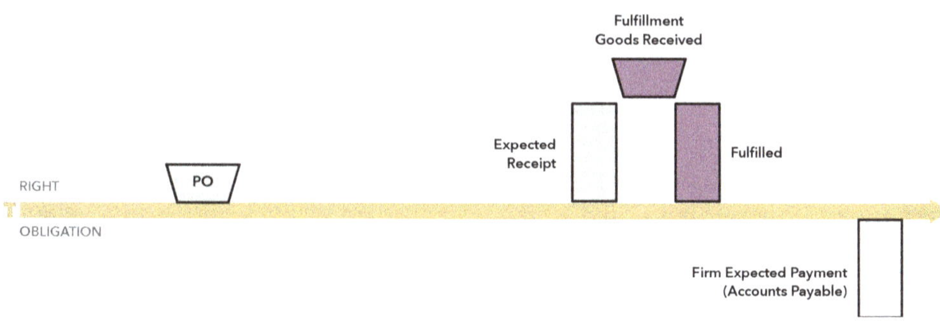

Figure 5.14: **Fulfilling the Delivery**

In these diagrams, we will show the fulfillment event as a berry-colored trapezoid, and the amount of the commitment that is now fulfilled as a berry-colored rectangle. In this case, the vendor fulfilled their obligation by delivering the product, which we record as a product receipt. Notice two things: first, the receipt did not happen on the day it was planned. Second, the receipt satisfied the commitment. The original commitment is still there but we want to make sure we don't double count it.

What we want to highlight is what happened to the commitment to pay, shown on the bottom half of the diagram. We call this the *reciprocal* agreement. When one commitment is fulfilled, its reciprocal undergoes a state change: it "firms up."

Consider what was happening prior to the receipt. We had an order for a part: a right to receive it, and an obligation to pay for it. We call these commitments "soft" because they are relatively easy to unwind.

As soon as we receive the product, however, our commitment to pay "firms up." Indeed, virtually all accounting standards say that it is the act of receipt that creates our payable. We tend to think it is the receiving of the bill, but that is a convenient fiction.

The receipt itself did not change our commitment; it merely recategorized it. Later in the reporting section, we are going to recategorize this from a "committed purchase payable" to "accounts payable." Thus, the rectangle is now shaded with a green diagonal pattern, indicating it is firm.

Completely Fulfilled

When the reciprocal commitment has been fulfilled, we say the whole agreement is fulfilled.

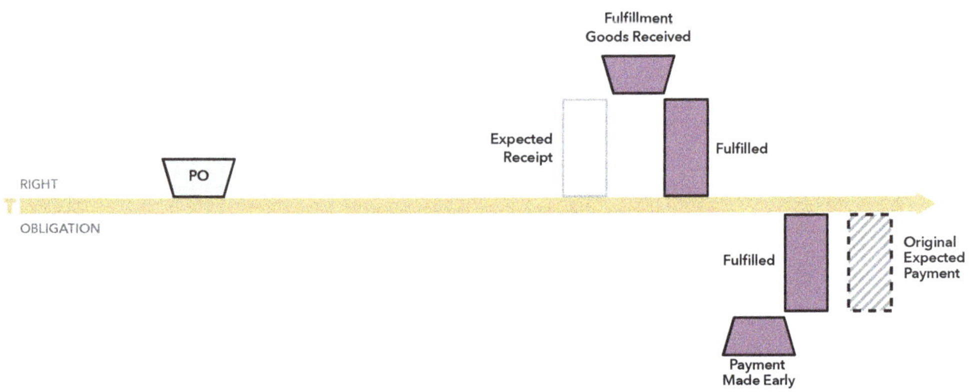

Figure 5.15: **Completely Fulfilled Agreement**

In this case, we make a payment. As the diagram indicates, the payment may have occurred earlier than originally planned, but in any event, once it is made, the obligations are done. There are no more counterparty considerations, and the lingering effect of these transactions is in the resources, which is reflected in the completed commitment. We now have an inventory part we did not have before, and we are out the stipulated amount of cash.

Partial Fulfillment

Either side can also partially fulfill their commitments. For example, the vendor may only ship a portion of the ordered parts, or we may make a partial payment on the obligation to pay.

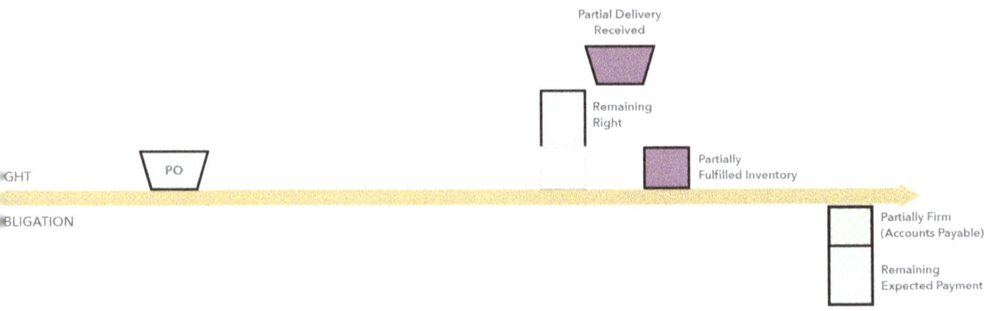

Figure 5.16: **Partially Fulfilled Agreement**

When this occurs, two things happen. First, the commitment is only partially satisfied, so the remaining portion is still outstanding. Second, the reciprocal commitment is only partially recategorized. If the vendor ships half the parts, half of our soft commitment to pay becomes accounts payable, and the other half remains committed payable.

Non-Typical Sequence

For procurement, the most common sequence is: purchase, receive, get bill, and pay. This is the basis of the "three-way match" we mentioned earlier, where the bill is matched with the receipt and the purchase order before funds are approved for payment. That discipline tends to keep many transactions on that happy path.

But other sequences are possible—and when they occur, they usually generate extra work for accounting departments. One such path is: purchase, pay (with or without a bill), and receipt.

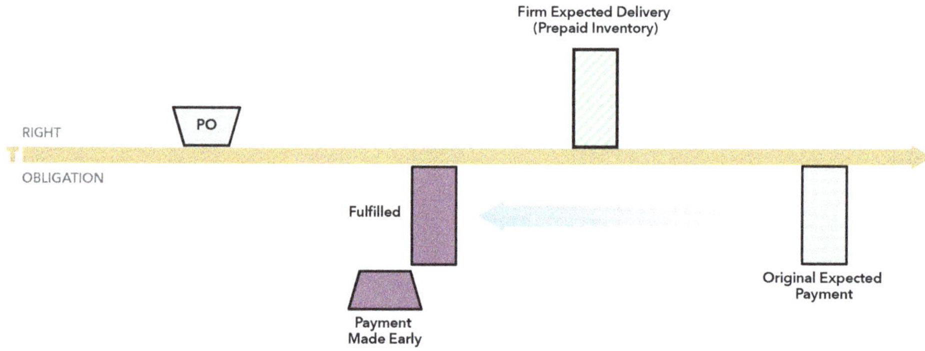

Figure 5.17: Paying Before Receiving

In Figure 5.17, the fulfillment of the payment obligation created a state change in the right to receive the goods. Most accounting policies will classify this newly firmed-up commitment as *prepaid inventory*. That label is a bit of a misnomer—it isn't actually inventory, as we can't issue it to any production orders yet. But it's right in that it is an asset.

We will say that the right to receive was a committed asset, but paying for it firmed it up. And now, it should show as prepaid inventory.

Income Statement Recognition

So far, all our examples dealt only with the balance sheet. We've been buying inventory with cash, so all our events only affected assets—cash, inventory, prepaid inventory, and the new "committed right to receive"—plus accounts payable (on the liabilities side).

Accountants use the term *recognition* to indicate recording something on a financial statement. They contrast recognition with *realization*, which means a transaction is complete. In traditional accounting, some transactions get reported on financial statements before they are realized—for example, revenue should be recognized when goods are delivered even though the cash for those hasn't yet been received (after which the entire sale transaction will be realized). While accountants may talk about recognizing something on the balance sheet, most often they use recognition to talk about something getting to the income statement.

From this point forward, when we talk about recognition, we are talking about an event being recorded on the income statement. In traditional accounting, the decision about whether and when to recognize revenue or expenses is mostly a judgement call based on accounting policy and applicable standards. In Chapter 4, we were able to automate most of the determination by knowing the combination of event type and intention.

Now, we shift the determination to the commitment event, which is then carried through the life cycle of the financial agreement. In most cases, there will only be one sensible default choice, based on the agreement type and resource type.

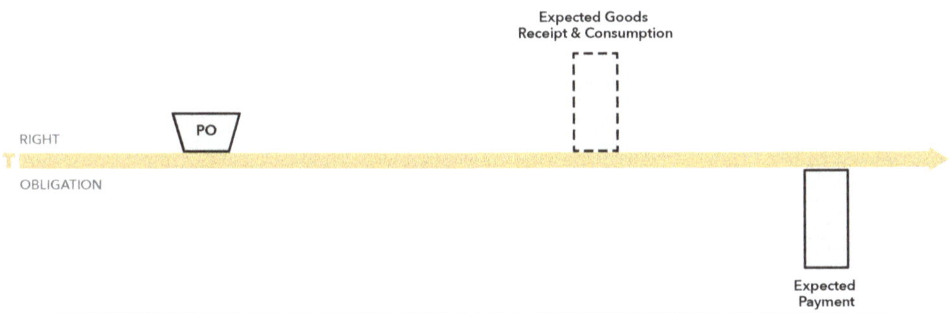

Figure 5.18: **Recognition**

In our graphic conventions, recognition will be shown as a bold box. In this case, we are still buying some goods. Unlike in the previous examples, here we are declaring that we will consume the goods immediately rather than store them for future use or sale.

It is this notion of consumption that separates the previous example from the current. Often consumption occurs over time, and we will get to that later, but to keep this as similar as possible, we consider the case where we consume the procured item immediately.

We haven't received the goods yet, so in the traditional accounting world, we would not have "recognized" the expense. What we're doing instead is setting everything up so that when we do receive it, the expense will immediately be recognized. Additionally, we will be looking at some "committed" income statement categories. These act as early indicators of future profit by reflecting commitments we've already made that will eventually flow through to recognition.

Receiving a Recognizable Good

When the good arrives, we treat it mostly as we did the inventory, with the exception of how the accounting is treated.

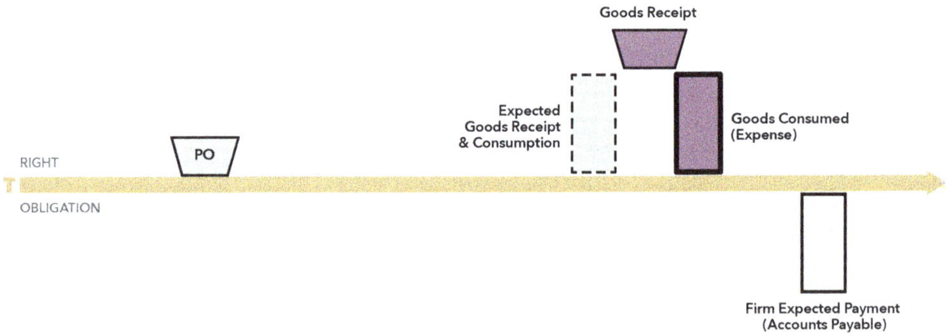

Figure 5.19: **Recognition at Time of Receipt**

The receipt still causes the state change of the obligation to pay to be a full-fledged payable now.

But instead of an asset, we now recognize the expense.

If we pay before the goods arrive, in an analogous fashion to the prepaid inventory, we cause a state change in the right to receive goods to become an asset called *prepaid expense*.

Services

There are a couple of key differences between services and goods. One we noted earlier: services cannot be inventoried. Another is that services are usually temporal—they are consumed or earned over time, rather than in a single moment. By contrast, cash and inventory are typically received and issued at a point in time, while the use of a rented item is received and consumed one day at a time across a long period.

Because services cannot be stored, they are consumed as they are acquired. And for the same reason, services are not assets. There are a lot of things on balance sheets that look like services (accrued wages, capitalized leases, prepaid expenses) but on closer examination, these represent obligations where the reciprocal commitment was fulfilled. That fulfillment temporarily firmed up the right that qualifies as an asset. Services are almost always "recognized" as revenue or expense.

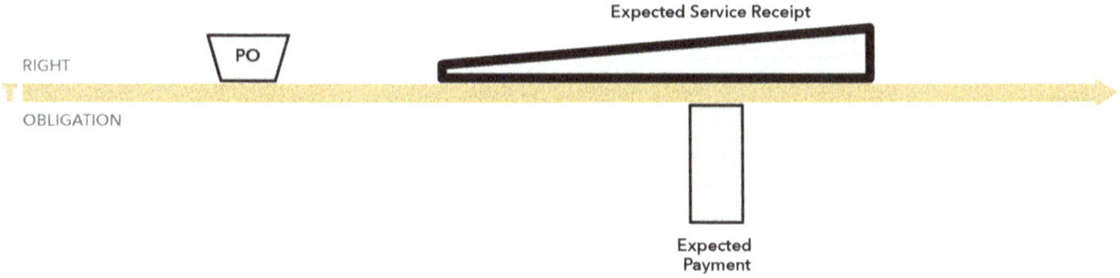

Figure 5.20: **A Procured Service**

This will be our diagramming technique for procured services. These could be subscriptions, landscaping, rent, labor, insurance, bookkeeping, or any number of activities delivered as services. In our diagram, the bold outline suggests that this is a recognized expense. The triangle represents how it is acquired over time. The light green box underneath indicates our obligation to pay—an obligation that doesn't always have to be settled up front.

When we started down this path, we wondered whether services should be treated as a special case. Traditional accounting does not. It deals with services transactionally, booking them at a single point in time. As we've noted earlier, in order to approximate the flow nature of many revenues and expenses, accountants will occasionally resort to splitting the transaction into multiple ones. This is extra work, and only roughly approximates the economic activity.

As we were considering the value of making services a special case, we reviewed the state of the US economy[25]. According to the Federal Reserve, services account for 72 percent of the US economy. In some industries, services make nearly up to 100 percent—on both the revenue and the expense side. So rather than making an exception for services, we now think this might be the predominant model and point-in-time purchases and delivery the exception.

[25]"The Rise of Services in the US Economy," *FRED Blog*, Federal Reserve Bank of St. Louis, July 15, 2024, https://fredblog.stlouisfed.org/2024/07/the-rise-of-services-in-the-us-economy/

By the way, a world obsessed with international trade deficits is missing a large part of the story. In 2022, the US exported $2.1 trillion worth of goods and $926 billion worth of services[26]. Focusing solely on goods—say, when calculating trade deficits—misses a very large part of the story.

A Service Partially Received

Imagine we've already received part of the service we contracted—for example, three of the twelve monthly newsletters that were promised.

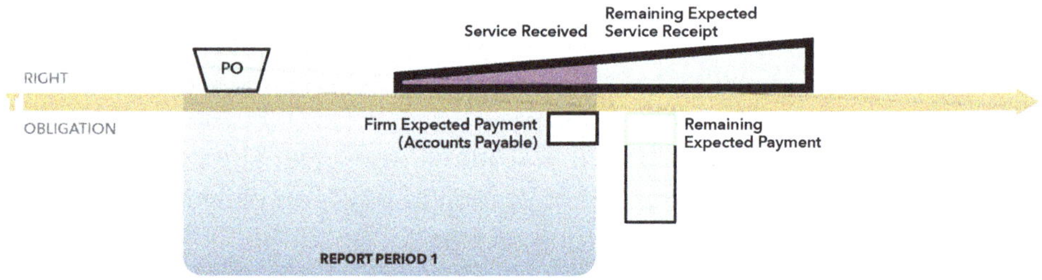

Figure 5.21: **Partially Received Service**

The berry-colored area in the triangle represents the amount of the service we've already received. Much like the goods example, the receipt of the service creates a state change in the obligation to pay. In this case, the cross-hatched section is meant to be the equivalent area as the berry color in the triangle—it shows how much of the committed payable has now been firmed up.

In many cases, services require payment up front. In those situations, the accounting is often set up to happen the other way around: there is less likely to be accounts payable and more likely to be prepaid expense. Service vendors still send bills, but these usually just confirm what we already know—and serve as a nudge to make the payment.

[26]Countries & Regions, United States Trade Representative, accessed September 1, 2025, https://ustr.gov/countries-regions#

Implied Receipt

We don't record the explicit receipt of many services. We don't go into our systems every day and say, "Yep, got another day's worth of all this insurance I bought, another day of rent, and another day of utilities." The fact that we don't do this is likely one of the reasons that most companies do their accounting based on bills and invoices rather than receipt and delivery, even though, from an accounting perspective, receipt and delivery are the true events that should be measured.

We propose treating many services as having *implied receipt* at the time they're procured. This approach assumes that the service has been received unless informed otherwise.

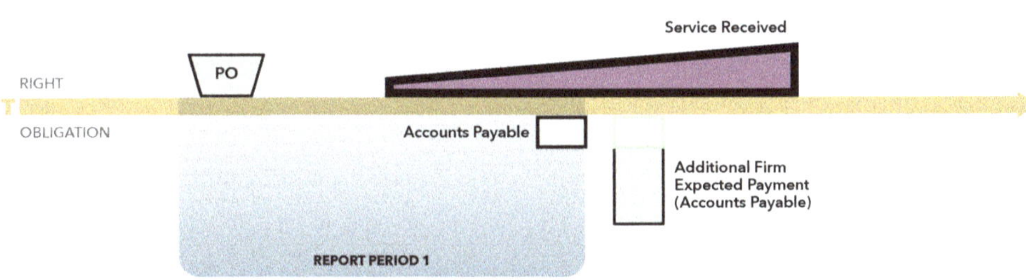

Figure 5.22: **Implied Service Receipt**

In this case, we set up the service—say, rent—and assumed it is received at a constant rate over the rest of the year.

Notice that it is the reporting period that determines how much has been received. Up to the end of a given reporting period, we recognize the portion of the service received so far. Depending on our payments, this results in either accounts payable or prepaid expense.

Exception to Implied Receipt

If we have implied receipt, we will need to have a receipt exception. These exceptions are usually obvious—like if your landlord breaks a water main, or if your insurance company sends a cancellation notice.

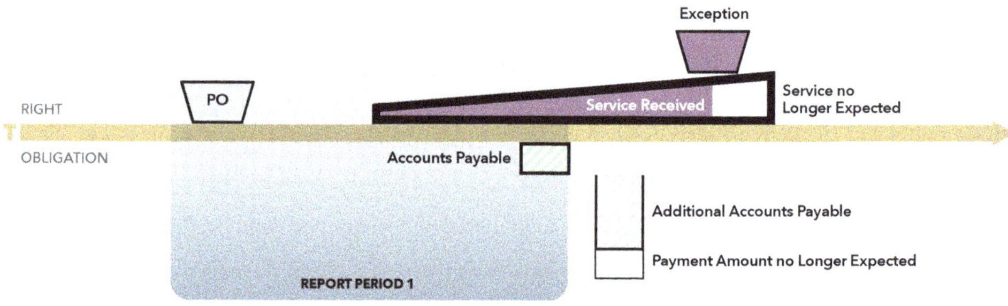

Figure 5.23: **Implied Service Receipt with Exception**

The receipt of the cancellation notice just stops the accumulation until the exception is reversed.

Interest as Service

Earlier, we said that cash was a resource. Most of the time, it is. But there are cases where it behaves more like a service. One such case is interest. Let's take a closer look at the loan we set up earlier.

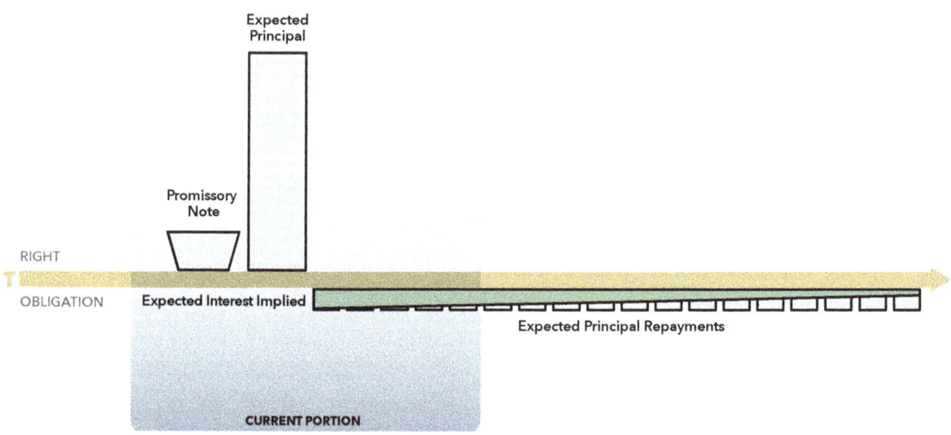

Figure 5.24: **Interest as a Service**

The green triangle represents the amount of interest implied over time. This looks pretty much like a loan amortization schedule: equal payments where the early payments are mostly interest.

Selling a Product

Selling a product is similar to buying one, with just a few interesting differences. The first is that a sale is always "recognized." With purchasing, there's a chance that the inventory we bought isn't immediately expensed but instead is posted to the balance sheet. With sales, however, there's no equivalent scenario—all sales are immediately recognizable.

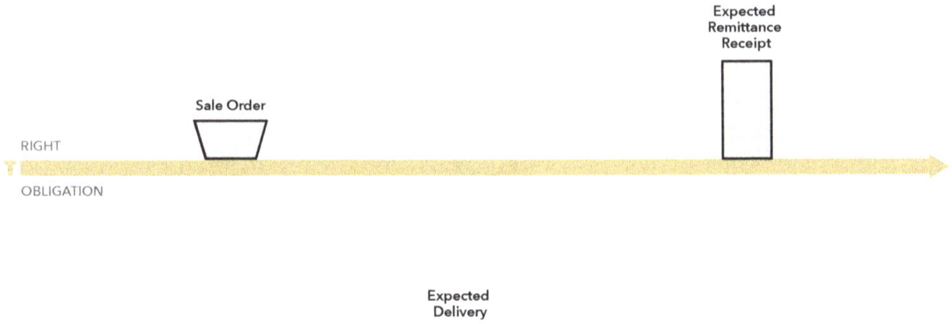

Figure 5.25: **Selling as an (Eventually) Recognizable Event**

The other difference involves an interesting asymmetry that makes business possible: the value of your obligation to deliver can be—and generally should—be less than your right to be paid.

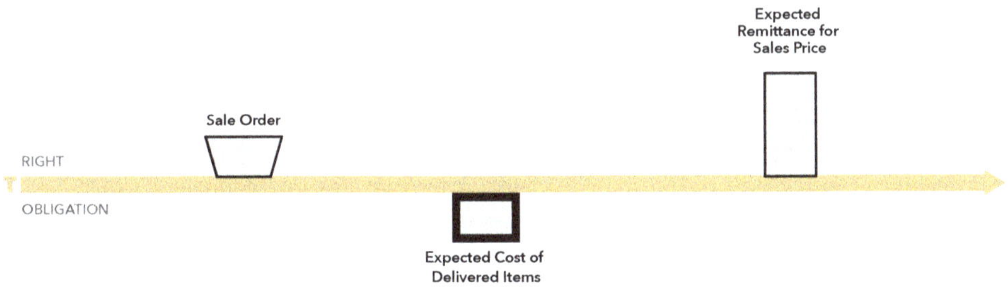

Figure 5.26: **Cost Asymmetry in Sales**

This asymmetry shows up as different heights for the two rectangles. If we leave this unaddressed, the books won't balance. Our recommendation is to build in committed profit at the time the agreement is recorded. This will be a *committed* profit as it hasn't been earned yet—it hasn't been delivered yet—but we've found this approach works better than any alternative.

For example, imagine you sold a widget for $1,000 and you know with a great deal of certainty that the only widget you had on hand cost $400.

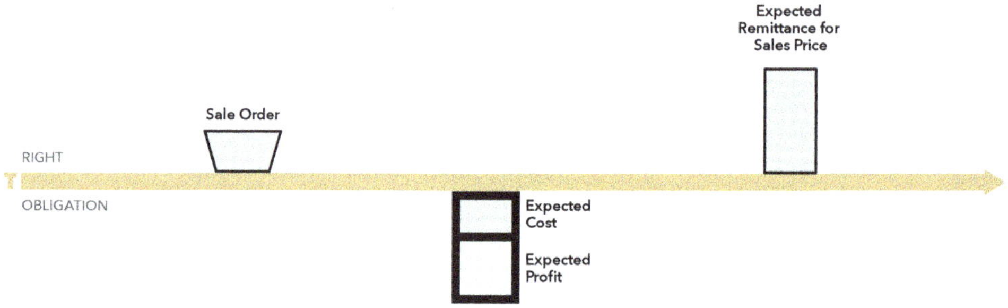

Figure 5.27: **Sales with Profit Built-in**

In this case, you already know the profit will be $600 as soon as the widget is delivered. We set up two obligations: the obligation to deliver the widget (at its $400 cost) and the obligation to deliver the $600 profit. It sounds odd to talk about an obligation to deliver profit, but it works.

Here's why: if the client prepays, both obligations change state and become deferred revenue. Deferred revenue is a delivery liability (in other words, a liability that requires you to deliver what the customer paid for). This is important because if the client prepays $1,000, even though the widget obligation is only $400, you must record the deferred revenue liability at the amount the customer prepaid. Because if you don't deliver the widget, you owe the customer a $1,000 refund. By viewing the committed obligations to deliver the $400 widget to the customer and the $600 profit to itself, if the commitment state changes because the customer prepays, the state of both obligations changes to the deferred revenue liability, which will show up as the full $1,000 on the balance sheet.

For companies that have cost-plus fixed fee arrangements—where profit is built into their contracts—this is straightforward. You can stack the profit and cost to equal the selling price.

For companies who don't know how much profit is built into their commitments, estimates are needed. Some may decide to "back into" the calculations by first recording the obligation to deliver the widget at the full selling price. Later, once the actual profit is known, they can record a negative obligation to deliver for that built-in profit amount. The math works out the same. In industries where costs aren't known until shipment—such as make-to-order or engineer-to-order—this approach can actually reduce the amount of work required, even if the idea of a negative obligation sounds unusual.

Summary of Fulfilling Commitments

We've covered a lot of detail here, but our goal was to address all the possible cases and introduce the language we'll be using in the next section on reporting.

No Chart of Accounts

Hopefully, Chapter 4 helped you get comfortable with the idea that you only need a small number of accounts—and they don't need to be hierarchical. We're going to take that one step further.

As we described in Chapter 4, only two types of accounts need running balances: counterparty accounts and resource accounts. Historically, there are two types of counterparty accounts:

> **Receivables** – where the counterparty owes you money.
>
> **Payables** – where you owe the counterparty money.

But even these essential accounts aren't truly accounts in the General Ledger. Instead, the General Ledger uses control accounts: *Accounts Receivable* summarizes the balances of all the customer accounts that have receivable balances and *Accounts Payable* summarizes all the vendor accounts that have payable balances.

Our recording of the obligation to deliver goods or services—and the right to receive goods or services—set up a couple of financial reporting line items that are rarely shown. Although they are rarely explicitly tracked and almost never show up in traditional accounting systems, their usefulness will soon be obvious.

> **Due In** – the financial value of goods or services you've purchased but not yet received or paid for
>
> **Due Out** – the financial value of goods or services you've sold but not yet delivered or received payment for

At best, the account numbers are now just codes, sometimes used in reporting. But as we'll discuss under reporting, there are other more principled and efficient ways to create the distinctions you need.

Ultimately, the concepts of fulfilling commitments are sufficient to provide all the distinctions expected in modern accounting—and more.

Accounting Policy in Fully Data-Centric Accounting

In fully data-centric accounting, policy choices are made at the time of the originating commitment event. While there may be exceptions for certain industries, we believe organizations would benefit from starting with the default framework outlined here, and then allowing for justifiable exceptions as needed.

Three main factors drive these policy choices:

> **Financial Agreement Type** – Is the agreement a purchase, sale, production order, project launch, fine, pledge, or transfer?
>
> **Temporality i.e., Are the Goods to Be Immediately Consumed?** – If the resource being acquired is physical, will it be treated as a service and consumed upon acquisition? On the selling side, there is no comparable decision to make.
>
> **Event Type** – As discussed in Chapter 4, events affect the accounting, but here they don't generate individual transactions. Instead, they change the nature of commitments, which are then valued according to their type.

Intention	Financial Agreement Type	Event Type	Treatment
Consumable	Purchase	Purchase	Increase right to receive consumable and obligation to pay
Inventory	Purchase	Purchase	Increase right to receive inventory and obligation to pay
	...		
Any	Purchase	Explicit Receipt	Increase fulfilled for good or service, and firm up obligation to pay

Figure 5.28: **Defining and Implementing a Fully Data-Centric Accounting Policy**

Automating the accounting policy in fully data-centric accounting will be a matter of implementing this table in a machine-readable format. The three financial agreement types are already explicit in the model. We now need to make the actions described in the treatment column into selectable and implementable options. This is an exercise left for the implementor.

Anticipating Events (and LLMs)

This approach can take us from merely responding to events to anticipating them. For example, once a purchase order is issued, we can expect shipping notifications and bills to follow.

This has two key implications:

> **Event monitoring** – We can set up systems that not only expect events but also report when they don't occur.
>
> **Simplified event processing** – Incoming events become easier to handle because we're already prepared for them.

Large Language Models (LLMs) or NLP (Natural Language Processing) can be trained to extract small bits of information from incoming messages—such as dates, product numbers, organization names, amounts, or order numbers—and match against a small number of attributes. We only need an 80 percent match rate to get major benefit from this approach.

We've already seen how third-party services like Expensify and Tripit use NLP or LLM to interpret semi-structured emails. In our case, we hold a major advantage: we can anticipate these messages in advance and only need to match them to a much smaller set of possible events.

Financial Reporting in Data-Centric Accounting

The structure of traditional accounting systems depends on the financial reporting needs. The chart of accounts is based on the line items of the balance sheet and income statement. The choice of accounting method (for instance, cash-basis or accrual accounting) drives the line items for those financial statements and for the chart of accounts. Companies that choose cash-basis accounting will not be able to generate accrual-basis financial statements. Companies that choose accrual-basis accounting might be able to back into cash-basis figures to produce cash-basis financial statements—but it won't be easy.

Data-centric accounting systems will capture and store data in such a way that financial statements—whether cash-basis, accrual-basis, or commitment-basis—can all be derived based on application of policies and event types application of event type/intention driven polices, as described in Chapter 4. The difference is, each reporting basis will have its own policy table.

Figures 5.29 through 5.34 illustrate cash-basis, accrual-basis, and commitment-basis income statements and balance sheets, all reflecting the same underlying business events. These examples are not prescriptive; rather, they illustrate the flexibility companies can have in financial reporting through data-centric accounting. In particular, the commitment-basis statements provide insight as to the kinds of information that could be available to users who wish traditional financial statements had more predictive value.

Income Statement
January 1-31

Revenue	
Sales Revenue	$776,000
Cost of Revenue	
Direct Materials	$59,000
Direct Labor	$70,000
Total COGS	$129,000
Gross Margin	$647,000
Operating Expenses	
Sales & Marketing	$75,000
Other Indirect Labor	$40,000
Equipment & Occupancy Expense	$452,000
Insurance	$20,000
Operating Expenses	$587,000
Operating Income	$60,000
Other Income (Expense)	
Interest Expense	($50,000)
Net Income	**$10,000**

Figure 5.29: **Cash-Basis Income Statement**

Income Statement
January 1-31

Revenue	
Sales Revenue	$976,000
Cost of Revenue	
Direct Materials	$230,000
Direct Labor	$140,000
Total COGS	$370,000
Gross Margin	$606,000
Operating Expenses	
Sales & Marketing	$70,000
Other Indirect Labor	$40,000
Depreciation & Occupancy	$10,000
Insurance	$20,000
Operating Expenses	$140,000
Operating Income	$466,000
Other Income (Expense)	
Interest Expense	($50,000)
Net Income	$416,000

Figure 5.30: **Accrual-Basis Income Statement**

Statement of Earned and Committed Income

	Earned January 1-31	Committed February 1-28	Committed March 1-31	Earned and Committed January 1 - March 31
Revenue				
Sales Revenue	$976,000	$750,000	$530,000	$2,256,000
Cost of Revenue				
Direct Materials	$230,000	$330,000	$180,000	$740,000
Direct Labor	$140,000	$70,000	$30,000	$240,000
Total COGS	$370,000	$400,000	$210,000	$980,000
Gross Margin	$606,000	$350,000	$320,000	$1,276,000
Operating Expenses				
Sales & Marketing	$70,000	$65,000	$45,000	$180,000
Other Indirect Labor	$40,000	$35,000	$25,000	$100,000
Depreciation & Occupancy	$10,000	$10,000	$10,000	$30,000
Insurance	$20,000	$20,000	$20,000	$60,000
Operating Expenses	$140,000	$130,000	$100,000	$370,000
Operating Income	$466,000	$220,000	$220,000	$906,000
Other Income (Expense)				
Interest Expense	($50,000)	($49,000)	($48,000)	($147,000)
Net Income	$416,000	$171,000	$172,000	$759,000

Figure 5.31: **Commitment-Basis Income Statement**

Notice that the first column of the Commitment-Basis Income Statement—the *Earned* column—provides identical results as the Accrual-Basis Income Statement. The committed columns are additional information that represent the financial business events to which the organization has committed with at least an originating event.

Balance Sheet
As of Jan-31

Assets	
Current Assets	
Cash	$1,010,000
Total Current Assets	$1,010,000
Total Assets	$1,010,000
Liabilities and Equity	
Current Liabilities	
Current Portion of Long-Term Debt	$130,000
Total Current Liabilities	$130,000
Long -Term Liabilities	
Loans	$770,000
Total Long-Term Liabilities	$770,000
Equity	
Capital Contribution	$140,000
Retained Earnings	$10,000
Distributions	($40,000)
Total Equity	$110,000
Total Liabilities & Equity	$1,010,000

Figure 5.32: **Cash-Basis Balance Sheet**

Balance Sheet
As of Jan-31

Assets	
Current Assets	
Cash	$1,010,000
Accounts Receivable	$300,000
Prepaid Expenses	$35,000
Deposits on Fixed Assets	$42,000
Inventory	$200,000
Prepaid Inventory	$29,000
Total Current Assets	$1,616,000
Non-Current Assets	
Equipment (net of Depreciation)	$400,000
Total Non-Current Assets	$400,000
Total Assets	$2,016,000
Liabilities and Equity	
Current Liabilities	
Credit Cards Payable	$30,000
Deferred Revenue	$100,000
Current Portion of Long-Term Debt	$130,000
Accounts Payable	$470,000
Total Current Liabilities	$730,000
Long-Term Liabilities	
Loans	$770,000
Total Long-Term Liabilities	$770,000
Equity	
Capital Contribution	$140,000
Retained Earnings	$416,000
Distributions	($40,000)
Total Equity	$516,000
Total Liabilities and Equity	$2,016,000

Figure 5.33: **Accrual-Basis Balance Sheet**

Balance Sheet
As of Jan-31

Committed Rights and Assets	
Committed Rights to Receive	
Committed Cash Receivable	$550,000
Goods & Services Due In	$450,000
Long-Term Assets Due In	$50,000
Total Committed Rights to Receive	$1,050,000
Current Assets	
Cash	$1,010,000
Accounts Receivable	$300,000
Prepaid Expenses	$35,000
Deposits on Fixed Assets	$42,000
Inventory	$200,000
Prepaid Inventory	$29,000
Total Current Assets	$1,616,000
Non-Current Assets	
Equipment (net of Depreciation)	$400,000
Total Non-Current Assets	$400,000
Total Committed Rights and Assets	$3,066,000
Committed Obligations and Liabilities	
Obligations to Deliver	
Committed Cash Payable	$500,000
Goods & Services Due Out	$400,000
Total Committed Obligations	$900,000
Current Liabilities	
Credit Cards Payable	$30,000
Deferred Revenue	$100,000
Current Portion of Long-Term Debt	$130,000
Accounts Payable	$470,000
Total Current Liabilities	$730,000
Long-Term Liabilities	
Loans	$770,000
Total Long-Term Liabilities	$770,000
Equity	
Committed Earnings	$150,000
Capital Contribution	$140,000
Retained Earnings	$416,000
Distributions	($40,000)
Total Committed Earnings & Equity	$666,000
Total Committed Obligations, Liabilities & Equity	$3,066,000

Figure 5.34: **Commitment-Basis Balance Sheet**

Notice that the Commitment-Basis Balance Sheet includes the same subsections as the Accrual-Basis Balance Sheet—such as current assets, non-current assets, current liabilities, long-term liabilities, and equity. One could, if desired, include subtotals for total traditional assets and total traditional liabilities and equity, to show the same information as the accrual-basis balance sheet. The Commitment-Basis Balance Sheet provides additional information about rights to receive and obligations to deliver, representing transactions that have been originated but are not deemed certain enough to satisfy traditional accounting requirements.

Regarding that uncertainty, once a company has sufficient history, it would certainly be feasible to provide a comparison of reported rights to receive with those that eventually were fulfilled and a comparison of reported obligations to deliver with those that were eventually fulfilled. Companies could report the percentage accuracy of those reported commitments or they could report allowances for an anticipated portion of originated transactions that will likely go unfulfilled—similar to how companies currently report allowances for uncollectible accounts receivable.

Summary of Fully Data-Centric Accounting

This chapter concludes what we started in Chapter 4, explaining how we can maximally streamline and automate the creation of financial reports directly from business events.

We have put almost all financial business events in the context of a longer-running commitment that prescribes their accounting treatment and makes it easier for us to predict and automate the receipt of subsequent related financial business events. Keeping the events in context with the commitments has allowed us to automate some of the more difficult to manage parts of accounting: dealing with prepaid and unearned income, for instance.

By capturing the start and end date of resources and services that are acquired and consumed over time, we now have a straightforward, automated way to track resources that were previously difficult to track.

We have also introduced new reporting that helps integrate cash, accrual, and commitment reporting. These tools fulfill the requirements of most enterprise accounting.

In Chapter 7, we'll look at common variations on these themes. But before that, we'll turn to accounting in scenarios where the scope extends beyond a single organization.

CHAPTER 6

Data-Centric Accounting in the Multi-Organizational World

Traditional accounting is subjective—not in the sense of being arbitrary, but in that it reflects only one entity's point of view. This perspective is very subtly embedded in traditional systems. For example, our accounts receivable ledger lists customers, but nowhere does it say *whose* customers they are. This is just assumed: because they are in our database, they must be *our* customers.

This myopia creates a great deal of unnecessary work—but it is also very easy to address. Even if you're not ready for multi-organizational accounting, we recommend incorporating some of the concepts from this chapter to future-proof your systems.

Looking at Transactions from Someone Else's Point of View

Remember this illustration from the previous chapter?

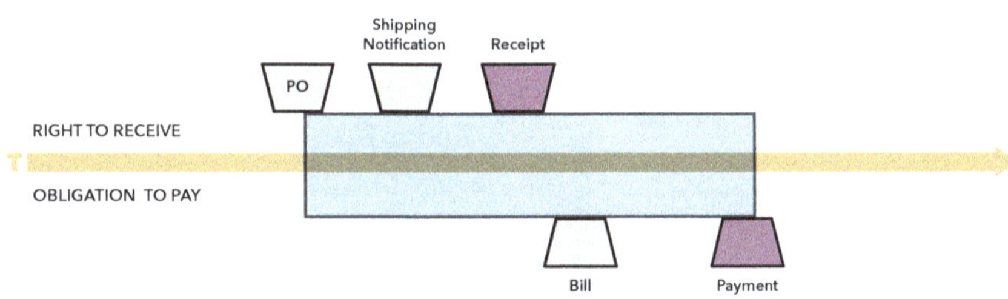

Figure 6.1: **Rights and Obligations**

Let's break it down a bit then put it back together.

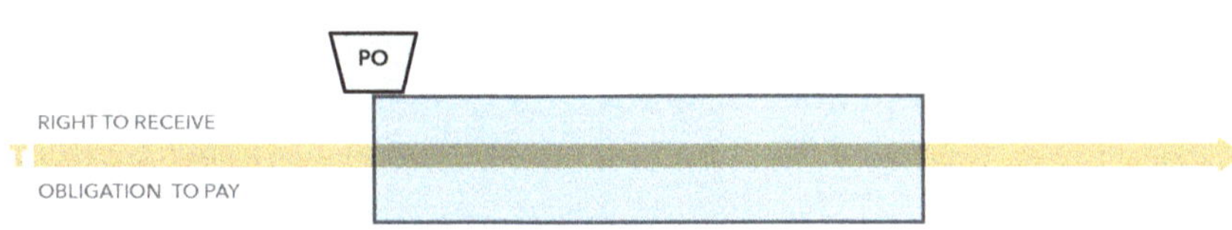

Figure 6.2: **Placing a Purchase Order**

We began with a purchase order (PO). The PO established reciprocal obligations: our obligation to pay and the vendors obligation to deliver, which we recorded as the right to receive. But that raises an important question: what did the vendor do?

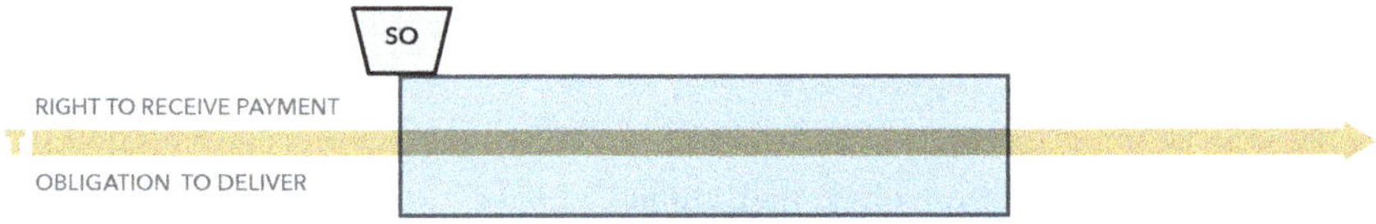

Figure 6.3: **Vendor Makes a Sale**

The first thing they do is cheer, "Yippee, we made a sale!" They might even ring a gong—yes, some of our clients have literal gongs they ring when they make a big sale. What they *don't* say is, "Here's a purchase order." Instead, they look at your PO, declare it a sale, and enter the key details into their sales order system.

Entity Resolution is a set of techniques for determining whether an "entity" (Person or Organization, most commonly) is the same as one you've already dealt with before and therefore have in your database.

Several amusing bits of sleight of hand are going on here. They look at your purchase order, which may have identified them as Vendor BB104. Of course, they don't think of themselves as Vendor BB104, especially since every one of their customers has given them a different number. That doesn't really matter, though, because vendors don't put themselves in their own database.

Meanwhile, the customer didn't give their customer number—because they probably don't know it, and even if they did, they would likely find the idea odd. Instead, you take their name and address, run it through your entity resolution system, and discover that you have indeed done business with them before. You even have a credit report on file, and you know them as *Customer GZ123*.

You enter this into your system as a sales order. In this case, instead of creating a "right to receive" and an "obligation to pay," you set up "right to receive payment" and "obligation to deliver."

So far, we've described this as if you were an organization with fully data-centric accounting that isn't multi-organizational. Most traditional firms would enter this information into a non-accounting sales system and only a partially complete version of the above.

This interesting mirror world property isn't just in the setup.

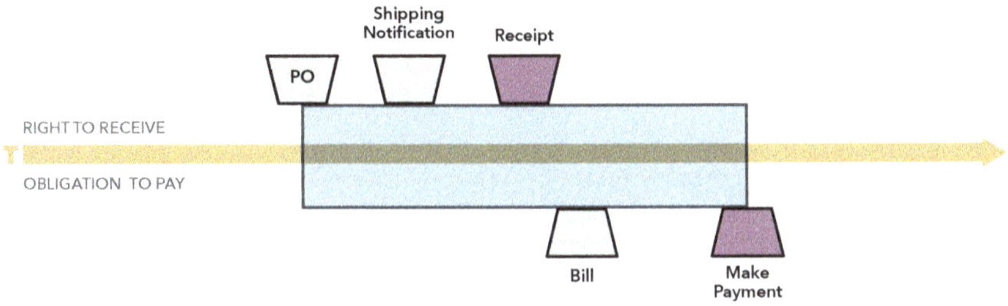

Figure 6.4: **Events in the Life of a Purchase Order from a Buyer's Viewpoint**

Each event in the buyer's P2P (procure-to-pay) process has a mirror counterpart in the counterparty's O2C (order-to-cash) system.

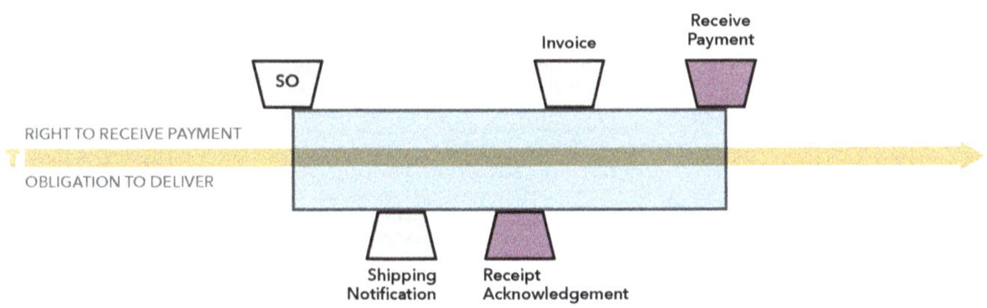

Figure 6.5: **Events in the Life of a Sales Order from the Seller's Viewpoint**

These events aren't just coincidently similar. In each case, they are the exact same event, interpreted differently by each party. One side may choose to ignore certain events. For instance, the seller will often have a "shipping" event that they record when the item leaves their warehouse. The buyer receives this as a *shipping notification* (think of those Amazon emails) and usually just files it away. What the buyer really cares about is the actual receipt, which happens a few days later.

At that point, the buyer may have a quality assurance function and not accept the receipt until they are convinced it meets the specifications. Only then do they record the receipt. They might even send a receipt acknowledgment back to the vendor—but the vendor usually only reviews exceptions, such as items that failed QA. From the seller's perspective, the shipment was already recorded, so unless there's a problem, they're done.

The key takeaway is this: a huge amount of unnecessary duplicate data entry exists because accounting systems are inherently subjective. This duplication is the root cause of reconciliations and other non-value-added activity.

Putting Ourselves in Our System

Up to this point in the book, we've been careful to distinguish *invoices* from *bills*, because confusing them would cause all manner of problems. But here's the deeper truth: they're actually the same thing—it's only perspective that makes them different. What we call our *bill* is simply someone else's invoice, just as *our* purchase order is someone else's sales order.

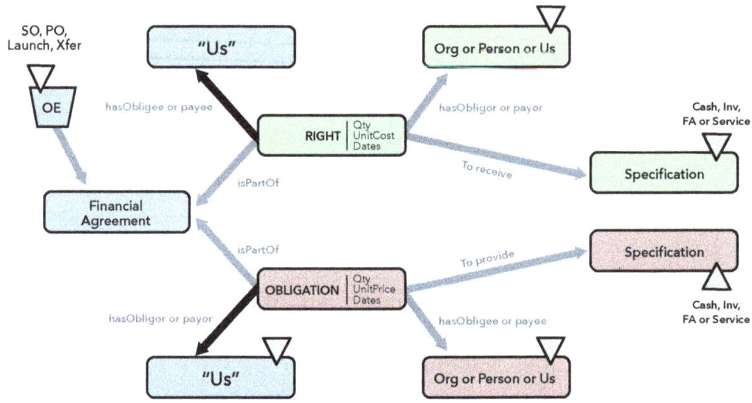

Figure 6.6: **Putting Ourselves in Our Obligations**

Here is the first step in rectifying this. Recall this diagram from the last chapter Figure 5.3. The only change here is the new arrows with the black lines. All we've done is make explicit what was already implied. Where another party (the obligor) had an obligation, of course we assumed we were the obligee—it was in our system, after all.

Now, we make this explicit. In your own system, this really doesn't change anything; we have just taken something that was implicit and made it explicit. In a moment, we will explore how this benefits us in the multi-organization scenario. But first, let's drill down a bit more on why this isn't done traditionally.

Why Don't We See This?

We can understand, at a conceptual level, that my purchase order *is* your sales order. But when it comes time to actually implement this, we still end up with two different versions—ours and yours—that hardly look related.

Why are they so different? There are two main reasons.

For starters, we have vastly different systems. We have a purchasing system from one software vendor, while our vendor has a CRM or order-taking system that they bought from a completely different software vendor. Their models are different, their terms are different. They call us a *customer* and assign us a customer ID in their CRM. We call them a *vendor* and assign them a vendor ID in our purchasing system. Every field, every code, every category—different.

And it doesn't stop there. It's not just this one supplier's system that doesn't match ours—*all* of them are different. Even when two companies happen to use the same software, their implementations are customized enough that reconciliation is still messy and difficult.

The second reason is each side attaches information the other doesn't need—or shouldn't see. On our end, that might be the budget, our reasons for the purchase, or the alternatives we considered. On their end, it might be salesperson commissions or internal cost structures.

This is, roughly, what is going on. Even in this simplified explanation, we've aligned some of the terminology just to make it readable. In reality, not only are the labels different, but the data structures themselves are entirely different too.

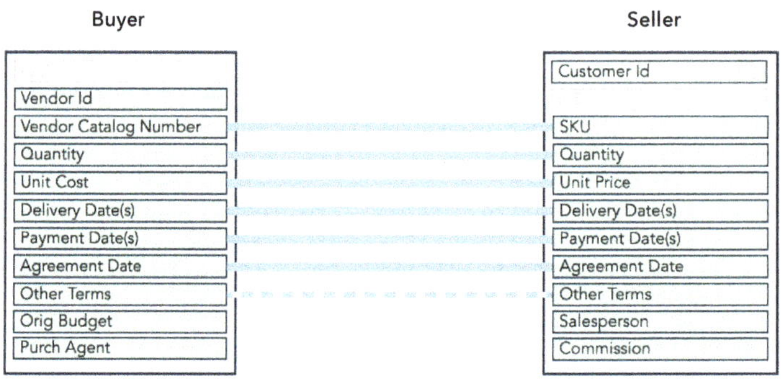

Figure 6.7: **Different Perspectives Yield Different Terms**

These are the essential elements of the agreement—each party extracts from the contract and enters them into their own system. At the bottom, you can see examples of information that each side might want to attach to the agreement but not necessarily share with each other. This gets a bit in the way of sharing, but we'll find a way around this.

The Integral Aperspectival

At first glance, it looks like there are two points of view that we need to deal with. In reality, it's more useful to think in terms of three. Borrowing a term from 20th-century philosopher Jean Gebser[27], we'll call this the *Integral Aperspectival*. Instead of constantly mapping between two subjective points of view, we propose a single, integrated point of view.

Integral Aperspectival is the point of view that combines (integrates) all other points of view, from a single non subjective point of view (the aperspectival).

[27]deep-psychology.com/jean-gebser-structures-of-consciousness/

To make such an approach practical, we need to establish these sharing points:

- Shared data representation
- Shared communication protocol
- Shared meaning of concepts
- Shared identifiers

There are many options for the first two items. For example, we can send data in JSON (a data representation) over HTTPS (a communication protocol—the same one your browser uses to communicate with a web server). The important thing is for the participants to agree on them.

In the next section, *Industry Standards*, we'll look at solutions that industries have relied on for decades. Then, in the follow-on implementation guidebook, we'll introduce what we believe to be the best current candidate for universal interoperability today.

Regardless of how the first two points—data representation and communication protocol—are resolved, we still need to tackle the last two: shared meaning of concepts and shared identifiers.

Fortunately, there are a limited number of concepts that need to be agreed to. The shared concepts are a subset of those introduced throughout this book and include:

> **Dates and Date-Times** – In most accounting systems, the lowest level of time granularity is a calendar date. There are certain domains—finance for instance—where there needs to be coordination at the sub-second level.
>
> **Quantities** – The big issue with quantities is achieving agreement on units of measure, including currencies, and therefore, achieving agreement on the meaning of prices and costs.
>
> **Parties** – In most domains, the parties to an agreement can be either people or organizations.

Specification – This is the idea that a good or a service can be specified in an independently verifiable way.

Terms – There are a limited number of contractual terms that need to be agreed upon. A common example is payment terms, such as how many days from an invoice date is payment due. Other terms that must be shared unambiguously include whether penalties or interest apply, and if so, when they begin to accrue.

Events – In any given industry sector, there are a limited number of events that the participants need to agree on. They need to agree what they mean and how they impact their mutual commitments. The events described in this book are a very good starting point.

Relationships – A small but essential set of relationships needs to be defined clearly. Four common ones—payee, obligee, payor, and obligor—were introduced in the previous chapter. Others that may be needed situationally are relationships like beneficiary, guarantor, or assessor.

The final requirement is for parties to agree on shared identifiers for certain concepts. In most cases, this involves delegating the assignment to a neutral third party for the identifiers. Two main concepts need resolvable shared identifiers: parties and specifications.

Examples of good candidates for parties include:

Dun & Bradstreet – for legal entities.

GLEIF – for legal entities.

Lexis Nexis – for lawyers (individuals) and law firms (organizations).

American Medical Association – for physicians (US persons).

Candidates for product or service specifications include:

> **GS1** (Global Standards 1) – bar codes and other identifiers based on the Global Trade Item Number (GTIN) system, for products, assets, and locations worldwide.
>
> **CUSIP** (Committee on Uniform Securities Identification Procedures) – unique identifiers for financial instruments (such as stocks, bonds, and derivatives) and their issuers in the US and Canada.
>
> **ISBN** (International Standard Book Number) – global standard for uniquely identifying book editions
>
> **CPT** (Current Procedural Terminology) – American Medical Association's code set for medical services and procedures.
>
> **NDC** (National Drug Code) – unique identifiers for human pharmaceuticals in the US, used by the FDA (Federal Drug Administration).

The right choice of identifiers will depend on the industry and context. Almost every industry has shared identifiers for interchangeable products and services. Identifiers for people, however, are more complicated. Past abuses of tax IDs and risks of identity theft have made universal personal identifiers problematic. Still, many industries have developed workable shared identifiers, often tied to membership in professional or regulatory bodies.

These identifiers give us the vocabulary we need for the integral aperspectival view on agreements.

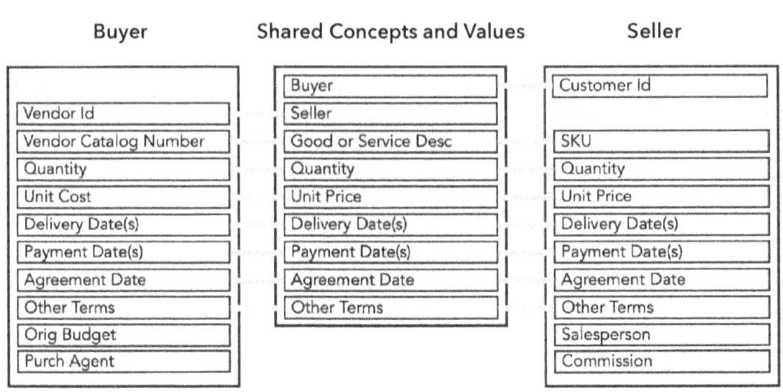

Figure 6.8: **A First Level of Integration**

Rosetta Stone: Archeologists were long baffled by hieroglyphics found in the Egyptian pyramids until Napoleon's soldiers stumbled upon a boulder with the same message in both hieroglyphics and Greek. The discovery of this boulder they called the Rosetta Stone gave researchers the decoder ring they needed to unlock an entire language.

This neutral, shared vocabulary and set of identifiers, becomes the *Rosetta Stone* for agreement information. Each party can agree to this shared representation and then map to their own internal representation. Many industries already do something similar, as we will see in the industry standards section—but here, we take it several steps further.

As we will elaborate in the implementation guidebook, it is now possible to literally share this representation in the middle, our integral aperspectival.

To understand the difference and the significance, we must first look at what organizations with shared standards currently do. Take health care insurance, for example. The industry has standardized on HL7 as their intermediate format for decades. HL7 comes with a comprehensive set of codes for procedures, drugs, diseases, and providers.

But here's the catch: they don't actually share this information as is. Instead, they copy and transform it. And in the copying and transforming, they introduce both added cost and the possibility for error.

Here's how it usually plays out: the provider records information in their medical records system (which, sadly in almost every case, has been over-engineered to support the payment function and under-engineered to support patient health—but that's another rant). To generate an HL7 message, the relevant data must be pieced together from thousands of database tables, copied, and packaged into HL7's format.

When the message arrives at the insurance company, they unpack it, copy fields into various adjudication systems, and only then begin their process of allowing or denying the claim and pricing it.

The 21st century solution to this problem is to share information at a deeper level. Imagine if we had a well-established way to share all four of the elements that we opened this section with: shared representation, shared protocol, shared concepts, and shared identifiers. Truth is, we already do.

The W3C has had mature standards (RDF, SPARQL, and OWL) for more than 20 years that cover all four concerns. We'll dig into the details in the implementation guidebook but for now, consider two usage scenarios that we'll call *caching* and *federating*.

Sharing by Caching

The first principle is that there is a neutral, standards-based way of expressing the commitments you have with a counterparty—your agreements. This shared representation captures everything about the agreement in an unambiguous format that you can consume directly, without transformation.

For example, if the agreement represents the party responsible for paying as ":hasPayee," then as long as your accounting system consistently uses that term, you can combine these shared agreements with the ones you've entered manually, such as purchase orders or bills.

What's significant here is that the representation does not need to be changed or transformed—it simply is what it is. You can still attach your unshared information to it (such as the RFP you issued or

> Caching, as practiced in web browsers and many other types of systems, is copying without transforming. The idea of caching is to selectively bring a subset of data closer to the consumer of the data as to reduce network delays. It works as well as it does because it does not transform the data. Data in the enterprise is almost always transformed in some way almost every time it is copied.

the competing bids you considered.) But this shared constellation of data itself remains unchanged. This is powerful. It eliminates the costly transformations, along with the possibility of error and cost.

It may be hard to imagine how this works in practice—but it does. We will detail the mechanics in the implementation guidebook. Most efforts that attempt to implement the principles of this book without following the best practices in the companion guidebook will fall short here, as well as in other key areas.

Sharing by Federation

While copying and caching are powerful techniques, they have a couple of downsides. Chief among them: caches need to be refreshed. When something changes in the shared representation, we need to push those updates to the cached copy. In this case, caching is far preferrable to sending updates through an ingest pipeline that will only further transform it.

The good news is that this technology allows us to go one step further—and even blend approaches—with only minor changes to consuming applications.

A shared representation of an agreement can be hosted in an environment that supports federated access, allowing the agreements to be queried *in situ*. There are many implementations that conform to W3C standards, and at least one[27] that conforms and does so on an immutable ledger (more below under blockchain).

In practice, you need not copy these shared agreements. You can leave them where they are and still incorporate them with the rest of your data—for instance, to get a complete up-to-date picture of your obligations at query time.

[27]One such implementation is Fluree, an immutable RDF graph database that conforms to W3C standards while persisting data on a blockchain-backed immutable ledger. https://flur.ee/fluree-products/intelligent-database/

Multi-Entity Organizations

Most large companies are not a single legal entity. Instead, they often consist of dozens, hundreds, or even thousands of legal entities.

From the outside, when you are selling to a large organization—say McDonald's—you may think of them as a single entity. In reality, most large firms are constellations of legal entities. A company like McDonald's, for example, may be composed of thousands of franchises, each operating as its own separate legal entity.

You may launch campaigns to sell to a large company, or maybe you want to buy something from them. Until you consummate a deal with them, this level of vagueness is sufficient. If you transact without extending credit—say, you buy a Big Mac at the corner McDonald's—you can continue to deal with them as an anonymous collection of legal entities that claim to be one.

But as soon as you consummate a transaction that involves granting credit, whether financial or in delivery, you will find out which specific legal entity you are dealing with. That entity's name will be on the contract. Regulators discovered this when they went into Lehman Brothers after their bankruptcy that triggered the Great Recession: there wasn't just one Lehman Brothers, but hundreds of separate legal entities. In practice, you may not care much, until something happens. But once credit is extended, you must have a relation with a specific legal entity.

The fact that many large companies are not single legal entities but rather constellations of legal entities—with either identical or very similar ownership—is not usually problematic. This is completely legitimate and even required in some cases. Some jurisdictions require companies to have local entities in their countries to do business there. Many people who work for these firms are often not aware which legal entity they work for. And these legal entities often have transactions with each other.

Recall our earlier discussion on ownership. In the world of multiple organizations, we have the concepts of *subsidiaries, controlled entities,* and *related entities*. In most cases, the key is whether one organization owns (directly or indirectly) more than 50 percent of the equity in another company. There are some additional circumstances where one company may be considered a controlling entity even with less than half the equity if there is sufficient overlap in management or boards. In the case that they do, there are many additional accounting and reporting requirements to comply with. Fortunately, the data-centric approach makes all this easier.

Non-Arm's Length Counterparties

When a company sells its output to another company it owns, that transaction is technically a counterparty transaction. On paper, it may look like an arm's length deal, but economically it isn't.

The first level of the solution is to treat such transactions as if they were at an arm's length. Since the bank accounts of the various subsidiaries are already distinct, we must recognize this separation in order to get each legal entity's books balanced. By including "ourselves"—that is, both legal entities that are different in form but collectively part of the same organization—in the obligations as described above, we have everything we need to report related party transactions as well as consolidations.

Reporting for Related Entities

When it comes to financial reporting, each entity can and should separately report related-party transactions. This is simple enough and was hinted at when we discussed the financial report model. A sister company, for example, can and should be indicated as such in the categorization of counterparties. The one legal entity can thereby report as a separate line item, revenue from related parties and expense to related parties. We need these transactions to be called out separately so that consumers of the financial reports can distinguish market-based transactions from those that are between controlled entities.

At some point, the constellation of legal entities will prepare consolidated financial reports. The central task in this process is to eliminate intercompany revenue, expense, payables, receivables, and even our new concepts of *due in* and *due out*.

Consolidations and reported entity transactions are just a simple variation on the integral aperspectival.

Mergers and Acquisitions

For some companies, acquisitions (and divestitures) are common occurrences. Certain companies do dozens of such deals every year. For them, an acquisition is like another financial business event. As we work through this, we will find that even for companies that only occasionally engage in these activities, we should still treat this as their own type of financial business event.

Merger Pursuit as a Project

The first thing to recognize is that many of these transactions never come to fruition. In this regard, they are similar to procurement teams spending time on RFPs and RFQs that don't result in contracts. What makes these M&A transactions different is the sheer scale of resources involved, whether they succeed or not. Investment bankers, outside accountants, and analysts are retained, war rooms are created, and significant expenses are incurred long before any commitments are made.

We recommend treating the pursuit of an acquisition as a project. Until there is a signed deal, there are no commitments with the target company (or companies). By treating it like an internal project, we have a vessel to capture the costs and keep track of the obligations we have with the investment bankers and outside analysts.

A Letter of Intent (LOI) is considered more of a moral obligation than a legal or financial one. There may, however, be some binding aspects of an LOI, including earnest money or a provision for covering expenses. In the event an LOI includes such binding financial obligations, we believe that it should be treated as any other financial obligation.

If the due diligence process concludes successfully and the parties agree to all the terms, they will *close the deal*—that is, finalize the merger, acquisition, or divestiture agreement. At that point, the lawyers and bankers are done. But just because the documents are done, it doesn't mean all the commitments are fulfilled.

Consummating the Deal

Part of any final deal is a value—or a formula for establishing the value. The commitments can go in either direction but often include the commitment to deliver the equity (the stock) of the acquired company in exchange perhaps for equity in the acquiring company, cash, or some combination of the two.

As mentioned earlier, most acquisitions result in the acquiring organization paying far more than the book value of the acquired organization. The result of this, which must be reflected in the acquisition accounting policy, is to book the difference as goodwill.

Integrating the Acquired Company

Two other aspects of M&A are especially important in the context of data-centric accounting.

First, the M&A process is the primary source of the multi-entity organization that we described in the previous section. Many acquired companies (especially those only partially acquired) maintain their legal entities and contribute to the size of the consolidated reporting burden.

Second, the integration process itself. Many acquisitions are justified on the basis of *synergy*. Often, this synergy is hard to realize, due to the difficulty in integrating systems. For example, we have worked with many companies that acquired other companies where part of the justification was the synergy, but the complexity of both the acquired and acquiring systems delayed their data integration not for months but in some cases, for decades.

> Synergy is the increased value that is expected to be realized when two entities combine. It is primarily expected to come from economies of scale in overhead activities, or increased revenue through cross selling.

A data-centric firm faces far fewer of these obstacles. It is surprising how much economy there is in simplicity. For instance, we worked with an industrial electrical device manufacturer, who acquired another firm in their industry. After converting their product specification and offering data to a data-centric representation, they asked if we could do the same for their subsidiary. It took about six weeks to conform and combine the subsidiaries' product data. It was only after the fact that we learned the subsidiary had co-existed for over a decade without being integrated because "it was too hard."

Cross Company Timing

When a small business receives a large check on December 31, the temptation to wait until January to deposit it can be strong. (Not legal advice—and certainly not a confession!) For a company on a cash basis, postponing the deposit means postponing the tax bill for a full year.

The IRS, however, is clear: if one company records the payment as an expense in December, the receiving firm should recognize it as income in December as well. In traditional systems, there is no coordination mechanism. Most larger firms are typically on an accrual basis, while many smaller firms are on a cash basis (at least for tax purposes) so the coordination doesn't necessarily apply.

Moving forward, this arrangement that is based on interpreting what you thought other firms did will be eliminated. Both the commitment date and the fulfillment date will be in the shared representation, and there will be no occasion for these timing differences.

Blockchain and Crypto

Blockchain is an architecture for decentralized digital ledgers. Many people conflate blockchain with Bitcoin and other cryptocurrencies, as they are the most popular application of blockchain technology. We will distinguish them here.

There are two interests in immutable ledgers, of which blockchain is the archetype.

Immutable ledger is a data storage approach where data is never overwritten. In a traditional database (or even an Excel spreadsheet), new data updates the previous data in a cell, and the previous data value is gone. In immutable approach, all updates are "adds." A new record will supply the new value, and may reference that it replaces the previous value, but the previous value is still there for anyone to interrogate.

The first interest is in the value of immutability in maintaining an audit trail. Traditional systems allow data to be overridden (updated in place). This presents a problem to anyone looking at the resulting data, "Was it changed? If so, what was the prior value, and who changed it?" In traditional systems, an audit trail is a separate data file that records all changes. Someone interested in the history of the data value must find and interrogate this other data set. And there exists the not discountable possibility that the audit trail itself was tampered with. An immutable ledger, by contrast, never deletes or overwrites records. The original entry remains, and new records are appended to indicate subsequent changes. Historical data stays intact and directly accessible—no separate audit file required. Data-centric design already tends toward immutability, but an immutable ledger enforces it at the architectural level.

The second interest in blockchain is with the implementation of the integral aperspectival and the ability to share mutual commitments. In this regard, we are interested in the potential for blockchain to implement smart contracts.

Smart Contracts

A smart contract is a contract in which trigger events are automatically detected and executed by computer software.

You could think of automatic credit card payment or overdraft alerts as very simple versions of smart contracts. In each case, you have set up an automation that surveilles the environment: when the end of the statement period occurs, it initiates a transfer in the amount of the balance; or when a withdrawal would overdraw your account, it sends you a notification or automatically transfers the funds.

When people talk about smart contracts today, they generally mean bespoke code that executes when certain conditions exist. At the moment, the most popular environment for smart contracts is the Ethereum ecosystem, with programming languages like Solidity and Vyper.

The difficulty with current generation smart contracts is that the participants must understand its code in order to understand the commitments they have agreed to. If you thought legalese was dense, wait until you get to this. The positive side is that most legalese is ambiguous at some level. Smart contracts are not ambiguous. They execute the script that was written when the event that triggers them occurs.

Looking ahead, we believe that the future of smart contracts will move beyond bespoke code. Instead, it will rest on architectures that support families of contracts, with semantically precise ways to express the parameters of each specific contract. This will be a Domain Specific Language (DSL), though not necessarily a programming language. We think the more powerful way to implement smart contracts will be via smart models, not code. Exploring this in detail is well beyond the scope of this book, but it points toward a more usable and trustworthy contract environment.

Crypto

Cryptocurrency is blockchain technology applied to money. While it may not be the most efficient use case, it certainly has been very popular. The challenge lies in scale: cryptocurrencies involve an enormous number of transactions. Like traditional money, crypto coins are fungible (within a coin type or currency). When you withdraw $10 at a bank, you don't care which specific $10 bill you receive. The same principle applies to cryptocurrency—you don't care which particular coin fulfills your transaction, as long as it does.

Bitcoin, the original and still the most popular cryptocurrency, is now routinely split into "satoshis"—units equal to 1/100,000,000 of a bitcoin. But accounting for millions of transactions across thousands of coins, often down to the satoshi level, risks overwhelming these supposedly immutable ledgers.

One last thought on crypto: in some contexts, it will be treated as a *commodity*—as a store of wealth, much like gold. In other contexts, it will function as a *currency*, allowing buyers to purchase products or services directly with their coins, just as sellers accept Euros or Japanese yen. In these cases, sellers will need to know the relevant currency "exchange rate" to price the transaction in cryptocurrency relative to their base currency.

Industry Standards

Some industries routinely interact with another, and, as a result, have developed standards—usually messaging standards—to grease those interactions. However, we are not aware of any standards that support the kind of "as-is" intercompany data consumption described earlier in the sections on *Sharing by Caching* and *Sharing by Federating*. Current messaging standards are meant to move data from one organization to another, with the assumption that the receiving organization will transform it to suit their own internal systems.

We will outline a couple of these industry standards to create a baseline and then suggest how they may evolve over time.

FIX / FpML

Companies in the Financial Services Industry, along with its regulatory agencies, are in constant highspeed communication using a series of standard messages called FIX and FpML. While these formats are well-defined, the content they carry is less so. The industry is continually inventing new financial instruments, particularly derivatives, whose exact obligations may only be fully understood by the transacting parties.

As noted under the *Integral Aperspectival* section, there is an ongoing need to extend the work on identifiers. Many identifiers—ticker symbols, CUSIP codes, and FIGIs—generally refer to the same thing (a tradeable financial instrument) but must be mapped to each other because there isn't a current universal identifier. The same is true with entity identifiers. This is why financial institutions have large KYC (Know Your Customer) programs: counterparties are not universally known or consistently identified.

HL7 / FHIR

As we earlier noted, healthcare delivery organizations—hospitals, clinics, and individual providers—communicate with each other and with payers (insurance companies and government healthcare agencies such as Medicare and Medicaid in the US) through a set of messages called HL7, and more recently, FHIR.

Providers have some form of Electronic Medical Record (EMR) system, which replaced those old manilla folders with their colored bar indexes. Every night, the system figures out what procedures were performed and on which patients, then assembles the appropriate HL7 messages to send to each patient's payer (insurance company or government agency). The US healthcare industry is primarily "fee-for-service," so these transactions are essentially bills for services provided.

Unlike a typical industry where the bill is sent to the entity that initiated the service, healthcare is different. The insurance company didn't order the patient's treatment; the patient presented at the emergency department, the physician treated them, and then the provider sent the bill to the insurance company. Because of this, the provider often doesn't know exactly how much they will be reimbursed. (Reimbursement rates are negotiated at high levels, but the exact payment for each claim can be uncertain.)

Payers ingest these HL7 messages and run them through programs that convert them into formats that will feed into their claims adjudication systems. Fields may be recast, combined differently, and different message types may even be processed by different systems.

Once the payer determines what will be paid, they send additional HL7 messages back to the provider to inform them. Paper copies of these messages are often sent to patients under the title *Explanation of Benefits*.

MARC

Even relatively small industries, such as the library sector, have developed communication standards. One widely used standard is MARC 21, which encodes bibliographic records for libraries worldwide. Names and terms are drawn from authority records maintained under another standard called RDA (Resource Description and Access).

Industry Communication Standards

Not all communication between members of an industry is accounting-related, but much of it is. In the next few paragraphs, we will suggest how industry accounting communication could evolve, and from there extrapolate to non-accounting interactions.

A prerequisite for accounting transactions between organizations in an industry is the existence of agreements. In the industries mentioned above, these agreements are often complex paper contracts. The complexity contributes to their opaqueness.

The first step to frictionless communication between organizations is to reduce these agreements to simple models, models that can be understood by all parties and, at the same time, executed directly by machines.

On top of these models, event representations that affect these agreements can be layered. In each case it should be possible for organizations in an industry to consume these models and events directly, as they are. They may augment them, but they should not need to transform them.

Supply Chains

Your immediate "supply chain" consists of the vendors from whom you procure your raw materials and other resources, as well as customers who buy your finished goods.

Your supplier also has its own immediate supply chain, and your customer may not be the final consumer of your goods—they too have an immediate supply chain.

When we snap these immediate supply chains together, we get a more complete picture of how an industry works: a complete supply chain.

Figure 6.9: **A One-Level Supply Chain**

Most companies don't just have one supply chain. They have different supply chains for each industry or line of business they operate in. For example, Coca-Cola's Minute Maid Orange Juice Division has a very different supply chain from its Dasani Water Division: the former is dominated by citrus farmers, while the latter relies on freshwater suppliers.

Two companies competing in the same narrow industry will have similar supply chains. They have the opportunity to work with the same citrus growers. But their actual supply chain is the set of citrus growers they actually have agreements with.

Industry Knowledge Graph is a subscription-based data provider that has a wealth of information on the entire world economy at the level of detail where companies compete.

Disclosure: Semantic Arts built the knowledge graph version of this data set and has an economic stake in the enterprise.

Readers interested in pursuing this further may wish to review a company called Industry Knowledge Graph[28] which has compiled a granular list of the 24,000 industries that represent this level of detail where supply chains are actually constructed.

Unless you have considerable leverage and power in your industry, you may struggle to produce such a complete picture at any level of accuracy. Your suppliers are reluctant to tell you who their suppliers are, partly because you may use that information to exclude them from the supply chain altogether.

[28]www.industryKG.com

Despite the lack of full detail, there are many parts of the supply chain you can—and should—assemble. You may not know all the intermediate suppliers for your lithium batteries, but you might know that they are all ultimately sourcing from the same mine. In supply chain circles, this is a phenomenon known as *concentration* and is considered a significant risk.

Another possibility that the technology we advocate in the implementation guidebook enables is the creation of an interesting third-party business model—one that, as far as we know, does not currently exist. Imagine a company that could collect agreements from all the participants in a supply chain while keeping the data separate and secure. Each participant could then subscribe to certain types of events that may have a bearing on their firm.

For instance, a participant might receive reports on the degree of geographical concentration of various upstream materials, notifications of price shocks entering the chain, alerts about changes in ultimate consumers demand patterns, or evidence of stockpiling at various points in the supply chain.

While some of these services are currently being provided by industry analysts, it seems that there is an opportunity to take this to an entirely new level.

Summary of Multi-Organizational Data-Centric Accounting

Multi-organizational data-centric accounting takes accounting beyond the boundaries of a single organization, treating it instead as part of a broader ecosystem.

This approach allows us to handle multi-entity firms with the same constructs that we used for single-entity implementations. Beyond internal reporting, it allows for true sharing with counterparties—whether in a smart contract environment, across supply chain partners, or even throughout an entire industry. Over time, we expect that the next generation of industry intercompany messaging standards will be replaced with truly shareable concepts as described in this book.

CHAPTER 7

Applying Data-Centric Accounting in Various Contexts

The previous sections laid out a major shift in how accounting information can be integrated with the rest of the enterprise and challenged us to think differently about accounting processes and financial reporting.

You may be thinking: "This all sounds interesting, but how does it apply to me? I have special circumstances that I'm not convinced could be covered by these methods."

Accounting is used in many contexts and for many goals, and each of these will be impacted differently by the data-centric approach. In this section, we'll touch on each context—but keep in mind that each of these subsections could easily be a book on its own.

Management Accounting

When people talk about accounting reports, they are typically talking about the income statement and the balance sheet. As used in annual reports for investors or in reports for banks to secure credit, these reports tell a story.

For investors, the story is typically something like: "We are a well-run, predictable enterprise, improving in certain areas, and worthy of your investment." The reports must be truthful (that's the auditor's job), but they aren't a "tell-all." Maybe revenue is broken down by region and costs by vendor type. In some ways, it is remarkable how little detail there typically is in published financial reports, given the detail that exists in a traditional chart of accounts.

Small- to medium-sized companies tend to use their financial reports to run their businesses on a day-to-day basis. This isn't a bad idea, as improving the financial accounting results on a monthly basis will generally improve the annual report to investors or creditors.

But eventually, this isn't enough. As the organization delegates financial responsibility to divisions and departments, upper management needs something more fine-grained to improve financial results.

This is the birth of management reporting in an organization. As this idea takes hold, it becomes obvious that management reporting is no longer just about storytelling.

The audience shifts from third parties to the managers themselves.

The emphasis shifts from storytelling to detailed benchmarking and management exploration.

This shift—from storytelling to exploration—means we need completely different tools. Traditional financial reports are hand-crafted, often with a great deal of narrative explanation. Management reporting, in contrast, starts with a few key metrics and allows the report consumer to drill down, search, explore, and look for correlations.

A second distinction is that management reporting often adds transactions to allocate overhead to lines of business or departments. Most businesses are comprised of revenue-generating lines of business, supported by shared cost centers such as HR, legal, purchasing, and accounting. To ensure profitability, the contribution from all lines of business has to more than cover the shared costs. One way to manage this on a day-to-day basis is to allocate some of the overhead costs to the lines of business.

Management accounting is also far more focused on budgets and budget attainment than financial reports. Indeed, very few investor or creditor financial reports include budgets at all.

Because financial reports are often significantly delayed, management accounting often relies on *flash reports*—informal, up-to-date summaries of activity.

Finally, management reporting incorporates a wide range of metrics. Evaluating business activity often involves involves correlating revenue or costs to non-financial metrics. For instance:

> **retailers** measure revenue per square foot of retail space.
>
> **hotels** measure cost per occupied room.
>
> **restaurants** measure average cover (revenue per seat).
>
> **airlines** measure cost per available capacity, with and without fuel.
>
> **startups** measure customer acquisition costs.

Traditional management accounting often builds up from the transactions in the General Ledger, augmented by allocations and adds in metrics from other sources. Management accounting is usually done from a separate system, often a data warehouse, that must be periodically reconciled to the General Ledger to prevent it from drifting away from the official record of financial events.

In data-centric accounting, management reporting is built directly from the same transactions and events that feed into the financial reports. This ensures both remain in sync, eliminating reconciliation issues. There is also no need for flash reports, since any information known to the organization is available for management reporting.

A facet is a small, often flat, taxonomy. A taxonomy is usually a large "tree" with thousands of leaves and branches descending from a single root. (And yes, it is a little odd that in taxonomies, the roots are always at the top!)

Facets (sometimes called dimensions) replace a large single-rooted tree, with several orthogonal facets.

Management accounting is not nearly as concerned with whether we are ahead or behind on a commitment, or with determining whether items are prepaid or unearned. In data-centric accounting, the management reports will primarily be built from the transactions as we described in Chapter 4.

Additional metrics will be part of the database and can be used to report costs and revenues per metric.

The allocations will be based on internally generated financial business events that allocate overhead to lines of businesses. These transactions will be ignored by financial reporting.

The report models for data-centric management accounting will be based on the facets that are attached to transactions. These facets are very similar to dimensions in data warehouses. Commitments and budgets will be available for management reporting, as we'll discuss in the next section.

Closed Loop Budget Management

We believe data-centric accounting will make budgeting—and controlling expenses to budget—far easier than it is today. Budgets exist because resources are limited, and we wish to deploy them in the most strategic way possible.

For a for-profit company, that means investing resources in niches where you can gain market share or in processes that improve profit margins. For a non-profit, it means channeling resources to maximize your mission reach.

Once you have set your budget, which is a strategic determination, you need to manage that budget, which is an operational activity. This involves several aspects, beginning with prediction. Prediction is about the unknown. Most businesses treat budgeting as prediction, because in part, that's exactly what it is.

Prediction Is Hard

As the 20th-century philosopher and three-time American League MVP Yogi Berra once said,

> "Prediction is difficult, especially about the future."

Prediction is hard because many events are uncertain. In most businesses, the greatest uncertainty lies in whether customers will buy their products or services, and in what quantity. The degree of uncertainty is quite different across industries. Retailers, for example, don't know what tomorrow's sales will be. But companies that work on multi-month contracts often know with confidence what revenue looks like weeks or even months ahead. In their case, the future isn't really being predicted—it's already baked into events that have already occurred.

In data-centric accounting, many of the things that are being predicted have already been committed to. We don't need to predict them; we just need better bookkeeping.

Tracking Commitments

In traditional systems, tracking commitments is hard because they live in many different systems—procurement, hiring, inventory, sales, and more. Just adding up the total commitments is challenging enough; determining how much has already been spent against them is even harder.

Delays in getting reliable spending information only add to the ambiguity over where we stand regarding outstanding commitments. As we showed in Chapter 5, however, we have a way to combine all the commitments that have been made and net them against receipts and payments. This integrated view of commitments is a crucial step in making budget management truly practical.

Budget Management as Behavior Control

There is one key moment when budget availability is effectively reduced: the moment an employee commits the organization. Hiring someone, placing a purchase order, or even accepting the terms of a sales order—all of these could affect overall budget attainment, and reduce the amount of outstanding budget available.

Controlling spending, then, is primarily about controlling the act of committing the organization. If there are hundreds of places in the organization to exert this control, it is hard. If there is only one, it is pretty doable. When you have control over commitment-making, you can tighten or loosen the thresholds as situations dictate. Typically, tightening is needed when non-controllable incidents arise—such as sales not materializing or unforeseen cost overruns in other areas.

Flexible Budgeting

Some parts of the organization (if they have budgets at all) should have very flexible budgets. If sales double, you shouldn't be constrained because you didn't budget enough raw material purchases. Anything that is directly variable with sales should scale up—or down!—alongside sales volume. When sales go down, automated procedures should prevent unnecessary stockpiling of inventory.

But many aspects of a business aren't quite so flexible. Most so-called "overhead" is not pure overhead—if it were, it could be eliminated without too much repercussion. Instead, most controllable expenses are tied to functions that support the organization's long-term competitiveness.

The Unit of Budget

One of the trickiest aspects of budgeting, especially in larger organizations, is deciding the right level of granularity. Exactly what should budgets attach to, and how those pieces combine to meet strategic objectives.

Most organizations use two main mechanisms to set and manage budgets: cost centers (based on the organization structure) and financial line items. This is yet another reason why organizations add more line items to their chart of accounts—to give more fine-grained budget management.

Department-based budgets generally work because most organizations have functional organization charts; giving or withholding resources at the department level can influence the effectiveness of those functions.

But we've recently been experimenting with something more direct: goal-based budgeting, which links the strategy of the organization with its spending.

Goal-Based Budgeting

We've recently had good results with something we call *goal-based budgeting*, a method that seems especially well-suited for small to medium-sized businesses. The basic idea is that the discretionary expenses might be better prioritized if they are directly aligned to the organization's goals.

The strength of goal-oriented budgets is that well-defined goals can be tied to metrics that indicate whether the related spending is making a difference. For example, one of our goals is *Increase Brand Awareness*. Progress toward this goal can be measured, for instance, by surveying a general population and, even in the absence of hard data, one can evaluate and discuss whether the spending is effective and whether funding should be diverted toward other goals, such as *Employee Retention* or *Refine Methodology*.

The goals can be broad, as in the examples above, or very specific. Regardless of how the budget is allocated, once set, the next task is trying to stay within the budget.

Goal-Based Budgeted Income Statement
From Apr 1 - Apr 30

Forecasted Revenues	
Consulting	$310,000
Subcontracting	$90,000
Training Workshops	120,000
Total Forecasted Revenue	520,000
Budgeted Cost of Services Provided	
Provide Service with Qualified Personnel	156,000
Host Workshops at Quality Venues	42,000
Quality, Cost-Conscious Travel for Personnel	55,000
Total Budgeted Cost of Services Provided	253,000
Budgeted Gross Margin	267,000
Goal-Based Budgeted Expenses	
Maintain Comfortable, Clean Workplace	50,000
Mitigate Risk from Theft or Natural Disasters	15,000
Increase Brand Awareness	20,000
Increase Reachable Contacts	30,000
Create New Training Workshops	10,000
Maintain Employee Morale	10,000
Improve Employee Skills	15,000
Total Goal-Based Budgeted Expenses	150,000
Budgeted Operating Income	117,000
Other Budgeted Income (Expense)	
Interest Expense	(50,000)
Budgeted Net Income	$ 67,000

Figure 7.1: Goal-Based Budgeted Income Statement

Notice that this is not the same as budgeting more money for the marketing or HR department. Instead, the focus is on measurable outcomes. Once budgets are formed at that level, organizations can adjust allocations even if the org chart doesn't neatly line up with those goals.

For instance, suppose your main organization structure is geographic (US, Europe, and ROW) and your next level is line of business (product lines). You can still say we like to allocate $x or x% of our revenue toward improving customer satisfaction. We will apportion the budgeted spending by sales and expect to see comparable improvements in customer satisfaction by both region and by product line.

What's powerful about this approach is that it avoids the trap of micromanaging line items. Instead, it gives departments the freedom to experiment with different strategies. One group may invest in more customer service representatives, another in new systems, and another might spend its budgeted amount on efforts to improve products and product instructions. It will be relatively easy to compare spending against results—and then see which approach works best.

Temporal Budgets

There is one more arrow in the budget management quiver: temporal budgets. Just as commitments can be spread out over time, so can our budgets. This approach helps avoid the classic "spend it before you lose it" problem, where people try to spend their budget as fast as they can.

With temporal budgeting, the system doesn't only check whether a new commitment would exceed your budget overall—it checks whether it would exceed your budget *at that point in time*. For example, a purchase might push you over budget in May, but if you wait until July, the allocation for that period kicks in and makes the spending feasible.

This approach also offers flexibility for companies that have shorter horizons for predictability of revenue. Instead of an annual budget, they can set expense budgets for just a few months. As sales materialize (or don't), the organization can adjust the expense budget up or down accordingly.

Summing up Budget Management

Taken together, these considerations strongly suggest that a data-centric organization not only has far better day-to-day control of spending, but can also spend in ways that can be traced to the organization's goals.

Cash Management

The traditional financial reporting package contains a *Statement of Cash Flows*, which provides an after-the-fact account of where cash came from and how it was used. Like other investor- or creditor-focused reports, it tells a story: how much cash flowed into the company, the sources of that cash (operations, borrowing, etc.), and how it was spent. From this, it is hoped, one can infer likely future sources and uses of cash.

To use the term we introduced earlier, the statement of cash flows is a lagging indicator. You do not use the statement of cash flows to manage cash.

Many companies, however, do manage cash on a daily basis. Even those not facing tight liquidity monitor cash closely to optimize investments. Traditionally, this process is ad hoc.

As we discussed in Chapter 2, there are two ways to report cash-based activity on the Statement of Cash Flows: direct and indirect. These are cash reporting methodologies, not management tools. While the accounting standards encourage the direct method, most firms stick with the indirect method, as it requires less work, at least for generating the Statement of Cash Flows.

But effective daily cash management requires the direct method.

Data-centric cash management goes a step further. It is more complete, precise, and operates at the level of every commitment—not just aggregates. Every obligation to pay or right to receive payment will eventually become a cash flow.

The most immediate and precise place to begin is with accounts receivable and accounts payable. Each transaction has a due date on it, which is a reasonable starting point. But we can go further. For existing customers, past payment behavior gives you a clear picture of when cash will actually arrive. For new customers, you have access to customers of their type, and how long they typically take to pay.

You have control on the payables side. You can pay each bill whenever you choose. Most companies choose to pay bills on or around the last day before penalties begin to accrue or before a discount expires. Armed with these two inputs, we have a fairly precise, day-by-day cash flow forecast, for typically about two months.

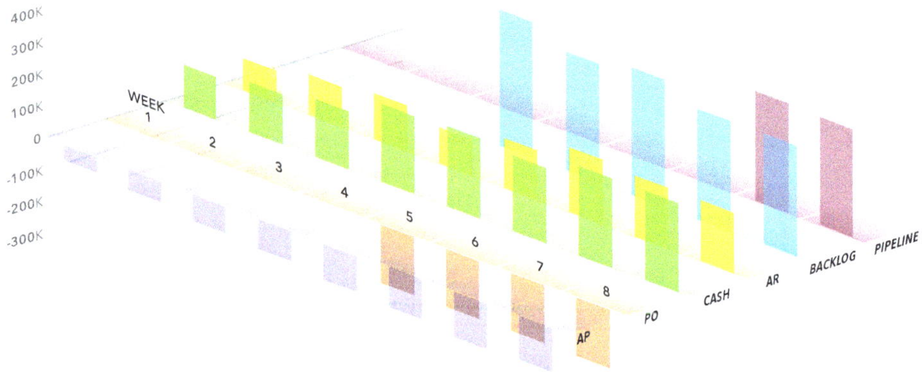

Figure 7.2: **Cash Management Histogram**

This chart illustrates the next eight weeks of projected cash activity. The current week is week 1, shown in the back. The bars below the plane represent planned outbound cash, on a weekly basis for the next eight weeks. The lavender boxes are scheduled Accounts Payable payments, but the orange ones are Purchase Orders where we have not yet received the bills.

The yellow-green bars predict our week-by-week receipt of cash from Accounts Receivable. Behind this are future cash flows from the backlog (sold but not yet invoiced) and the pipeline (high probability work not yet sold). Generally, the effect of Purchase Orders and the Pipeline have little effect on the very short-term cash flow, but factor into the two- to six-month cash planning.

The net of all this is shown in the green predicted cash balance.

Depending on the nature of the industry, a data-centric organization can plan out its cash commitments on a weekly basis for months into the future. Indeed, if you have all your commitments captured, there are no other cash outflows you need to consider. If you have control of your commitment authorization process, you can staunch any future outbound cash before it is committed.

Tax Accounting

There are several key considerations in the domain of tax accounting:

- Tax motivated transactions
- Different policies for tax reporting
- Different categorization of financial results for tax purposes

Let's take these up in turn.

Tax-Motivated Transactions

There are events you might not have indulged in, if not for the tax advantage. These are called *tax-motivated transactions*, but we still call them *financial business events*. We will generate transactions from the events' value of the outstanding commitments, exactly as we would any other commitment and event. We flag the source of the originating commitment in case someone needs to get credit for initiating it. In some cases, the transactions will be exactly the same for financial and tax reporting purposes, but in some cases, they will be different.

For example, an organization might choose to realize capital gains during a year when tax authorities grant favorable treatment, or it might open a branch in a government-designated area that offers tax incentives to spur local development.

In each of these cases, the motivation for entering into the event may be the tax advantage that accrues. Even so, they are still events, no different in structure from any other event. Most organizations rely on a tax advisor to stay apprised of opportunities to initiate these events.

You may want to flag these events to give credit to those who initiated them, but beyond that, they are treated identically as any other transaction.

Different Policies for Tax Reporting

Tax law allows us to have different policies for tax reporting purposes. One common example is depreciation. Tax codes typically allow capital assets to be depreciated more quickly than their useful life would suggest. In the US, purchases of property, plant, and equipment not exceeding a certain dollar value may even be expensed entirely in the year of purchase. This accelerated deduction, known as Section 179, enables organizations to reduce taxable income immediately, even though the assets will be used for years.

Some organizations use different inventory costing methods for tax reporting and for financial reporting. While US GAAP generally allows flexibility, it requires that companies using LIFO for tax purposes must also use LIFO for financial reporting. Outside that exception, a company might use FIFO for tax reporting while employing weighted average costing for financial reporting—or vice versa.

And if you think about it, using cash basis accounting for tax reporting is literally an alternate policy to accrual accounting for financial reporting. The tax code says you can use a different policy for revenue and expense recognition. Instead of recognizing revenue at invoicing or shipping time, the IRS says you can recognize it when you receive payment (remittance, in our terminology).

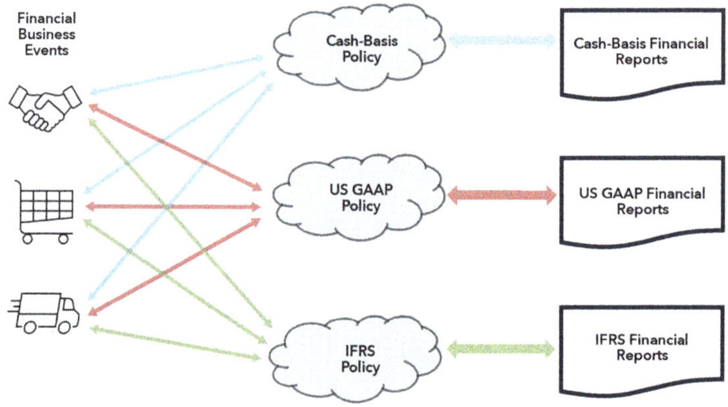

Figure 7.3: **Multiple Policies Applied to the Same Data to Produce Different Financial Reports**

Figure 7.3 illustrates that the same financial business events (captured once) can be interpreted differently through the lens of each policy. The policy then leads to financial reports, that conform to the policy. Auditors can trace reports back through the policy and transactions to the originating events. (Although not shown in the diagram to avoid clutter, the audit trail explicitly connects events, policies, and resulting transactions.)

It's easier to think of two or three complete sets of transactions. In practice, 90 percent of the transactions would be identical between the policy groups. Most implementations would therefore use a category on each transaction to indicate whether it should be included in tax reports, financial reports, or management reports.

One final note: tax reporting usually doesn't need to be as frequent—or as detailed—as management reporting.

Other Types of Tax Reporting

The previous discussion focused on corporate income tax obligations. Companies are liable for several other types of taxes, many of which often act as stewards and pay taxes on behalf of others.

This section provides a brief outline of the non-income related tax obligations and indicates how data-centric accounting handles these obligations:

> **Property tax (real estate):** Businesses pay property taxes on real estate, similar to individuals, though rates on commercial property are typically higher.
>
> **Property tax (inventory):** Many states also impose taxes on non-real-estate property, sometimes called an *inventory tax*.
> This category can include not only inventory but also equipment, machinery, and other operational assets.
>
> **Sales tax:** A tax on sales levied in some jurisdictions; sellers are obligated to collect a percentage of sales made on behalf of customers and remit it to the appropriate jurisdiction.

Use tax: A companion to sales tax, imposed when buyers in a taxable jurisdiction purchase from sellers who are not required to collect sales tax. In this case, the buyer must remit use tax to the sales taxing jurisdiction.

Excise taxes: These are additional taxes imposed on specific goods such as cigarettes, alcohol, fuel, and ozone-depleting chemicals. Unlike sales tax, excise taxes are typically calculated per unit (e.g., cents per gallon or per pack) rather than as a percentage of sales. These taxes often serve the dual purpose of generating revenue and discouraging consumption.

Stamp duties: These are a variety of transaction-based taxes, common in the financial services industry and imposed on financial services firms. Examples include Section 31 fees that fund the SEC in the US.

Value Added Tax (VAT): Common outside the US, VAT resembles a sales tax but is collected at every stage of production on the value added at that stage. VAT taxes the value added at each level. For example, if a wholesaler adds a 20 percent markup to the goods they buy, their VAT will be on the added 20 percent, not the full price.

Tariffs[29] and duties: Essentially taxes levied on goods as they cross international borders.

Payroll tax: In the US, there are three main species of payroll-related taxes.

> ***FICA (Social Security/Medicare):*** Employers and employees share the cost, each contributing 7.65 percent of wages. Self-employed individuals must pay both shares (12.4 percent for Social Security and 2.9 percent for Medicare), totaling 15.3 percent. For employers, this effectively increases labor costs by 7.65 percent.
>
> ***Unemployment taxes:*** Employers also contribute to federal and state unemployment funds. Rates vary depending on the employer's history of layoffs and terminations.
>
> ***Withholding taxes:*** Employers are responsible for withholding employees' income taxes (federal, state, and sometimes local) as well as the employees' portion of FICA and remitting these taxes on the employees' behalf.

[29]We wrote this section in 2024, before the debate about whether tariffs are taxes on consumers heated up. Semantically, they are.

Anyone in business recognizes the number and significance not only of the cost of these taxes but also the burden of reporting and complying. A data-centric approach does not eliminate these obligations, but it can reduce the complexity of meeting them, as we will discuss.

The obligation to pay taxes generally comes from one of two primary sources: things you own or things you do. In data-centric accounting, these map directly to the two fundamental concepts: resources and events.

In the former category are the various property tax categories. Real estate ownership is registered with the local tax jurisdiction, which periodically assesses its value and issues a bill. You will treat these property taxes as procured services. When purchasing the property, you also establish the equivalent of a purchase order without a corresponding right to receive anything, to represent follow on tax obligation. This is handy in that you can track (approximately as you don't have clairvoyance onto the jurisdictions valuation assessment methods) the long-term commitment that continuing to own the property places on the organization. Other property taxes are similar, except that part of the obligation is the obligation to self-assess periodically and pay based on that information.

Some taxes—such as use taxes and excise taxes—are essentially taxes on activities an organization performs. As such, they are part of the cost of doing business and should be reported as expenses. In a data-centric model, we will create event templates for these types of activities. When triggered, these events can generate an additional event that reflects both the expense and resulting liability implied by conducting this activity.

A template is a reusable data structure. In this case, it will be a template of a business event, that generates other business events. A sales order template will generate two financial business events, one concerning the sales transaction between you and your customer for the goods, and the other between your customer and the tax jurisdiction, which you are intermediating.

By contrast, other taxes, such as sales tax, are not a cost of doing business. They are the customer's liability, not the company's. Accordingly, sales taxes should never be reported as revenue or expense. The correct accounting treatment (data-centric or not) is straightforward: record the selling as revenue and the cost of providing the goods or services as a cost of goods sold. Sales tax is a separate transaction, even if it appears on the same receipt as the sale itself. It is simply money collected on behalf of the taxing authority. From an accounting standpoint, it is booked as accounts receivable until collected from the customer and as sales tax payable until remitted to the jurisdiction.

In a data-centric model, this secondary transaction is generated from a template based on the primary transaction.

Employer taxes are activity-based taxes, where the activity being taxed is the work performed by your employees. The tax is a cost of doing business and is recognized as additional expense as soon as it is calculated. Withholding taxes, on the other hand, operate more like sales taxes. They are not recorded as additional expense to the employer—the employer's expense is simply the employees' gross pay. The withholding template apportions the obligation to pay between the employee and the tax jurisdiction on behalf of the employee. An important difference between sales tax and payroll withholding is in the reporting requirements. For sales tax, you are only required to report the aggregate: total taxable sales and the corresponding tax remitted. Whereas with payroll withholdings, reporting is individualized. You must track and report the specific individuals' tax identifiers, and the amounts remitted on their behalf when you pay the tax jurisdiction.

Financial Reporting Compliance

Most financial compliance reporting boils down to this: you already have the financial information, but regulators want it categorized and slotted into very specific fields on their predefined forms.

Take the W-2 form as an example. In the US, employers must provide this report to both federal and state governments—as well as to employees—within a month of the year-end. This is a classic financial compliance report. Don't let its small size fool you, there is a lot of information packed into those little boxes.

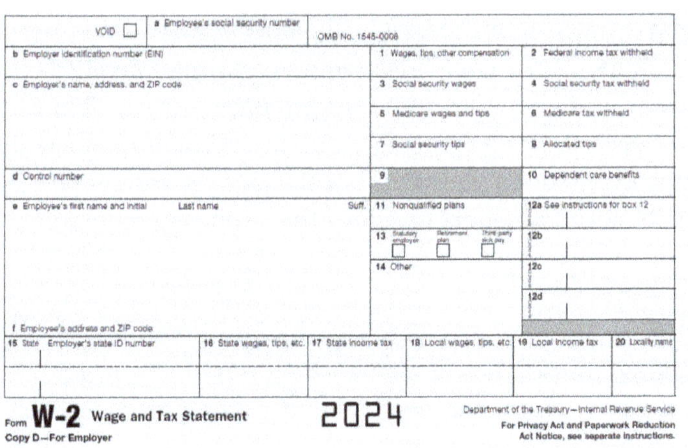

VOID ☐
a Employee's social security number
OMB No. 1545-0008
b Employer identification number (EIN)
1 Wages, tips, other compensation
2 Federal income tax withheld
c Employer's name, address, and ZIP code
3 Social security wages
4 Social security tax withheld
5 Medicare wages and tips
6 Medicare tax withheld
7 Social security tips
8 Allocated tips
d Control number
9
10 Dependent care benefits
e Employee's first name and initial
Last name
Suff.
11 Nonqualified plans
12a See instructions for box 12
13 Statutory employee ☐ Retirement plan ☐ Third-party sick pay ☐
12b
14 Other
12c
12d
f Employee's address and ZIP code
15 State Employer's state ID number
16 State wages, tips, etc.
17 State income tax
18 Local wages, tips, etc.
19 Local income tax
20 Locality name
Form **W-2** Wage and Tax Statement
2024
Department of the Treasury—Internal Revenue Service
For Privacy Act and Paperwork Reduction Act Notice, see separate instructions.
Copy D—For Employer

Figure 7.4: W-2 Form

Essentially, the IRS is asking you to take information you already have—wages and deductions are the big ones—and categorize them in ways you wouldn't have imagined if not for the reporting requirement.

Traditionally, the way to accommodate this has been to add account numbers in your financial system that correspond directly to the boxes on the forms. At year-end, you map from the account numbers to the reporting boxes.

The problem? It doesn't scale very well. Each regulatory jurisdiction has its own way of asking you to categorize information to suit their reporting purposes. That said, these requirements aren't completely arbitrary. Each category is based on some underlying principles.

For instance:

> A corporate tax return (another form of compliance report) requires that you segregate meals from other sales expenses (lodging or airfare for instance).
>
> It also has a special category for skyboxes and similar excessive marketing expenses. It separates them because they don't qualify as tax deductible at the same rates that the more prosaic expenses do.

But here's the thing: in a data-centric database, you've already captured the source information about the event that gave rise to the expense transaction. You know whether it was airfare, a meal, or entertainment. You could also require your sales department to provide any other specifics with their expense reports. That way, you don't need to teach employees obscure account numbers just for compliance, nor do you want bookkeepers wasting time moving balances between accounts to satisfy this reporting requirement.

Banking

The banking industry has its peculiarities, but once you get used to them, it's clear that they fit neatly into the data-centric approach.

The biggest difference is that there are no goods or services being exchanged. Well, there are a few services, but they mostly involve money. In a typical non-banking transaction, you have an obligation to deliver goods or services on one side and a right to receive payment on the other. In banking, however, both sides of the transaction are money.

Take originating a loan, for example. It's much like a contract to sell a capital asset over time. Imagine signing a sales contract to deliver a $1 million piece of earthmoving equipment, with the buyer paying it off over 10 years.

Figure 7.5: **Buying a Tractor**

The exchange looks like this: it starts with an obligation to deliver (the tractor) and a corresponding obligation to pay (over time).

Now substitute a pile of cash for the earthmoving equipment. In banking, that's essentially what a loan is. Underwriting is the process of determining whether the bank will do the deal at all (is the borrower creditworthy?) and at what interest rate (the equivalent of pricing).

Once both parties commit to the loan, the transaction moves to closing. At that moment, the bank fulfills its obligation to deliver—not a massive piece of machinery, but rather a bag of money.

Figure 7.6: **Acquiring a Loan**

This is why we've grouped loans into a P2P (procure-to-pay) process for the recipient of the loan and an O2C (order-to-cash) process for the bank.

Another key difference in banking is how bank accounts are viewed. From your perspective, you think of your bank account as an asset, more specifically as a resource you can use to write checks or pay bills. From the bank's perspective, however, your bank account is a liability. They call it a *demand deposit* because you can demand your money at any time. This is the liability aspect of it.

But here's the catch: they still have your cash. As we discussed earlier in the context of ownership, the bank possesses your money but does not own it. Thanks to the fractional banking system, banks enjoy a special privilege: they can use the money they possess—but don't own—to issue loans.

Another oddity is the way banks use the terms *debit* and *credit*. Their meaning depends entirely on which side of the transaction you're viewing. To you, your cash is an asset, so you record your cash increases as debits. To the bank, your cash account is a liability (they owe it back to you), so the bank records increases in your cash account as credits. Both are accurate, but the different perspectives can seem confusing. Whenever someone in the financial industry tells me they are going to *credit* my account, I always ask: *does that mean you are putting money in or taking money out?* It is almost comical how often the same term produces a different result.

All these banking aspects are completely compatible with data-centric accounting—the only adjustment needed is to think of the commitment to deliver goods as a commitment to deliver funds.

Investment Accounts and Wealth Management

Wealth management is the practice of entrusting your spare money to professionals who can often put it to better use than you might on your own. In many ways, wealth managers operate like banks—and many are directly affiliated with them. The similarity is that they hold your assets but do not own them.

The key difference is that, beyond cash, your assets also include investments in financial instruments such as specific stocks and bonds.

Opening an investment account is a lot like opening a bank account, except you can direct someone to use the funds to buy financial assets. A broad industry of professionals exists to guide and support you in making these investment decisions.

This wealth management industry is divided into two main groups: the *buy side* and the *sell side*. Both aim to improve the financial returns on the money invested.

> Buy-side organizations include hedge funds and asset managers. They are primarily focused on buying financial assets that they think will outperform the market as a whole. Some invest for their own accounts, while others package this expertise into funds or other tradable financial securities that investors can buy.
>
> Sell-side organizations include broker dealers and market makers who are primarily focused on helping a client (an investor) choose financial products or investments that best match their needs.

Everything described here is completely compatible with data-centric accounting. Still, a few things are worth elaborating.

The first is that a financial instrument is a special case of a product specification. In our discussion of product specifications and the item of supply concept, a central consideration was their fungibility but at the same time the requirement that they meet the specification.

Take stocks, for example. When you buy a share of IBM, you don't get to choose which specific share—you simply receive one that meets the defined specification. In the case of stocks, the specification is the prospectus, which spells out exactly what rights you have. This is much like buying a standardized widget: you don't care which widget you get, only that it meets the spec.

As with physical products, there are cases in which you do buy non-fungible, specific items. When you buy a used car, you are buying a specific VIN number. Replacing it with another "equivalent" car—say, a different 1952 Studebaker Commando—would not be allowed because no two are identical. In finance, exchange-traded financial instruments are fungible, while certain Over-the-Counter (OTC) financial instruments are not and cannot be freely interchanged.

Second, the financial world mirrors the concepts of commitment, obligations to deliver, and obligations to pay. When you buy a stock, you create a commitment—and that's exactly what the industry calls it. You owe payment, while the seller owes delivery of the stock. A whole industry exists to ensure these obligations are fulfilled. Traditionally, the settlement period was T+3 (three days after the trade date) to complete both sides of the transaction, which has recently moved to T+1.

Other Financial Industry Considerations

Beyond banking and wealth management, another major branch of the financial industry is investment banking. Investment banking is about helping companies raise capital—whether through an Initial Public Offering (IPO), a bond issue, or facilitating an acquisition.

From an accounting perspective, each of these activities can be viewed as a project. These are highly complex projects. For example, when a company retains an investment bank to execute an IPO, it is rarely handled by a single organization. Instead, a syndicate of banks typically divides the duties and responsibilities.

The obligations in these projects are also much more complex. The organization going public commits not only to paying fees, but also to allocating a certain portion of their equity that will subsequently be offered to the public. Meanwhile, investment banks earn their compensation partly from client fees, but more significantly from allocations and spreads on the equity offered. Still, at its core, each engagement remains a project.

Other aspects of the financial industry include highly complex instruments being offered, particularly derivatives. There is a huge industry buying and selling these instruments, though historically these have often been opaque—understood mainly by industry insiders.

After the Great Recession and its aftermath, however, demand has grown for greater transparency in how these products are structured and traded.

Fortunately, there is no shortage of standards in the area of defining and identifying financial instruments. Initiatives such as:

- International Swaps and Derivatives Association Taxonomy 2.0 or ISDA[30]
- Financial Industry Business Ontology or FIBO[31]
- Financial Instrument Global Identifier or FIGI[32]
- Financial Product Markup Language or FpML[33]
- Financial Information eXchange Protocol or FIX®[34]
- CUSIP for identifying specific financial instruments[35]
- Algorithmic Contract Types Unified Standards or ACTUS[36]

All of these standards are useful and necessary. One of the most promising for the future is ACTUS. Unlike traditional approaches that describe or categorize financial instruments, ACTUS defines them mathematically through a few dozen algorithms. These algorithms cover the entire spectrum—from simple loans to complex derivatives—and are available as open source.

Before digging into any of those sources, consider that all the *financial instruments* are just different bundles of obligations and rights. Take a *call option* as an example: it gives the holder the *right* (but not the obligation) to buy a stock at a specific price within a set time frame.

[30] www.isda.org/2019/09/04/isda-taxonomy-2-0-finalized/
[31] spec.edmcouncil.org/fibo/page/ontology-tools
[32] www.openfigi.com/about/overview
[33] www.fpml.org
[34] www.fixtrading.org/what-is-fix/
[35] www.cusip.com/index.html
[36] www.actusfrf.org/about

Suppose Apple stock is currently trading at $200 per share. You might purchase a call option with a strike price of their stock for $225, exercisable at any time in the next month. Obviously, you wouldn't exercise this option right away—it would make no sense to pay $225 for something you can buy on the market for $200. But stock prices fluctuate, and if Apple's stock rises above $225, the option could become valuable. Options are described as *out of the money* when the strike price is higher than the current price, *in the money* when it is lower. In the latter case, the option's value is at least the difference between the strike price and the current price.

We bring this up in this context to tie this back to our discussions about rights and obligations.

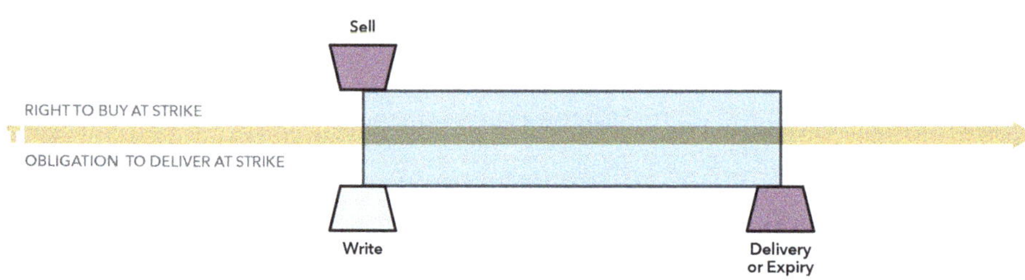

Figure 7.7: **Rights and Obligations on a Call-Option**

When you purchase a call option, you are buying a right in the exact same sense as we've been discussing throughout this book. And, as with so many other rights, it exists only because someone else first created an obligation.

Prior to your being able to buy the option in the open market, someone—known as the *writer* of the option—committed to sell that stock at a particular price within a particular time. The writer might already own the stock or be confident they can acquire if the option is exercised. At the moment they make the commitment, they create an obligation to deliver the stock, which in turn creates your right to buy it. As we explored in the "word to world" discussion in Chapter 6, a promise generates a reality.

The right they created is usually immediately sold. The writer or seller receives their money, but their obligation is not yet complete.

Selling it creates a tradeable instrument in the world, which traders can buy and sell all day long. However, what is being traded is only the right—the obligation remains with the entity that originated it until the option is exercised or expires.

Another, slightly more complex, family of instruments are derivatives. One of the simpler types of derivatives is a *swap*. Take a currency swap as an example: two parties agree, "I'll pay you $1,000,000 USD per month for the next year if you agree to pay me €950,000 EUR per month over the same period" (assuming the exchange rate is 0.95 Euros to the dollar at the time).

This doesn't mean a million dollars and almost a million euros are crossing the Atlantic every month. Instead, it means there are mutual obligations that mostly net out. If the nominal amount of a contract is $12 million USD ($1 million x 12 months), the amount of money that actually changes hands may be only a few hundred thousand (depending on the exchange rates' volatility). Each party is hedging a position they may have in the other currency.

But let's dig a bit deeper. Half of the swap is one party's obligation to pay $1 million per month to the other party. The second party, in turn, has the right to receive that $1 million per month. The right was purchased by the second party by making what is called the *second leg* of the swap—offering an offsetting obligation in euros, which in turn created a right for the second party. Unlike the call option example, these rights and obligations are harder to untangle. As a result, most swaps are bespoke OTC instruments that typically don't trade in the open market.

One last thought. Most complex financial instruments are different packages of monetary obligations and rights, but there is one type that deals with *non-cash* resources—commodities. Commodities are tangible goods and therefore count as non-cash resources.

Futures contracts are just a variation of our *due in* and *due out* discussion. At some point, someone takes delivery of actual oil, gold or wheat, at which time the contract is fulfilled.

Hopefully, this discussion sheds a bit of light on the arcane world of high finance, and at the same time, shows in principle how all the complexity can be reduced to the same few primitives we're dealing with throughout this book: obligations, rights, and resources.

Non-Profit Accounting

There are two big differences between non-profits and traditional organizations.

The first difference is the non-bilateral nature of many non-profit transactions. In any business—whether for-profit or non-profit—when a purchase is made, there is usually a corresponding right of equal value: the right to receive what was purchased. Similarly, when they commit a sale, the right to receive payment is coupled with an obligation to deliver, something of equal value.

In contrast, when someone pledges a donation (pledge being a non-profit's fundraising analog to sale and donation being the analog to remittance) there is no direct quid pro quo. Instead, the pledge results in a mostly vague, non-quantified commitment to do something good with the donation.

While this doesn't violate any data-centric conditions, it is just that people may find it odd to have special kinds of events that are unilateral in terms of their obligations.

The second major difference for accounting in non-profits is the fund accounting requirements. With fund accounting, each transaction may be earmarked to a given *fund*. There are restrictions on the use of funds. Usually, the funds align with aspects of the mission of the non-profit. A donation may be restricted to a certain set of uses. For example, a donor may specify that their donation may only be used solely for tree planting, not for herbicide treatment.

This requires treating money as if it were non-fungible. In government accounting—which we pick up in the next section—they often refer to the *color of money*, which is a way to think through the fund restrictions. Essentially, you can't pay for blue services with green money.

In a data-centric system, we need to set up separate resources. Much like the *item of supply* concept gives us different SKUs for inventory, we will have resources that are sub-resources of cash.

One straightforward—but tedious—way to do this is to have a different bank account for each fund. This way, any commitment to pay becomes tied not just to generic cash, but to a specific resource, such as "Fund A cash from Bank Account A."

However, having a separate bank account for each fund becomes unworkable. An alternative is to have a two-stage payment. Here, the payment is made with the virtual resource representing fund A. This virtual resource is essentially an obligation to pay, which is eventually settled from the actual bank account where funds are comingled. This approach satisfies both the fund restrictions and audit requirements.

Government Agencies

Government agencies face many of the same issues as non-profits—they are, after all, non-profits themselves.

They also have unilateral commitments, but rather than being inbound and initiated by third parties, as non-profit donations are, theirs are outbound and non-voluntary. When a government agency levies a fine, there is no corresponding obligation for the agency to deliver anything. Fines and taxes are basically unilateral transactions. That is, the government has a right to receive payment without the corresponding obligation to deliver. Yes, governments have obligations to deliver something, but it is usually not specific to the person or organization that paid the fine or tax.

Government fund accounting issues are much more draconian than those of non-profits. Most restrictions come from appropriations and are written into law.

Also, government agencies are on the other side of the compliance reporting issues we've discussed earlier. As we mentioned before, companies that are obligated to submit compliance reports are reading a bunch of text and are trying to find out how to recategorize economic activity they have already engaged in, in order to be compliant with the regulators' categories.

Regulators

What if regulators could—and did—define their categories not in natural language, but using attributes or pre-existing categories that the reporter is likely to already have encoded in their system?

Let's use the W2 reporting example from earlier. Any given employer primarily deals with three expenditure categories:

> **Wages** – Every month, they calculate the gross wages for each employee.
>
> **Deductions** – These are amounts that are reduced from gross pay. Some deductions are removed before calculating withholding taxes, while others come after. For our purposes, tax withholdings are a form of deduction. Note that these deductions are not actually the employer's expense—they are amounts included in the employees' gross pay that are redirected to taxing agencies, insurance agencies, and so forth. The gross pay amount minus the deductions is the employee net pay for which their paychecks are issued.
>
> **Contributions** – In addition to withholding money from employees' pay (which is later forwarded to benefit providers and tax authorities), employers also chip in some of their own money. These funds are called contributions.

There are hundreds of types of deductions and contributions, and dozens of ways to categorize wages. IRS regulations wax on about them for thousands of pages.

We can imagine a world where, instead of hundreds of thousands of employers—or their external accountants and payroll providers—poring over a vast sea of unstructured text to determine which box to put each portion of each deduction in, the rules could be defined unambiguously, semantically.

Take one example: HSA (Health Savings Accounts). These are often deductions, sometimes contributions, that an employer forwards to a custodian who holds these funds on behalf of the employee. The IRS has at least five publications that cover aspects of this deduction and where exactly it should show up on a W2.[37]

All this narrative boils down to establishing the rules for categorizing deductions or contributions that have already been accrued and paid. For example, regulations specify the *maximum annual contributions* that may be made to an HSA. Semantically, this really means the maximum amount that can be used to reduce wages that are subject to federal and FICA taxes, and therefore the amount that can be deducted from boxes 1, 3, and 5.

It seems possible—difficult for sure but incredibly useful—to reduce the ambiguous verbiage of this regulatory code to unambiguous, faceted categories that could streamline this type of reporting. This would remove most of the post hoc arguing that currently characterizes regulatory relationships.

Continuous Auditing

A financial audit is trying to establish that the financial results reported accurately reflect the activity of the organization. While this sounds simple, there are some deep problems hidden in there.

In order to make that kind of assurance, an audit firm has to establish:

> Any event that happened to the organization that should have been reflected in the books and records was, in fact, reflected.
>
> Policies and standards were applied—and applied consistently.
>
> No fictitious events were introduced.

Auditors use a variety of techniques to verify these points. For example, accounts receivable and accounts payable audits are classic examples of these which are meant to provide independent verification by sampling and obtaining concurrence from organizations not owned by the company under audit. Inventory reviews rely on the physical goods themselves to verify that information records are accurate.

[37]For detailed guidance on HSA and their reporting requirements, see IRS, "General Instructions for Forms W-2 and W-3 (2024), accessed September 3, 2024, https://www.irs.gov/instructions/iw2w3#en_US_2024_publink1000308298 and IRS, "Internal Revenue Bulletin 2004-2," accessed September 3, 2025, https://www.irs.gov/irb/2004-02_IRB#NOT-2004-2

> However, auditing is traditionally an after-the-fact, once-a-year affair. Many people long for continuous, automated auditing, and data-centric accounting can take us a long way toward that goal.

First, automating the application of accounting policy helps ensure consistency. In a data-centric organization, there should be very few "miscellaneous" transactions and little need for spreadsheets in the workflow between events and the financial reports. A limited number of special transactions reduces the scope of things the auditor needs to review.

Making sure each figure in the financial reports derives from a series of valid events is another area that gets improved with data-centric accounting. At the moment the event is created, the transaction is linked to its placement in the financial report. Rather than wait until the end of the year, any value being added can be randomly assigned for audit follow up shortly after it occurs. A lot of transactions are with third parties. We will need a mechanism for contacting all third parties that we extended credit to or who extended credit to us. This is an essential aspect of granting credit that is not present for vendors or customers where no credit was extended. Where no credit was extended, there is little need to verify as the commitment will not have been reflected on the books. It is not hard to imagine a rules engine that selects transactions for verification based on a combination of materiality and suspicious patterns.

Finally, the immutability of the audit log also makes it far harder for fraudsters to hide their tracks.

Publicly Traded Company Reporting

Publicly traded companies have a great deal of extra financial reporting and control requirements piled on them. Conceptually, there is nothing that would prevent publicly traded companies from adopting data-centric accounting. However, we believe inertia will cause them to continue with their very complex processes and high degree of manual intervention—at least until some privately held, data-centric companies go public and demonstrate to the investing public what is possible.

Startups

Startups are enterprises much like any other. They often seem obsessed with one particular aspect of the business: the equity statement—more specifically, the "cap table," short for capitalization table.

The cap table is a summary of all investment rounds and the specific investors from inception to date. It also includes details such as the valuation for each round and the rights associated with each round—and therefore each investor—including voting, non-dilution protections, and preferences in subsequent rounds.

Phenomenal Fun, Inc.
Capitalization

Common Stock		Preferred Stock Series A		Preferred Stock Series B	
Authorized Shares:	2,000,000	Authorized Shares:	500,000	Authorized Shares:	400,000
Outstanding Shares:	904,000	Outstanding Shares:	400,000	Outstanding Shares:	220,000
Stock Option Shares;	200,000	Stock Option Pool Shares:	0	Stock Option Pool Shares:	0
Remaining Unissued Shares:	896,000	Remaining Unissued Shares:	100,000	Remaining Unissued Shares:	180,000

Shareholder Name	Relationship	Common Stock	Stock Options	Series A Preferred	Series B Preferred	Total Shares	Percent Ownership
Maeve Kincaid	Founder & CEO	460,000	70,000			530,000	30.74%
Krista Madison	CFO	200,000	10,000			210,000	12.18%
Kyle Kessler	COO	150,000	10,000	10,000		170,000	9.86%
Lara Maier	Officer	45,000	5,000		10,000	60,000	3.48%
Joseph Ausherman	Investor	20,000		200,000	100,000	320,000	18.56%
Mark Vanderhaag	Investor	17,000		125,000	100,000	242,000	14.04%
Tom Perrin	Investor	12,000		65,000	10,000	87,000	5.05%
Employee Stock Options Pool	Employees		105,000			105,000	6.09%
Totals		**904,000**	**200,000**	**400,000**	**220,000**	**1,724,000**	**100.00%**

Figure 7.8: **Cap Table with Stock Options**

Stock Options

An adjunct to the cap table is employee stock options. Any firm can offer stock options, but they are especially prevalent in startups. Employee stock options fit the data-centric model perfectly.

When an employee is granted a stock option, the company has a commitment, although much of that commitment is contingent. Most stock options have a vesting period. At the end of a vesting period, if the employee still meets the conditions of the option (usually remaining an employee in good standing) the employee vests, which is equivalent to moving up a significant step in the degree of commitment.

Brokerage

Brokerage essentially means selling something you don't own, or in most cases, don't even possess. This covers real estate brokerage, stockbrokers, yacht brokers, many art dealers, and even a lot of produce.

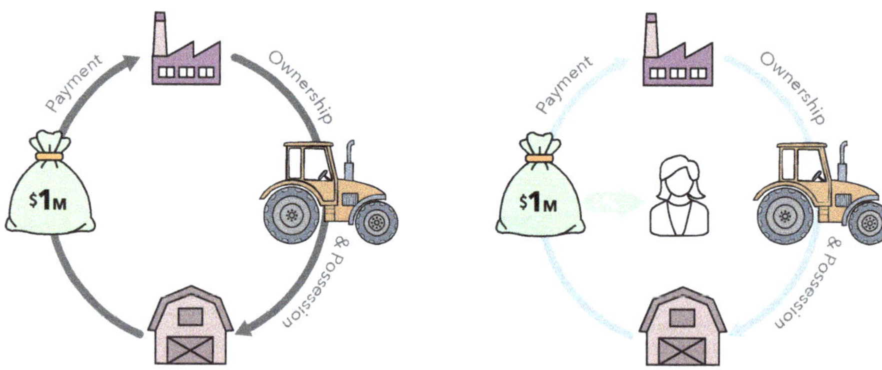

Figure 7.9: **Left Traditional Sale, Right the Broker Model**

The diagram on the left represents a typical purchase transaction. The farmer receives a $1 million tractor and pays $1 million for it. The manufacturer receives the $1 million cash as income and reduces their tractor inventory by the same amount. Both parties record $1 million in their accounts.

When a broker is involved (shown on the right), the broker doesn't take possession or ownership of the tractor, nor the money. The broker receives a fee—typically a commission—which could come from the buyer, the seller, or the transaction. The accounting difference is when the broker sells a $1 million tractor, they do not report $1 million as income. Their revenue is the commission, for example, 7 percent of $1 million, or $70,000. Their cost of goods sold is not the cost of the tractor, but anything they put directly into this transaction (for instance, amounts they paid for advertisements and the cost of the congratulatory hats and t-shirts they gave to the tractor's buyer and seller).

So how do we handle this in data-centric accounting? We want to capture the sales price without being tempted to treat it as income. This is a case where semantics must reflect deeper meaning and not merely define the terms. In this case, a single term—*sales price*—means two things.

In a non-brokered sales order, the *sales price* is simply the price the buyer is paying. We actually capture the price per unit and the number of units, but with brokered transactions, the number of units is usually one. We think the preferred way to handle this is to have the sale event be denominated as the full amount but not be a financial business event for the broker. It can be treated as a business event that spawns a financial business event, as described under composite events. The spawned event will be at six or seven percent of the sales price value. This gives correct valuation for the brokerage but maintains the selling price in a way that the brokerage can easily produce plaques for all their "$10 Million Club"—based on $10 million in sales, not $10 million in commission.

Consignment

Another interesting variation on inventory ownership comes in the consignment world. In consignment, one company has possession of the inventory without owning it. Note how most of these differences are variations in the degree or type of ownership, as discussed in Chapter 5. While there are pure consignment stores where (almost) everything is owned by someone else, there are many situations where companies have partial consignment inventories. Some manufacturing companies have MRO (Maintenance, Repair, and Operations) supplies on hand that they do not own. They issue the supplies as needed and the owner of the MRO items bills the company after the fact.

Consignment creates several interesting variations. First, the company with possession has no inventory value on its books. This does not mean the inventory has no value, but that the possessor is not carrying the value on its books because the possessor doesn't own the inventory. In most cases, they need to maintain some sort of replacement value, for if their facility burns down or if the item is damaged or stolen while in their possession, they will be liable. The consignment inventory system must have a mechanism for assigning value at the time of issue. It might be a negotiated price agreed on ahead of time, in some cases, it is a predetermined percentage of the sales price (e.g., cost will be 70 percent of the sales price).

Note that because the consignor owns the inventory, when the consignee makes the sale, the consignor is the entity that will record the sale and cost of goods sold on its books. The consignee will simply record their commission or markup on the sale as commission revenue.

Manufacturing

Manufacturing has a few extra wrinkles. First, all manufacturing involves inventory, so the discussion of inventory costing in Chapter 4 applies here as well. In fact, manufacturing typically tracks three types of inventory:

- Raw Material
- Work in Progress (WIP)
- Finished Goods

Finished Goods Inventory

Finished goods are inventoriable parts that are ready to be sold to customers. Wholesale and retail companies do not make the distinction because they rarely make anything. Instead, they buy finished goods from manufacturers (or from wholesalers) and resell the goods as they are. As such, wholesalers' and retailers' "on hand" inventory should be treated similar to manufacturing's finished goods.

There is an area that we think wholesalers and retailers could benefit from the distinction though. Generally, retailers, and often wholesalers, buy materials in one unit of measure and sell in another. A wine store may buy six cases of a recent vintage Château Lafite Rothschild for $18,000 ($3,000 per case) and then resell them at $500 per bottle. They could treat their input (cases of wine) as raw material, the process of breaking the cases down to bottles as the manufacturing process, and the resulting on-hand inventory as finished goods.

Raw Materials

One company's finished goods are often another company's raw materials. If you make bicycle saddles (seats), your raw materials are plastic shells, foam padding, vinyl for the covering, and metal tubes for attachment. Your finished goods are the bicycle saddles, but a bicycle manufacturer treats those saddles as raw materials while bicycles are their finished goods.

Raw materials and finished goods are recorded as assets on the balance sheet. Raw materials are only rarely converted directly and immediately into finished goods.

Work In Process

Any manufacturing process that takes time generates what is called "work in progress" or WIP.

Figure 7.10: Raw Materials, Work-in-Progress, and Finished Goods Inventory

As we explained in a previous chapter, when a manufacturing company decides to make something, they create a "production order." In data-centric accounting, we call this a *launch event*. A production order is very similar to a project. The production order creates a new species of inventory: WIP inventory. As raw material is added to the WIP, the cost of the raw material inventory is also transferred to WIP. Direct labor is also applied to WIP as the work is done. There can be many levels of WIP orders feeding into each other. Ultimately, the order is completed, inspected, and transferred to the Finished Goods inventory, along with all the costs it has acquired in its journey.

Raw material and finished goods inventory could use any of the inventory costing methods described earlier. When a production order is completed, normally, the whole order goes into finished goods, so there is not the same opportunity for the variety of methods to cost WIP inventory. WIP inventory itself has a policy-based variation: whether it is valued at *actual cost* or *standard cost*.

For relatively large, infrequent production orders, it may be feasible for workers and inventory clerks to charge time or parts directly to a WIP production order number. The more custom the manufacturing process is, the more likely this method, called *actual*, will be used.

For high-volume production line manufacturing, it is not feasible and may not even be possible for workers to assign their time to individual orders. In this case engineers calculate what they think each order will require in terms of parts and labor. Periodically, they add up all the labor, say on a given production line, and all the raw materials that went into the products on the line, and compare that to their estimates (and adjust their estimates based on what they find). This methodology is called *standard costing* as the labor and material costs associated with each WIP order reflect these standards-based estimates.

Two other distinctions in manufacturing have important accounting implications and will receive special treatment in data-centric environments: bills of materials and make-to-stock versus make-to-order.

Bills of Materials

A bill of materials (BoM) is usually presented as an indented list or a tree of the products that go into a finished good. When the production order is complete, sometimes this tree is collapsed into a simple list. For process-manufactured items, this list is often called the *ingredients*.

> In data-centric terms, a Bill of Materials (BoM) is a nested set of templates that describe internal and external commitments.

However, the BoM is more than just the list of parts. The structure of the tree mirrors the manufacturing process. Each indent is another manufacturing, inventory, or purchasing process. The lowest items in the tree or indented list must be completed first and then assembled up to the higher-level items.

Component ID	Description	Type	Total Qty	UM	Fixed Qty	Overage %
1080-000	Red Wagon	BOM	1	EA		0
8720-010	Sheet Metal. 10 gauge. 2.5 x 4. stainless	Item	1	EA		0
8110-010	Paint. Red	Item	0.25	GAL		0
1081-100	Front Undercarriage Assembly	BOM	1	EA		0
1081-110	Wheel Assembly - Front	BOM	1	EA		0
1081-200	Bracket. front. steering	Item	1	EA		0
1081-240	Axel Rod. 15 inch	Item	1	EA		0
1081-250	Axel cap, red	Item	2	EA		0
1081-260	Wheel Standard. metal hub. rubber tire	Item	2	EA		0
1081-130	Handle Assembly	BOM	1	EA		0
1081-220	Handle Bar. metal	Item	1	EA		0
1081-230	Handle Grip. metal	Item	1	EA		0
8420-010	Bolt 1/4 x 1. stainless	Item	1	EA		0
8430-010	Nut. 1/4. stainless	Item	1	EA		0
8440-010	Washer. 1/4. stainless	Item	1	EA		0
8410-020	Cotter Pin. 2 inch. stainless	Item	1	EA		0
8420-010	Bolt 1/4 x 1. stainless	Item	2	EA		0
8430-010	Nut. 1/4. stainless	Item	2	EA		0
8440-010	Washer. 1/4. stainless	Item	2	EA		0
1081-120	Wheel Assembly - Rear	BOM	1	EA		0
1081-210	Bracket. rear	Item	1	EA		0
1081-260	Wheel Standard. metal hub. rubber tire	Item	2	EA		0
1081-250	Axel cap, red	Item	2	EA		0
1081-240	Axel Rod. 15 inch	Item	1	EA		0
8420-010	Bolt 1/4 x 1. stainless	Item	8	EA		0
8440-010	Washer. 1/4. stainless	Item	8	EA		0
8430-010	Nut. 1/4. stainless	Item	8	EA		0
1081-270	Decal Set. wagon	Item	1	EA		0

Figure 7.11: **Bill of Materials**[38]

In principle, any item on the list—especially the "leaves" of the tree—might be pulled from raw material inventory or procured directly from a vendor. Intermediate assemblies could also be inventoried. Each process in this tree may take time, depending on the nature of the product; the duration could be weeks, months, or even years.

Bill of Material processing is a procedure that takes a BoM, such as the one described above, and "explodes" it. For example, if you want to make 20 wagons, you can do the math all the way down the tree and realize that 20 wagons will require, among other things, 220 quarter-inch nuts—one nut in the handle assembly, two to attach the handle assembly to the undercarriage assembly, and eight to attach the undercarriage to the wagon. While this is simple case, in

[38]East West Manufacturing. "Items You're Not Including In Your BOM But Probably Should Be." *East West Manufacturing Blog*, October 27, 2022, https://news.ewmfg.com/blog/items_to_include_in_a_bom

reality, these operations might be spread over a long period of time, and therefore some of these nuts might be required at a different time and possibly at different places.

For data-centric accounting, we take each component in the bill of materials as a commitment. You can see the parallel between a production order and a purchase order when you consider that any level in this BoM could have been procured. In fact, much of modern manufacturing involves final assembly of components that were previously manufactured elsewhere.

This parallel means that a production order is essentially a purchase order to and from yourself—often another department within the same company—but you still have a commitment where the counterparty is yourself. We treat it just the same. If an assembly needs bolts, they are *due in* from the raw material inventory department, until such time as they are *issued*, which is the fulfillment of that commitment.

All of the timing considerations work exactly the same, only there is no payment being made and no true external counterparty.

Make-to-Stock (MTS) versus Make-to-Order (MTO/ETO)

Another consideration with a very profound effect on accounting is the distinction between Make-to-Stock (MTS) and Make-to-Order (MTO) / Engineer-to-Order (ETO).

Make-to-stock is traditional manufacturing; you make goods in anticipation of later selling them. First, raw materials are purchased (1), then converted into finished goods (2), and finally sold (3). In this scenario, all accounting standards require that the finished goods are on the balance sheet; revenue and cost of goods sold are not recognized until the sale occurs.

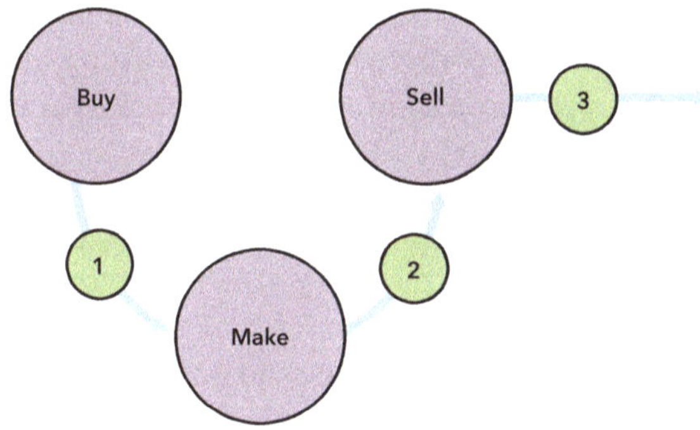

Figure 7.12: **Classic MTS Model**

However, it is possible—and usually highly desirable—to sell goods before you make them. This is especially true for products with a custom element. There is much more than a simple change in sequence of steps here. The real semantic difference has to do with the commitments.

With Make-to-Stock (MTS), you have no certainty whether, when, or for how much a customer will buy. With Make-to-Order (MTO), you know exactly who is committed to buy and at what price. In this case, you wait until you have a sale (1), then acquire the necessary resources (2), and begin production (3). This introduces a new challenge: you can't recognize the revenue for the sale at the time of sale as you did with MTS, because you haven't made the goods yet.

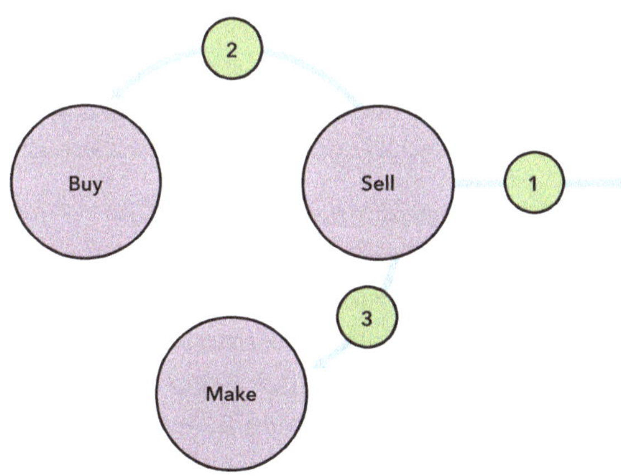

Figure 7.13: MTO Typical Sequence

Depending on the length of your manufacturing process, you may want to take one of two approaches to recognizing revenue. If the manufacturing process is short, you may opt to treat it like MTS. If you are selling polo shirts with company logos, as soon as you have an order, you have a commitment. If it only takes a few days to apply the logos and ship the goods, you can treat this like MTS and recognize revenue at time of shipment.

However, for long manufacturing cycle—such as building custom motor homes, airplanes, yachts, you have another option: recognize revenue as you complete the project. This is a policy choice, with multiple approaches. You may recognize revenue proportionately to the cost of material and labor applied. **Or you may recognize revenue based on known milestones.** In each case, we introduce a *progress event*. This event is the one that triggers revenue recognition.

Some companies are completely MTS, while others are completely MTO. Data-centric accounting makes it easier for hybrid organizations. By distinguishing MTS from MTO as an *intention*, different policies can be applied, allowing the same events to be treated differently depending on the intention of the order.

Construction

Construction is mostly Make-to-Order (MTO). The only Make-to-Stock (MTS) example we have identified is the building of a *spec home*. The term seems odd, as you are not building it to a specific customer's specifications but rather to a general model intended to sell easily. With a *spec home*, revenue is not recognized until the sale is consummated. Almost all construction, however, is MTO.

As such, construction accounting is very similar to manufacturing MTO. One difference is terminology: in construction, they do not refer to *production orders* but instead to *projects*. Similarly, what other industries call *sales orders*, the construction industry calls *contracts*, the creation of which involves much negotiation. In a data-centric model, a construction contract could be treated as either a sales order plus a project launch, or as the customer purchasing the project directly.

The construction industry also makes extensive use of *change orders*, which would be a new event type in data-centric accounting. A change order is an agreed-upon amendment to the specifications of the construction contract, including any revised selling price, adjustments to commitments, obligations, and rights, and any completion date extension.

Extractive Industries

Extractive industries include oil and gas, mining, forestry, fishing, and agriculture.

Many companies in these industries have long-running commitments, primarily to themselves rather than to third parties. For instance, a mining company may have a mine development plan, which is like a long-running construction project. A forest products organization may have sustainable harvesting or may treat logging more like farming. In addition to the commitment to develop the ore body or the forest, there is often an even longer-term obligation: the obligation to return the site to something similar to its original condition, often called *reclamation*.

Some oil and gas companies are permitted depletion allowances which are like depreciation for other types of assets. Most land is not depreciable, as the salvage value is expected to be higher than the initial cost value. However, land that contains natural resources such as oil deposits is likely to decline in value as the natural resources are extracted. The depletion allowances spread the value decline over the time the company expects to use the land. The deduction amounts allowable for tax purposes have declined over the past 50 years, and some organizations are not permitted to deduct depletion allowances at all anymore.

Most of these organizations are equipment-intensive which necessitates preventative and breakdown maintenance (which are variations on projects) and consume the equipment toward the processes of development or extraction.

Extractive industries will often have long-term contracts with customers to buy their output at pre-negotiated prices, which will be a fairly standard data-centric sales order. In cases where markets set the selling prices, the commitment may be in estimated tons or gallons and then valued based on recent commodity prices.

Services

There are many types of service industries. The main distinction we are interested in are those that are fulfilled on the same day that they are purchased (such as restaurants, tattoo parlors, and beauty salons) versus those where the payment may be settled later (such as health care), where the service is paid for but delivered later (such as lodging or travel), and those where both may be fulfilled later (most professional services).

The main differences, beyond labels for events, lie in the kinds of compound events that need to be set up. Most retail transactions are sales orders that are committed and fulfilled all at once. Exceptions include cases like catering, where the commitment and partial or full payment may be weeks ahead.

Most professional services (such as consulting, accounting, marketing agencies, or architecture.) are a lot like construction without the heavy equipment.

They often have long-term contracts and the option to earn as the resources are consumed (time and materials) or set goals are achieved (milestones) or upon completion.

Law firms can have a lot of their income tied up in contingent fee arrangements, whereby the lawyers are paid a percentage of the client's settlement or court judgment if they win the case. Some of the accounting challenges for law firms include distinguishing what they call *Hard Costs* (such as external fees or expert witnesses) from *Soft Costs* (such as photocopies or research time) and *Advanced Client Cost* which are hard costs associated with a contingent case but will be due from the client irrespective of the outcome.

The longer-term the commitments of a services industry are, the more advantage they will gain from data-centric accounting from commitments as described in Chapter 5. Because of the short-term nature of their client commitments, a nail salon will not benefit to the degree a consulting firm or law firm will.

Mass Markets

Here we are interested not so much in the sheer scale of the market, but how some industries have a different take on accounting based on how they deliver.

In the section on laterality in Chapter 5, we noted that in most industries, most agreements are bilateral. That is, they have one buyer and one seller, and the seller delivers their goods and services to the buyer.

But in some cases, mostly certain kinds of services, and some data or content-oriented products, one delivery can satisfy many buyers. Concerts are like this; beauty salons are not. Platforms such as Facebook or a cellphone network are like this, where selling cellphones is not. You cannot sell one cellphone to thousands of people, but you can sell access to one network to millions of them.

The biggest difference here is that when mass market revenue is recognized, cost of goods sold is less meaningful. The same or nearly the same costs are incurred with or without an additional incremental buyer; therefore, it is impractical to assign costs to revenue.

Insurance

The insurance industry is dominated by contingent events. When you buy an insurance policy, you have an obligation to pay (the premium) and they have an obligation to deliver indemnity. But indemnity is an odd service. There is value in having insurance even if nothing happens. Many contracts require insurance. If you buy a car or a house with a loan, the bank will require the property to be insured. In some ways, the value comes even if nothing happens. At the end of a year if nothing happened, both parties have fulfilled their obligations, and the commitments can be zeroed out.

But the other half of indemnity is covering the contingent events. Some small percent of insurance contracts will result in a claim. In data-centric accounting, when the claim occurs, it is a new event. It is tied to the contingent event the insurance was procured to cover. When the insurance was written, it may have included hail damage coverage for a particular house for a particular period of time. The claim is a business event, but not yet a financial business event. The insurance company is allowed to assess the damage and its cause, and review whether the policy was in force when the damage occurred. When all that has completed, a financial business event, an approved insurance claim, will be created that spells out the remedy and when it will be fulfilled.

Foreign Currencies

There are two scenarios for dealing with foreign currencies:

> When you make commitments to buy or sell that are denominated in a currency other than your home currency, and
>
> When you consolidate companies that report in different currencies.

The first scenario further breaks into two sub-scenarios:

> Where your exposure to the currency conversion is singular, and
>
> Where your exposure to the currency conversion persists.

An example of the singular is when your employees travel to Europe and incur expenses in foreign currencies, but you must reimburse them in their home currency. In this case, there was an exchange rate at the time of the transaction (often supplied by a credit card company if a credit card was involved). Your obligation to reimburse them is converted and maintained in the home currency. Even if the exchange rate subsequently changes, neither you nor the employee is affected.

The other case is where your obligation persists in a foreign currency. For example, you purchase maple syrup from Canada, priced in Canadian dollars. You will need to maintain exchange rates for all foreign currencies you deal in. Any report produced will need to interrogate these rates and for each outstanding obligation, reprice them as of the current exchange rate. This will be the equivalent of a price change and will change the economic value of the obligations.

The consolidation scenario is similar, except it does not operate at the level of commitments. The subsidiary has already resolved the value of all their positions in their base currency. You will adjust their balances and flows to your base currency, using the exchange rate as of the reporting date. Assets and Liabilities and all Equity accounts save the retained earnings, will be recast to the base currency. The activity, the Revenue and Expense for the period likewise will be recast, over the period to the value at the end of the period.

Summary of Applications

Hopefully, this section assured you that the data-centric accounting approach can be applied in all conceivable accounting situations. As we discuss in the follow-on implementation guidebook, we believe there will be separate implementations in different industries, to accommodate the variations described in this section.

The primary differences between industries will be accommodated by:

Additional financial business events – Some industries have events that do not occur in other industries.

Different composite financial business events – Even where industries share the same primitive financial business events, there will be differences in the templates. Companies that collect and pay sales tax on behalf of customers, for instance, will have a different composite event from those that do not.

Different policies – The difference between cash and accrual is a policy difference, as are many differences in revenue and expense recognition. Each industry has different norms that will be reflected in their different policy implementations.

Different financial report models – Each organization will have its own financial report model. As we discussed for investor reporting, this is often a highly curated model. Within industries though the starting point will be similar. Investors have become accustomed to seeing certain sections that they would not expect in other sections.

CHAPTER 8

Summary of The Future Of Accounting

We made some bold claims in the introduction. We hope we have provided sufficient evidence of the need for these new approaches as well as enough substance to understand the viability of this approach.

In an earlier draft, we had a great deal more detail, mostly implementation-specific detail. There is a tradeoff. On the one hand, the additional detail provides more evidence of the viability of the approach. But for those who are more interested in whether they should do this, rather than how, we thought it a distraction.

For those tasked with implementing, we have put a great deal more detail in the companion implementation guidebook. Please watch the Semantic Arts website for updates on a certification process. With the publication of this book, we anticipate that many software vendors and consultants will begin claiming to offer "data-centric accounting systems" without upholding most of the principles called out in this book.

Having read this far, two questions arise: (1) What will happen to accountants if the world adopts data-centric accounting instead of sticking with traditional accounting? and (2) Why would an organization adopt data-centric accounting?

Overall, the welcome answer to the first question is that the world will need fewer accountants. Why is that welcome news? Because for several years the world has faced a significant shortage of accountants[38]—a shortage that is expected to further intensify as the number of accountants approaching retirement age exceeds the number of those beginning their careers and the number of students pursuing accounting degrees. Reasons given for the declining supply of accountants include the perception of accounting as tedious and boring, as well as its reputation for burnout—requiring long hours and high stress, especially when financial reports and tax return deadlines are imminent. The long hours and high stress create a spiral: more accountants leave the workforce, leaving fewer behind to handle the same workload.

[38]Zank, Alex. "Accounting's talent shortage is undeniable—50% of industry leaders say it takes 60 days or more to fill jobs," *Fortune*, July 4, 2024. https://fortune.com/2025/07/04/accountings-talent-shortage-is-undeniable-50-of-industry-leaders-say-it-takes-60-days-or-more-to-fill-jobs/

As accounting becomes more integrated into the fabric of the business, as we suggest here, we think the job of being an accountant will become far less tedious. Less spreadsheet monkey, more governance and decision making. As for the firms contemplating making this shift, let's explore this further by revisiting the seven reasons we introduced in Chapter 1 for why organizations do accounting, and speculate as to how things may change. Recall the seven reasons:

> 1. Operational Accounting
> 2. Cash/Treasury Management
> 3. Resource Management and Valuation
> 4. Management and Incentive Setting for the Organization
> 5. Internal Control, Compliance, and Related Audits
> 6. Tax Minimization
> 7. Investor Reporting and Related Audits

Of these seven reasons, we believe operational accounting will change the most. In fact, if organizations become fully data-centric, operational accounting will become almost completely automated, with human intervention needed primarily to handle exceptions. Today, much of this work is done by bookkeepers and clerks, with oversight by managers, controllers, and financial executives. In the future, most operational accounting workers will need to retool their skillset to work in other areas.

Cash/treasury management, resource management and valuation, and management and incentive setting for organizations (items 2, 3, and 4) will still be necessary. We explained some of the changes in these areas in Chapter 7, in the sections on management accounting, closed-loop budget management, and cash management. Data-centric accounting will greatly facilitate these functions, as the data needed to support these areas of accounting will be more complete and more accessible, with the elevated focus on commitments and greater traceability of product and project inputs to revenue generation. We expect these areas to require fewer lower-level accountants doing clerical data-assembly work, but those in decision-making positions needn't fear impending unemployment.

Internal controls and compliance will always be important, as will audits of various kinds of measurement and scoring systems. Data-centric companies will require less of the tedious tasks involved in these areas. Reconciliation of reports produced by different internal systems will no longer be needed, as there will be a single source of truth. Compliance reports will be automatically generated from the data-centric system. Internal auditors will be able to focus more effort on fraud prevention and detection, as companies must always combat humans' inclination to exploit vulnerabilities and perpetrate scams.

The field of tax accounting could see huge changes if the world ever gets to the phase of multi-organization data-centricity described in Chapter 6. Taxing agencies such as the US Internal Revenue Service would certainly love to be able to match one entity's expense to another entity's revenue. While we don't anticipate this happening in our lifetimes, we did describe many of the advantages of data-centric accounting for tax planning and tax reporting in Chapter 7.

Investor reporting and related audits will undergo similar changes. As explained in our discussion of Figure 7.3, data-centric accounting will facilitate both the summarization and reporting of business event data according to multiple policies and the transparency of audit trails from the financial reports back to the business event data. Independent auditors will still likely be needed to maintain public trust. However, we expect the nature of their work to change such that it involves more forensic analysis, fraud detection, and system audits rather than financial statement audits. Such audits may be continuous—a concept that has been an academic research topic for decades—rather than done periodically at annual intervals.

The broader answer to the second question, the organization that adopts data-centric accounting will:

> **Make far better business decisions** – All the information that could bear on the decisions will be co-located and easily accessible. Flash reports and their inevitable inaccuracy will be gone, replaced by accurate, auditable, up-to-the-minute financial reports. Commitments and expenditures that occur over time (such as service, rent, insurance) will be visible at any time granularity.
>
> **Develop their budgets with far less effort** – Defining budgets, not at an accounting line item, but at a goal level will be far easier to do.
>
> **Control budgets** – Combining spent, committed, and outstanding budget on a report that is completely up to date eliminates guesswork. Additionally, assigning a single place (the approval of commitments) where executives can curb spending will provide the ability to immediately change course if need be.
>
> **Reduce the cost and complexity of IT systems** – Not only will whole categories of systems vanish, but so will the attendant systems integration and reconciliation.
>
> **Reduce the size and cost of the accounting department** – Most of the traditional accounting functions (such as bookkeeping, reconciliation, financial and management reporting, and compliance reporting) will be automated or self-service.
>
> **Reduce the effort the organization spends dealing with accounting** – There is a great deal of time spent understanding accounting codes and how to enter things just right to accommodate the accounting system, that will no longer be necessary.
>
> **Comply with regulators in an integrated fashion** – Regulatory reporting is currently often ad hoc and piecemeal. One side effect of this is that regulators often find discrepancies in regulatory reports which cause more work in their reconciliation. The single simple model integrates all the information that goes into regulatory reporting and provides reports that do not require reconciliation.

This is a major, but essential undertaking. We are committed to helping anyone who is on this journey. Feel free to reach out for advice or questions.

Phone: (970) 490-2224

Email: info@semanticarts.com

Website: www.semanticarts.com

Dave McComb

Email: mccomb@semanticarts.com
semanticarts.com
linkedin.com/in/davemccomb/

Cheryl Dunn

Email: dunnc@gvsu.edu or cheryl.dunn@semanticarts.com
linkedin.com/in/drcheryldunn/

Index

List of Figures

www.ingramcontent.com/pod-product-compliance
Ingram Content Group UK Ltd.
Pitfield, Milton Keynes, MK11 3LW, UK
UKHW021421091026
15624UKWH00010B/322

9 781637 352212